Ruling Culture

Ruling Culture

ART POLICE, TOMB ROBBERS, AND THE RISE OF CULTURAL POWER IN ITALY

Fiona Greenland

The University of Chicago Press CHICAGO AND LONDON

The University of Chicago Press, Chicago 60637
The University of Chicago Press, Ltd., London

Published 2021
Printed in the United States of America

30 29 28 27 26 25 24 23 22 21 1 2 3 4 5

ISBN-13: 978-0-226-75698-1 (cloth)
ISBN-13: 978-0-226-75703-2 (paper)
ISBN-13: 978-0-226-75717-9 (e-book)
DOI: https://doi.org/10.7208/chicago/9780226757179.001.0001

Library of Congress Cataloging-in-Publication Data

Names: Greenland, Fiona, author.
Title: Ruling culture : art police, tomb robbers, and the rise of cultural power in Italy / Fiona Greenland.
Description: Chicago : University of Chicago Press, 2021. | Includes bibliographical references and index.
Identifiers: LCCN 2020043888 | ISBN 9780226756981 (cloth) | ISBN 9780226757032 (paperback) | ISBN 9780226757179 (ebook)
Subjects: LCSH: Classical antiquities thefts—Italy. | Art thefts—Law and legislation—Italy. | Cultural property—Italy. | Italy—Antiquities—Law and legislation.
Classification: LCC KKH3183 .G737 2021 | DDC 364.16/2870945—dc23
LC record available at https://lccn.loc.gov/2020043888

♾ This paper meets the requirements of ANSI/NISO Z39.48-1992 (Permanence of Paper).

Contents

Map of Italy, showing approximate locations of principal research sites, "Campobello" and "Vergilia."

Introduction

THE WORLD'S GREATEST CULTURAL POWER

We tend to assume that Italian culture is eternal. As a body of art, architecture, and literature—to say nothing of cuisine, fashion, and film—it shows remarkable quality over many centuries. Its consistent influence should surprise us. Empires fall, territories contract, economic and political poles shift, and artistic styles fade in popularity. Italy's cultural heritage, broadly speaking, seems to have transcended all this. It consistently ranks high in international tourism surveys, and today Italy dominates the prestigious UNESCO World Heritage List. Instead of being surprised, we treat its value as inevitable. Studies of heritage despoliation and antiquities theft are numerous, but they tend to confirm that Italy's cultural heritage possesses a robust superiority that is natural and effortless—even providentially ordained as the fortunate outcome of the vicissitudes of civilization and nature.

A vocal critic of this view is also its most significant proponent. The Comando Carabinieri per la Tutela del Patrimonio Culturale—known colloquially as the "Art Squad"—is an elite military-police unit charged with protecting Italy's cultural treasures. Since 1969 the unit has deployed extensive surveillance and law enforcement tactics to eradicate looting and smuggling, and developed a worldwide reputation for its vigorous program of reclaiming purloined artworks and antiquities. The Art Squad and the state actors who preside over it do not take cultural heritage for granted. Affecting a performance of wary appreciation, the Art Squad does not rest on its laurels. While civilians and tourists admire the Colosseum, Renaissance churches, and the thousands of archaeological sites, the Art Squad is doing its part to maintain the country's cultural power. Its officers insist that this power is grievously imperiled by unscrupulous art collectors and rapacious thieves, chief among them the homegrown tomb robber, or *tombarolo*. Ironically, the very presence and notoriety of the *tombaroli* contribute to the unit's mystique.

Huaqueros and *Raubgräber, dao mu zei* and nighthawks: many cultures have specific words and phrases to describe people who dig for artifacts illicitly. In Russian-speaking regions, *tchorniye arkheologi* translates as "black archaeologist" and includes those digging for ancient relics as well as those using metal detectors to scavenge for jewelry and money from newly buried corpses. The term implies a contrast with "white" or legal archaeologists. It suggests that there are moral and immoral ways of digging, and that illicit diggers can be thought of as a type of archaeologist even if they lack formal training. The Chinese term *dao mu zei* makes clear the legal status of those who take tomb pots: *zei* is a thief, a cheat, and a sneak. Until 2010 the Chinese government executed tomb robbers on grounds that they threatened the intactness of the Chinese people. While the specific resonances of these terms are socially and culturally determined, what links them all is a sense of cunning, deceit, and magic.[1]

Because the tomb robber's treasure is buried in the ground, locating it requires, by definition, an extraordinary capacity for navigation—including exquisite sense perception of undulations in the landscape and changes in the soil quality, and a penetrating "vision" into the soil that can be learned only through years of living and digging in a particular field or valley or hilltop. Pietro Casasanta, whom the *Wall Street Journal* dubbed the "Prince of the Tomb Robbers," credited his stunning artifact discoveries to his deep knowledge of the land. Digging in the earth, he says, is an all-encompassing bodily experience. "It's like falling in love with a woman, it's hopeless" (fig. 1). The magic of the tomb robber is never limited to the ability to return from the underworld, however; it is also always aesthetic. Tomb robbers find and transform. They can plunge into the earth and emerge with jewelry, pottery, coins, sculpted jade or ivory, and skulls and bones. For this ability—taking the possessions of others, alive or dead—tomb robbers often stand accused of banditry.

Banditry, however, is in the eye of the beholder. Italian tomb robbers defend their digging and insist that they make little or no money from artifacts. They say they keep what they find or make gifts to family and close friends who will appreciate the objects as reminders of shared history. Money, they will tell you, is not the motivation for digging, and in any case the most substantial profits are said to be going to foreign archaeologists, private collectors, or Ministry of Culture officials. Given

FIGURE 1. "Prince of the Tomb Robbers" Pietro Casasanta talks during an interview near the ruins of a Roman palace in Anguillara Sabazia, near Rome, June 2007. Photo credit: AP Photo/Gregorio Borgia.

the power imbalance, my informants emphasized, why not allow them some leeway in digging on the side and pocketing a few artifacts that they will cherish and preserve? Unauthorized diggers, then, deftly play down financial motives yet insist that *someone* is making money. The interplay of history, land, and value—with the suspicion and status it confers—structures the discourse and practice of Italian cultural patrimony. The *tombarolo* is a persistent feature of the cultural landscape in Italy. There are alternative terms in the Italian language for a person who digs illegally at archaeological sites. A *saccheggiatore* is a "plunderer," and *clandestino* can refer to a clandestine digger. Both are serviceable phrases and readily comprehensible in context. The cultural trope of the *tombarolo*, on the other hand, has evolved so that it is imbued with a complex of meaning these other terms lack. Rather than a straightforward bad guy, the *tom-*

barolo is widely regarded as a swindler and a prankster who loots, in part, to mock state authorities. While the *tombarolo* is associated with certain negative cultural and political traits, it is also a romanticized figure who stands for a bygone age of local, pre-state community ties. Whom we deem a legitimate handler of antiquities changes over time. Among the disputed points in such a determination are who should have access to Italy's cultural resources, whom we regard as credible protectors of the country's patrimony, and whom we regard as a threat to it. Who is *in* the national community, in other words, and who is out.

I will argue that Italian state patrimony is prestigious and influential precisely because of internal dissension and threat. Tomb robbers play an especially important role in the face that Italy shows the world and in its aggressive claim to cultural superiority. *Tombaroli* exemplify what Michael Herzfeld (2016) calls "cultural intimacy," or the practices and discourses of a cultural identity that provide insiders with a sense of pride and belonging, but also embarrassment. Every national community has its version of cultural intimacy. Insiders are aware of outsiders' gazes, and they deploy discursive and practical strategies to downplay the embarrassing traits and construct a more palatable public image. Part and parcel of cultural intimacy is creative dissent, whereby insiders test and negotiate the terrain of official social identity and everyday life in the nation-state. This arena of dissent is alive with interpretations and sensory experiences that make national culture vivid, meaningful, and highly personal.[2] Every nation-state has culture-building projects, and in each of them the official version of nationhood must make compromises with local and regional idioms, as well as with actual practices that belie the smooth running of cultural narratives. Italy is in good company in this regard, yet it is also unusual for the extent of its reliance on internal Others—including *tombaroli*—to carry out the work of cultural patrimony. Artifact thieves are not a by-product of organized crime, and they are not a holdover of southern atavisms.[3] *Tombaroli* are a core component of patrimony in Italy. They are baked into the system. The mutually beneficial relationship between state actors and internal Others, including tomb robbers but also charismatic political leaders and celebrity archaeologists, sustains a vigorous narrative of cultural superiority.

Cultural Power: Defining the Problem Space

In a 2004 interview with national news magazine *Secolo d'Italia*, a top Art Squad official was asked whether, given his unit's successful record of repatriating stolen art and antiquities, it might serve as a model for other countries. Yes, he replied. It is only natural that Italy should do so. We have 60 percent of the world's artistic and historic patrimony, he said, citing data from the United Nations Educational, Scientific and Cultural Organization (UNESCO). Our artworks are admired by everyone. The antiquities trade pays top money for any Italian piece (*pezzo italiano*), he continued, but we have the best professionals fighting that trade. "Italy," he said, quoting former Italian President Carlo Azeglio Ciampi, "is the world's greatest cultural power."[4]

Reading that line stopped me in my tracks. What an audacious claim, I thought, impossible to confirm or refute. As a non-Italian person, I felt insulted. (*What does that statement imply about the rest of us?*) Once I'd regained my composure and thought about it further, I realized that Ciampi's statement offers a brilliant insight into the relationship between cultural heritage and state power in modern Italy. *Cultural power* is normally thought about in one of two ways. The first is through Joseph Nye's influential model of "soft" and "hard" power. Nye (2005) classified culture under the rubric of soft power, with "culture" standing for a broad category that encompasses novels, paintings, traveling ballet companies, piano competitions, and theatrical productions, among other things. The aim of soft power, according to Nye, is to shape nation-states' behavior in nonviolent ways by subtly influencing citizens' ideas and ambitions. The influence is subtle because things like piano competitions and literary exchanges are seemingly apolitical and passive. All parties have the opportunity to look good—to look *moral*—as they peaceably engage on a level of mutual appreciation. The second way to understand cultural power is as influence and imitation. Dominance in a particular artistic field establishes a place as a center of cultural activity, leading imitators and wannabes to follow the trends of that center even as they work to develop their own distinctive styles. As with New York City in the contemporary art world, or Josephine Baker's Paris to the avant-garde, this mode of cultural power is less about equal exchange and more about models and followers, centers and peripheries.[5]

What Ciampi meant, however, was yet something else. The way he said it in Italian (or, to be precise, the way the Art Squad official quoted him) suggested that cultural power (*la potenza culturale*) is not just something that a country has (like influence) or does (like soft-power exchanges). Instead, he meant that it is something that a country *is*. Modern Italy is a cultural power. Its polity has been built up through centuries of artistic superlatives. These are not absolute superlatives. I don't believe it is possible to compare, say, Navajo beadwork, Kabuki theater, the Benin bronzes, and the poetry of Sappho and arrive at a ranking of best to worst.

Ciampi may not have believed that, either. What he said, however, revealed the long-term effects on a polity of having its art, architecture, and archaeological materials celebrated and reified by outsiders, and being told by them that those are the most important things about the polity. Cultural power in this sense it not an ability or resource possessed by a country, but rather the logic through which the nation-state is structured. The type of state that Italy is, then, is a cultural power, and Ciampi implied that it is the best of that type. When a state is a cultural power, and its culture is definitionally inalienable (*it ceases to be a state without it*), then the art police take on a new urgency. They must fight tomb robbers and the art market because, taken together, those elements constitute an existential threat to the nation-state.

Still, isn't it risky for a nation-state with global aspirations to plant its flag in culture? It is, after all, an unruly domain. Raymond Williams famously wrote that *culture* is one of the "two or three most complicated words in the English language" because it is entangled with so many different historical ideas.[6] As soon as one starts to list examples of what should be included in it, counterfactuals and further examples present themselves. It is a wonderfully, frustratingly un-pin-down-able, expansive element of human societies. To be sure, for purposes of national heritage management, there are precise lists and inventories specifying what falls within the state's jurisdiction.[7] But those lists can be amended to suit the needs of culturally elite countries.[8] Culture's elusiveness and the flexibility of its content are its great advantages. More can always be added to the inventory, and so the state that calls itself a cultural power can, in theory, infinitely extend its reach through time, space, and object.[9] That is the basis of Italy's place in the world, and it starts to explain why the Art Squad can never rest on its laurels and must constantly combat tomb robbers.

❋

What are we talking about when we talk about tomb robbing? A helpful starting point is the definition offered by the archaeologist and criminologist Blythe Bowman Balestrieri:

> The looting of archaeological sites, which largely fuels the international trade in illicit antiquities, occurs when undocumented, illicitly obtained artifacts are ripped from the ground and sold, often on the legal market. Archaeology is a critical component in the study and understanding

> of human history, and the destruction of archaeological finds has both material and intellectual consequences. That is to mean, not only are archaeological resources finite but so is the cultural information they may yield. Looted archaeological sites and the orphaned objects removed from them (which are then bought and sold as commercial commodities) provide limited contributions to our knowledge about the human past and tell us little about the culture that produced them. In short, looted antiquities and archaeological resources retain little scientific value. As finite resources, once they are gone, they are gone forever.[10]

Balestrieri's definition distills the core features of the problem. When artifacts are ripped from the ground, scientific information that archaeologists rely on to study past human societies is compromised. When the artifacts are sold, that information vanishes along with the objects. "Once they are gone, they are gone forever": no other phrase better captures looting's material and epistemic consequences. Elected officials, archaeologists, and cultural heritage policymakers have invoked this fear—which I call *scarcity anxiety*—at various points in Italy's history. Finally, her definition stresses the role of the market. Whether the antiquities trade encourages looting or receives encouragement from it (and, indeed, whether it is accurate to speak of "the trade" in the singular sense of a discrete market space) is subject to lively debate.[11] One certainty is that the trade in artworks and archaeological materials has long been blamed for depleting Italy's cultural stock. We will see that the antiquities trade symbolizes a raft of social ills that the state denounces, in rhetoric and performance, as it asserts its authority and morality.

THE STATE AND THE ITALIAN MODEL

"State," "state actors," and "state patrimony" recur frequently in these pages. It is important to specify my terms at the outset. By state, I mean the constellation of policy institutions and networks of official actors that sustain a particular national ethos and act as primary spokespersons for Italy's artworks, artifacts and antiquities, and other cultural goods. They are "goods" because they have been constituted by law as property and commodities. The Ministry of Culture is one of the essential institutions in this constellation. Historically, it has had direct responsibility for the valorization and protection of culture, both ancient and contemporary.[12] In addition, important cultural functions are vested in the country's system of museums, archaeological superintendents, schools, and law enforcement agencies. According to article 9 of the Constitution of the Italian Republic, protecting the nation's cultural patrimony is a legal obligation of the state: "The Republic promotes the development of culture and scientific and technical research. It safeguards natural landscapes and the historic and artistic patrimony of the Nation" (my translation).[13] That principle was enshrined in text for nearly sixty years. In 2008, as part of a package of constitutional reforms initiated by Silvio Berlusconi, the state's obligation to patrimony was amended. Protection (*tutela*) and valorization (*valorizzazione*) were cleaved apart. The move was defended on grounds that the two activities, although potentially complementary, were essentially distinct. Italy's Constitutional Court explained:

> "Protection" rules are those aimed at safeguarding the good's cultural value and delimiting its range of uses in accordance with the public interest; but the aims of "valorization" are those of expanding the good's cultural value, through third parties' regulated use of it, as long as their activities do not diverge from the purpose inherent in cultural value and in its function of public interest.[14]

One outcome of the amendment was expanded opportunities for the state to accept money from private firms to invest in patrimony. Whether this is being done in a manner consistent with public interest is contested.[15] Public-private partnerships are now a dominant feature of the heritage landscape. There are numerous financial, political, and symbolic benefits in these arrangements, as I will explain in chapter 5.

In carving up and carving out the functions of cultural heritage development and care, Italy has altered what it means to be a cultural power. From an early twentieth-century vision of robust government support for cultural heritage and landscape preservation, the structure today is characterized by networks of capital flowing into patrimony development projects. This is patrimony as governance beyond the state, and while injecting new forms of capital into cultural heritage, it relies on longstanding ideas about authenticity, tradition, and value to do its work. The *performance* of state cultural power continues to project an image of national pride and civic belonging through the government's artifact protection. Through television news programs, press releases, conferences, in-house publications, museum displays, and educational films, Italian authorities broadcast their fulfillment of this obligation. A January 2012 press release from Italy's Ministry of Culture, discussing the return of purloined artifacts, is a representative example:

> All the masterpieces above have finally returned to Italian soil, from where they had been unfairly transferred, many years before, by dishonest, unscrupulous criminals [*criminali*] who, for sinister reasons of personal enrichment, attacked the spirit of cultural identity of the nation. The recovered assets, as well as having a commercial value of approximately €2 million, represent, each in its own characteristics, highly valuable historical and artistic expressions and are of particular value as testimony for future generations of consciousness and knowledge of their past and of the cultural identity of the Italian state.[16]

There is no hint in this text of the state's divestment from cultural heritage. Instead, the state is portrayed as inextricably bound to it. An attack on the nation's cultural identity is an attack on the state itself. This, combined with the putative commercial value of the objects, justifies the state's defending itself through a variety of law enforcement practices. Repatriating artifacts, prosecuting foreign art museums' directors, raiding and arresting tomb robbers, threatening legal action against auction houses and art dealers, and doing all this through combined and coordinated powers of law enforcement and public prosecutors: this is the essence of the Italian model of cultural patrimony.

The Italian model is characterized by an activist government, multilevel law enforcement, domestic and international surveillance, and a highly visible profile, with mass media often serving as the platform of choice to amplify the state's claims.[17] It has been praised by scholars and cultural heritage activists for protecting a national asset. It has also been blasted as a "hardball strategy" that relies on bullying tactics to wrest artifacts from unwitting foreign collections.[18] What everybody agrees is that, for better or for worse, the distribution, political valorization, and deinstitutionalization of cultural artifacts around the world is closely tied to the patrimony policies promulgated and prosecuted by the Italian state and its considerable arsenal of legal, investigative, scientific, and rhetorical strategies. This term, *Italian model*, will appear numerous times in these pages, and I use it to reflect ongoing, active practices rather than to reify a static policy apparatus. What keeps the model dynamic and changing are the relationships that form through it—relationships within the constellation of state actors, with third-party private firms, and between patrimony goods and "ordinary" Italians. I ask how concrete interactions involving people and artifacts construct ideas about the Italian model of national patrimony and help produce a belief in Italy's cultural superiority that is socially dominant, though internally inconsistent.

The Distributed Sovereignty of Italian Artifacts

Much has been written about commodifying cultural heritage, or leveraging cultural objects for capital accumulation. In addition to their symbolic and epistemic properties, artifacts are resources for developers, planners, citizens, and politicians.[19] Today it is the promotion of homegrown culture to the status of global masterpiece that constitutes the most vigorous competition for cultural capital.[20] Social scientists have examined the economic payoff of promoting national culture.[21] Through nation-state branding, for example, state officials work with the private sector to advertise the excellence of the country's artistic production and the uniqueness of its historical sites.[22] Whether the monetary payoff is actually significant is less important than the *perception* that it is. Concomitantly, there is potential for revenue from global elites who may consider countries' cultural prestige when choosing where to situate private residences and principal firm sites. But these economic analyses do not always capture the mechanisms by which culture is evaluated as "national" in the first place, or how material encounters and everyday relations keep national culture afloat.[23] The intersection of these lines of inquiry is the point at which sites and objects from the distant past are given meaning by and for contemporary audiences.

Scholars of nationalism have generated a robust literature on national ideologies of belonging and the ties of solidarity that are shaped by significant, collectively esteemed symbols and images. One of the most emblematic authors of this tradition is Pierre Nora, whose influential work on *lieux de mémoire* (realms of memory) emphasized the importance of landmarks and artifacts in crystallizing collective memory—particularly the memory of national groups. In Nora's argument, *lieux de mémoire* is best understood as a replacement for *milieux de mémoire*, the premodern manifestation of collective identity that was more deeply rooted in landscape and practice.[24] What his model introduces, among other binaries, is a distinction between traditional and modern societies' reliance on symbols to make sense of the community's spatio-temporal status. Ideas of belonging and communal identification did appear in my fieldwork data and can sometimes be traced back to a speaker's sense of connection with a premodern object that symbolizes the modern nation-state. I am less interested in the iconographic meanings of particular objects, however, than in the chains of relationships linked by antiquities. Modern nations boast numerous interpretive and performative strategies for making sense of symbols. But to regard archaeological artifacts only as texts to be read or puzzles to be deciphered is to risk losing sight of their extensive capacity to suture people to nation and nation to state. It is this framing, I argue, that gives access to the "idioms of relatedness" through which Italians make sense of their place in the world.[25] Autochthony, fictive kinship, and the mantle of past glories are examples of such idioms and emerged frequently in my interviews. Italians may not believe in or legitimize autochthony or fictive kinship on the individual level. It is through social practices and habits of nationhood, however, that these idioms are reproduced and entrenched in community life.[26] Archaeological artifacts make it possible to stretch the meaning of those idioms and then harness them to national and even transnational projects.

One way to think about all this is to say that archaeological artifacts do different kinds of work in the world.[27] Semiotic pictorial interpretation—or unpacking the visual elements of a statue, painted vase, coin, or other symbol-bearing artifact—is one avenue of work. It is a favored analytical route and one that I pursued in earlier projects.[28] Iconographic interpretation provides useful analytical tools, particularly for scholars with full access to the setting and audience reception of a certain case. There are many cases, however, in which reception dynamics are unclear or the physical features of an artifact are ill-equipped for iconographic interpretation. In such cases, the Italian Republic has sought to imprint itself, or more precisely to extend its presence, through the blunt physicality of the objects. In sum, we unnecessarily delimit the expressive possibilities of state patrimony if we focus exclusively on visual interpretations and the semiotics of cultural heritage.

To expand the expressive capacity of artifacts, and to capture what my fieldwork and archival evidence revealed about the state of ancient culture in modern Italy, I build an analytical framework that draws on several theorists whose ideas are not normally brought to bear on the study of national patrimony. Because archaeological materials are physical objects that generate powerful emotional and physical responses in people, concepts including materiality, presence effects, and landscape phenomenology are woven into my analysis. As status-conferring symbols that situate people in imagined communities, antiquities link ideas from nationalism studies and global cultural fields. The capacity of antiquities to stand in for the Italian nation-state calls for a theory of cultural power that connects object with sovereignty. I have found it helpful to adopt Alfred Gell's (1998) theory of distributed personhood to argue that archaeological artifacts are vehicles for distributing Italian authority. To paraphrase him, artifacts can act as "fictional mini-states within the state" and carry out broader political projects.[29] Precisely because they are not texts, artifacts have different ways of drawing significant connections between people and things. None of the artifacts discussed in this book can be said, on their own, to look like or "be" Italy. But when Italian artifacts are displayed abroad, Italy looks like them because they visibly represent the country. In 2006, when the Metropolitan Museum of Art was forced to repatriate an iconic ancient vase to Italy, for example, the vase was allowed to remain on public display in the Met for two additional years. The display's signage, however, had to include the words "Lent by the Republic of Italy."[30] The text functioned both to affix Italian ownership over the vase—making Italy look generous—and to assign authorship to it. A very Greek-looking, fifth-century BCE pot was now the creative work of Italian society. Finally, the agency of the Italian state—its will and capacity to act—was conducted by the pot itself.

In line with Gell's work, my theory of distributed sovereignty posits archaeological materials—particularly those considered sufficiently beautiful or special to be called "antiquities"—as carrying the authority of the state by abducting the authorship of the national community. My framework understands sovereignty as taking symbolic form: it spills over territorial boundaries and moves into circuits of value where "state effects" may occur with no obvious link to artifacts.[31] Sovereignty, to paraphrase Gell, refers not to a discrete space of decision making but to all the objects in the milieu from which authorship and state control can be abducted.

Central to this theory is the originary relationship, as I call it, between the soil and the artifact. Over the years, archaeologists have had various terms for describing the substrates they excavate: "interfaces," "contexts," *luoghi* (positions), and, more generically, "sites." Generally speaking, when contemporary archaeologists excavate a site, they adopt a method of temporal succession of archaeological contexts, called stratigraphic layers or features, and operate on the basic assumption that "younger" or more recent layers lie on top of older layers. Those layers and the soil in which they are embedded constitute the matrix. *Matrix* is the Latin word for womb and is evocative of the notions of relationality that have long been associated with the soil. Modern stratigraphic tools arrived several decades after the unification of the Italian nation-state, but some of the ideas they build on are ancient.[32] Matricial thinking holds that contexts of formation are inalienable. People never shed their roots, we might say, and neither do artifacts shake off the dirt that once enveloped them. In this thought system, the soil is capable of being nationalized and sacralized. Antiquities, being the works of long-dead authors forgotten or unnamed, begin to make sense as products of the soil.[33] When the life-giving quality of the soil is directed to cultural authorship, the reach of power is validated in new terms: wherever there are Italian artifacts, there is the state.

The Road Map

Italy is a country whose artistic and archaeological legacy enjoys universal visibility but where state authorities struggle to sustain a coherent meaning of that legacy among the very people whose heritage it is said to be. Tomb robbers, in this regard, would seem to be particularly disruptive to the project of state patrimony. It is tempting to frame the case as a paradox, wherein meaning making and cultural identity persist in spite of aberrant practices and ideas. Instead of approaching tomb robbers as disruptive to cultural power, however, I suggest they are constitutive of it. My analytical interest is whether this figure, the *tombarolo*, has something to teach us about state power. To this end, I tried as much as possible to understand the diverse actors and audiences who make artifacts meaningful. Professional archaeologists, museum staff, and government cultural officials are the sorts of people most of us would associate with this work. They are certainly part of the story. But ordinary, everyday Italians—some of whom care a lot about antiquities, some of whom do not—are also important. Over a four-year period, I conducted open-ended and semi-structured interviews with men and women in three primary sites: the city of Rome; the archaeological site of "Vergilia," in Lazio; and the Tuscan town of "Campobello." These regions boast a trove of Etruscan and Roman artifacts, and their archaeological discoveries have sparked some of the most contentious and influential debates about national culture in the history of Italy.

I wanted to know what it is like to live in a country that calls itself an "open-air museum," and how people navigate cultural protection laws in their everyday lives. I wanted to know, too, what Italians think about tomb robbers and their role in all of it. As explained in the methodological appendix, I attended carefully to confidentiality parameters. I use pseudonyms for individuals and places and refrain from describing my subjects in specific terms that could lead to their identification. This was especially important with individuals who were directly involved in illegally digging and selling archaeological materials, or who told me about family members involved in those activities. "Vergilia" and "Campobello," too, are pseudonyms. When I describe them, I include sufficient details to give readers a sense for the social and physical contexts. There are particularities that make these places special, though any archaeologist who has worked in Italy will, I think, recognize structures and dynamics recurrent in archaeological sites across the country. In this way I hope that my selection of field sites is representative of broader phenomena.

Because my questions about sociocultural contexts were deeply engaged with historical developments, I also draw on forms of evidence that reveal deliberative and interpretive processes from past periods. Nineteenth- and early twentieth-century scholarly reports, newspapers, legislative debates, and popular magazines sustain chapters 2 and 3. This effort culminates in my examination of the historical developments and ideologies that informed the watershed legislation, in 1909, to make the state the presumed owner of all artifacts in the ground and above it. Subsequent laws have affirmed the nationalization of cultural objects that are more than fifty years old; that are of interest to the national heritage; and that pertain "not only to art, but also to history, ethnography, numismatics, epigraphy, furniture, applied arts, [and the] history of science and of technology." From the early days of public discussions about nationalizing Italy's cultural assets, elected officials and scholars emphasized the inalienability of artifacts and artworks to the public body. With that principle concretized in law, state actors have been empowered to expand Italy's cultural influence through diplomacy, repatriation, and the prosecution of tomb robbers, smugglers, and buyers.[34] One revelation of the archival materials is that the cultural power of the state does not consist only in laws and their enforcement; it is also grounded in symbols, values, and myths about the nation's past. These are crucial to the maximal interpretive expression of the nation-state.

In the chapters that follow, I will show how Italy's version of cultural power relies on a synergy of intimate, backstage processes at the micro-, meso-, and macro-levels, from a child tomb robber's terrifying nighttime exploits with his father to the pristine displays in the Capitoline Museums and headline-grabbing repatriation ceremonies in the nation's capital.

To understand how the open-air museum factors into the belief in cultural superiority, I visited archaeological sites and museums, conservation labs and illicit dig sites, private homes and public parks, and the Art Squad headquarters in Rome. My study is based on firsthand conversations with Art Squad staff members, state-sector archaeologists, university archaeologists, museum curators, unauthorized excavators and collectors of art, and ordinary citizens whose lives are permeated with the sights, sounds, and political dramas of Italy's cultural treasures. I base my argument on the stories and perspectives of these individuals as well as on court cases and archival material reaching back to the early years of unification and extending through the struggle to nationalize Italian antiquities in the opening years of the twentieth century.

This range of settings opened a window onto the synergy, as I have described it, or the engagement of tomb robbers, everyday citizens, law enforcement, and cultural professionals. I look at how people mobilize different idioms and narratives to their benefit, as when tomb robbers emphasize their careful excavation and their self-taught indoctrination into formal field methods. At the same time, I ask how it becomes advantageous to overturn or question official narratives, for example, when the same tomb robber rejects professional archaeology for being a corrupt project of late capitalism, one intertwined with state efforts to privatize archaeological parks and historical landmarks. Recasting official idioms as personal goals is one way that cultural form serves as "a cover for social action" with significant play or leeway with cultural content.[35] It is the prerogative of cultural intimates to participate in this play, and tomb robbers are no exception. The approach described here suggests a triangulation of social actors, namely, state or official actors, everyday people, and Others. While that basic template is a helpful starting point for organizing a complicated social space, it does not capture the full story. Archaeologists, employees of the Ministry of Culture, and Art Squad agents are also "everyday people," and everyday people can become Others when they deviate from prescribed social norms and embarrass their neighbors and community members. This is particularly revealed in chapter 4, where the focus is on tomb robbers' own accounts of digging for artifacts. That chapter is part of an overall effort to trace the synergistic relations among soil, artifacts, and people from the formation of the Italian nation-state through Fascism and postwar recovery to the Berlusconi era and privatization of the cultural sphere. Throughout the book, I chart the role of the land—the mythologized *patria*—in generating cultural heritage. The land is a resource that Italians draw on to make sense of their entanglements with nationalism, localism, modernity, history, and culture. Just as the people I studied were multifaceted as social actors, so the patria emerges here as a nuanced collection of actors and ideologies that, over the long term, was invoked to describe the Italian nation as grounded in, and made possible by, cultural artifacts.

In the first chapter, "Art Squad Agonistes," I recount my first brush with tomb robbing and use it to map the trajectories of power and culture that pass through it. That episode was a failed performance of authority by Italian law enforcement. And yet, as I argue, there is more to the story. The state cannot be actively engaged everywhere at once. To be believed in and respected, it makes itself felt and proved and seen through various mechanisms. Tomb robbers contribute one such mechanism by substantiating the perception of threat to state patrimony and hence state sovereignty. Chapter 2, "The American Price," traces the history of nationalized cultural heritage, culminating in the 1909 law that made all artworks and artifacts, movable and immovable, state property. Rich foreign collectors were said to present a grave threat to the nation's cultural stock. Even as they denounced the "American price," or the unfair, sky-high prices that US collectors were willing to pay, Italian state officials relied on the international art market to articulate the value of the national antique. In this way, *patrimony capital* and a specific, artifact-focused logic of accumulation were born. In chapter 3 I show how successive regimes enlisted patrimony capital in state projects and offered a personalized style of cultural politics—notably in the figure of Benito Mussolini—to fill the interpretive gaps left by the state patrimony apparatus. The Fascist reorganization of national patrimony in 1939, and the creation of the first Art Squad in 1969, expanded the possibilities for cultural authorship and state authority. Foreign collectors became a common enemy and bridged contrasting views about the appropriate role of antiquities in Italian public life. Tomb robbers take center stage in chapter 4. Through in-depth interviews with tomb robbers, I explain why they do it and how their digging activities shape their understanding of Italy's culture and history. Their own contributions to patrimony capital include the extraction of raw materials (artifacts) that, once unearthed, are exchanged and circulated at the community level. Chapter 5 brings the story to the present, analyzing the logic of accumulation in public-private patrimony capital, and through diplomacy and transnational cultural projects that distribute Italian sovereignty to new horizons across the Mediterranean and beyond.

✷ CHAPTER 1 ✷

Art Squad Agonistes

Lazio, Italy. July 2010. After the looters struck, the archaeological field school fell unnaturally quiet. Normally noisy with the pickaxes and trowels of sixty archaeologists, the atmosphere was tense as we absorbed the news. Corinna, the field boss, dragged irritably on her cigarette. She was angry because the looters had stolen irreplaceable artifacts and had pointlessly destroyed faunal specimens in the storage trailer. She was furious that the archaeology superintendent had failed to protect her site, "Vergilia," an ancient town of Etruscan origin that once sent orators and officers to the Senate at Rome. And she was raging, too, because the bureaucratic ritual of filing a *denuncia* (law enforcement report) and providing testimony to the Italian Carabinieri would cost precious time and was unlikely to help recover any antiquities.

On that hot July morning, I could see just one piece of the bigger picture. I had thought tomb robbers were a thing of the past, a matter of ghastly nighttime raids on churchyards and daring incursions into ruined temples. The looters' raid cast everything in a new light. Two officers of the Carabinieri arrived, and I watched as they inspected the crime scene with Corinna. Corinna was in charge of the network of trenches that sliced through the site, and she supervised a phalanx of trench masters and their rookie archaeologists. It was one of the most senior and respected positions in the team, and she had earned it. Born and raised in Lazio, Corinna had been digging in this part of the country for decades. She knew its archaeology intimately. Her colleagues praised her "dirt sense"—an innate understanding of what lies beneath the soil based on subtle variations in topography. Dirt sense is a valuable professional skill for archaeologists. It is also a prized form of knowledge in a country where the land is linked with cultural identity. Corinna had endured years of university study and low-paid rescue digs, routine gender humiliation in a macho discipline, and the grueling, multistage exam of the state's archaeological service. She was a force of nature with a pickax. Corinna brooked no fools, and more than once she had given the boot to team members who shirked or showed up too hungover to work. She was also the consummate professional, well versed in the diplomatic niceties expected by the excavation's patrons and the nattily dressed officials who occasionally descended on the site from their bureaucratic lairs in Rome.

The cops greeted Corinna politely and shook hands with her and Nino, a trench master who was born and raised in Bologna. Corinna led them to the crime scene, two portable cabins—the field offices (*uffici modulari*, or *mods*)—that had been broken into and ransacked. The officers took notes on a clipboard, nodding as they listened to Corinna's description of what had been taken. After a few minutes, one of the officers got back in the car to take a phone call. The second officer finished his notes, shook hands with the archaeologists, and joined his colleague. He opened the passenger door and, with great care and deliberate gestures, tapped his shoes on the door frame to shake off a thin layer of dirt. Their fact gathering complete, the officers drove off.

The theft was devastating. There was clear evidence of a crime—a crime against national culture, as it is encoded in Italian law. Why had the officers seemed so indifferent? Why hadn't they taped off the crime scene, put on gloves to collect evidence, or dusted for fingerprints? None of it made sense to me. Corinna and Nino sat slumped on folding chairs outside the *mods* and commiserated over cigarettes.

"Are they coming back?" I asked.

"Who?" Corinna said.

"The police."[1]

"No."

"Who will investigate? I mean, fingerprints or something."

"Ha! Not in this country. That *was* the investigation. It wouldn't surprise me if they knew who did it [but won't say who]."

Nino glanced at her reproachfully and looked at me. In small towns like this one, he explained, locals often knew about archaeological site thefts but were reluctant to come forward. "There's not much that can be done."

Later I was able to situate Corinna and Nino's mistrust of law enforcement in the context of cultural intimacy, a shared insiders' knowledge of how society really works "backstage," with the cringing self-consciousness that entails.[2] But at the time I was still operating within the public framing of national patrimony, a powerful idea that presents Italy as unified in its effort protect the country's cultural treasures. I'd joined the excavation team as a true believer in that effort. As a trained archaeologist, I was there to participate in the physical work of excavating while conducting fieldwork of my own: a study of the group processes that produce scientific knowledge. The state's cultural authorities had entrusted our dig team with the temporary care and study of the site—an enormous honor and responsibility. We dug and sorted, conserved and recorded. That was our job. Protecting the site from thieves and interlopers was the state's role. That's how it's supposed to work, I thought, and that's the version of the story Corinna and Nino later gave to my teammates, the press, and their donors. But the way it actually works is infinitely more complex and interesting.

Gratta e vinci is how Italians describe chance encounters with artifacts in the culturally rich land they inhabit, using the metaphor of a "scratch and win" lottery ticket. Dig in the right place and you might find something old. Chance finds are part of everyday life. In Italian homes today, it is common to find Roman amphorae, large ceramic containers designed for the ancient wine and oil trade, reused as planters and garden décor, or remnants of marble sculpture—a foot, say, or part of a head—casually displayed on a bookshelf. Possessing such objects is in most cases illegal, but Italians tolerate in-home artifacts within limits. Culturally, there is an important difference between a lucky find and an inheritance. *Ereditare*—to inherit—is the domain of family, or non-state relations. *Trovare*—to find—is more ambiguous, straddling private and public claims on the land and the objects it contains. Many Italians would agree that it is probably acceptable to keep an antiquity passed on from a relative. But most would be uncomfortable about finding an antiquity and keeping it rather than reporting it to the authorities. In light of this, *tombaroli* exceed the limits of tolerance by finessing the distinction between chance finds and planned ones. By selling artifacts for money, moreover, the tomb robber hits a nerve that is especially meaningful in Italian society. Cashing in for individual gain insults the collective spirit conveyed in the phrase *tutti insieme*, everyone together. That phrase is a floating signifier—invoked in politics, sports, community organizing, and labor—and it extends to the artifacts and ruins that populate the landscape. The minister of culture may be the official manager of the country's cultural patrimony, but in practice it is the public who, through countless day-to-day interactions and decisions about where to tread and what to preserve, provide custodial care. In Italy, tomb robbers are despised for violating the trust that makes the "scratch and win" work, and for personally profiting from a shared good.

If *gratta e vinci* conveys the good fortune of a lottery windfall, another common phrase, *museo a cielo aperto*, casts the country's artifacts and the soil that contains them in the aspirational role of an immense "open-air museum."[3] It is a powerful metaphor that highlights the pride people feel about living in a country where antiquities and monuments are part of the everyday fabric of social life. Given the scale and scope of Italy's cultural patrimony, with densely packed layers of history that spill over their modern containers, it makes intuitive sense. But think about it a little longer and the sensibility evaporates. How can a museum be in the open air? The very premise of museums of art and antiquities, since their inception three centuries ago, is that they are quasi-sacred spaces of quiet reflection and a retreat from the grind of everyday life.[4] A museum is by design hermetically sealed, with clearly articulated spaces of privilege and access marked by vitrines, locked cabinets, and Do Not Touch signs. Museums do something else important: they teach people how to behave by instilling civic virtues and commanding bodily self-control through the rules of gallery decorum.[5] The pedagogical impact of the museum has always relied on its being demarcated from the open air. It makes even less sense that an entire country could be a museum. How could anyone *live* in a museum? Who would want to, given the discipline and stifling protocol? If the museum is everywhere, how are the objects in its "collection" made special or distinctive? Finally—and these were the questions that eventually led me to abandon my research plans and set out in pursuit of thieves—why do tomb robbers continue to burglarize the open-air museum despite years of government exertion to the contrary, and what might their persistence tell us about their place in the nation's cultural ecology? The answer to these questions, in brief, is that state patrimony has evolved in such a way that it draws symbolic benefit from the steady hum of tomb robbing. Tomb robbers produce a constant supply of artifacts that, when captured or repatriated by the state, stand as proof of the nation's cultural richness. They generate plausible market prices, which state officials can point to as evidence of their effectiveness in combating the art market. Tomb robbers, finally, provide a pretext for state action by sustaining the claim that Italy's cultural patrimony is under siege.

The National Antique

The idea that Italy has the best or largest cultural patrimony in the world is an operative part of Italians' everyday life. Ancient Rome and its antecedents and heirs are quintessential features of this idea. They are associated with the emergence of national consciousness and glorified as a foundation of civilization that transcends any particular contemporary polity. This idea—along with the sacralized soil, its countless artifacts, and its dazzling array of ancient ruins and monuments—constitutes the core of what I call the *national antique*. The construct of the national antique moved the country into pole position in the global hierarchy of value, the "homogeneous language of culture and ethics" that articulates a logic of unspecified, deracinated cultural "difference, heritage, local tradition."[6] By harnessing this logic to the national antique, Italy can call itself the world's greatest cultural power.

By Italian law, *beni culturali*—or "cultural goods" that are at least fifty years old and are of artistic, archaeological, or historic interest to the country—belong to the national government and are under state protection.[7] Coins, manuscripts, marble sculptures, wooden altarpieces, Neolithic tools, photographs, postcards, pottery, public squares and the stone benches that line them, urban cathedrals and rural farmhouses, furniture, medals, bridges, mines, and navigational instruments: all of these constitute *beni culturali fino a prova contraria*, "Cultural heritage until proven otherwise."[8] Private as well as public goods are potential assets in the proprietary regime of cultural heritage, and there are clear procedures for determining an object's heritage status. The procedures are spelled out in article 12 of the *Code of Cultural Heritage and Landscape* (*Codice dei beni culturali e del paesaggio*), the official law governing the use and protection of Italian cultural heritage goods. To judge if an object is patrimony worthy, the Ministry of Culture relies on experts to "verify" the national community's potential interest in it. Specific criteria establish how this is to be done, to ensure consistent evaluation of this question: How does the country's heritage benefit from having this object?[9] The answer to that question can change over time. A thing or building or place that was once tertiary to the national patrimony may become central after new finds are discovered, scholarly appraisal changes, and official priorities shift.

When I say "by Italian law," I am referring to more than a hundred years of legislation, with major statutes, adjustments, and reforms passed in 1871, 1909, 1939, 1969, and 2004. There is no single law that says, "This painting (or manuscript or statue, coin or pottery fragment) belongs to the government." Rather, there is a complex framework of laws, institutional policies, and administrative and scientific procedures that establish cultural goods as belonging to the nation.[10] The idea of state-owned cultural treasures, that all those *beni culturali* belong to the people as a public good, is so natural in Italy, so taken for granted, that it is easy to forget that the framework is the outcome of some three centuries of social change, massive political ruptures, seismic economic shifts, and a rise, decline, and rise again of the political influence of the Italian peninsula and islands. The law makes exceptions for works by living artists, for works less than fifty years old, and for works in certain technical media. But on the whole it is broadly encompassing, such that the state lays legal claim to cultural goods in the ground and above it, known and as yet unknown. Violations are prosecuted and can lead to jail time. If you own land in Italy and find pot fragments or an ancient structure on your land, the state can take those fragments or building remnants and send archaeologists to excavate your backyard. This is because, in addition to those cultural goods being property of the state, the territory of Italy is symbolically operationalized as a continuous archaeological site—the open-air museum unfolding in real time.[11]

Every country has culture, and the discourse of heritage is found all over the world. Every national community has its points of pride, its boasts and branding strategies.[12] France, like Italy, claims to be a dominant global cultural force. As far back as the early 1500s, when Francis I purchased high-quality replicas of Roman statuary for his hunting lodge at Fontainebleau, French rulers styled their regime a "second Rome." Under the reign of the Sun King, Louis XIV, all pretense of flattering imitation was dropped and France became simply "the New Rome."[13] In 2019, for the second time in three years, France was declared the world's number-one soft power for its cultural richness and influence, easily eclipsing its old rival Italy, which was number eleven on the list.[14]

Other modern nations compete with Italy's claim to the mantle of Western civilization. The Greek government used the 2004 Athens Olympics as an opportunity to broadcast the country's cultural heritage to a global audience, and like the Italian government it maintains a specialized archaeology law enforcement unit to protect artifacts and ruins from theft.[15] Turkey and Egypt, similarly, tightly control excavation permits and the export of historic cultural artifacts. And yet, for all these similarities, Italy is unusual in its practice of state patrimony, which combines a continuous insistence on cultural superiority with creative appropriation of internal dissonance. Internal Others sustain the collective belief in cultural superiority. Those Others include regional patriots who reject nationalism in favor of ultra-local cultural idioms based in specific landscapes and objects, and looters and tomb robbers whose thieving and smuggling generate cross-boundary practices and official nation-making projects. These Others are a source of embarrassment. They are also vital to the success of the national antique.

Patrimony and the Problem of National Culture

When I packed my bags for the field school, questions of national culture were not my priority. I intended to immerse myself in the daily practices of the excavation team and to observe knowledge being made—a bread-and-butter project within the academic field known as science and technology studies (STS). The STS literature regards nationalism as one of several factors that influence how scientific fields are structured, including funding priorities and hiring decisions, the organization of labs and academies, and ethical standards. That angle interested me; indeed, I chose Vergilia because its team was highly diverse in national background, gender, and age. I thought I was looking for "gotcha" moments when the archaeologists' masks of objectivity slipped and biases crept in—influenced by individuals' cultural backgrounds, perhaps even nationalist in character. But I had given little thought to the broader social and cultural milieu in which the field school operated. I eventually came to recognize in that milieu an intensive cultivation of cultural superiority on the national level. After all, according to some historians of modern Italy, this thing called "Italian national culture" is misleading.[16] National unity in this country, they argue, was a fraught endeavor from the beginning.

Uniting the peninsula's distinctive regions, islands, and city-states into a single geographic territory was the first step toward forming a nation-state. That step, beset by a decade of bloodshed and resistance both foreign and domestic, was easy compared with what came next: fusing the peninsula's diverse communities into a single people. Some have rejected the notion that national unity "failed" because no singular collective memory or identity emerged from it. Instead, they insist, we have to consider the possibility that having multiple possible memories or interpretations of cultural patrimony is *positive* because of the variegated ideas that result.[17] It is from this perspective that I approach cultural heritage and state patrimony. Unsettled meanings can make national identity richer rather than deficient or "failed," and divergent attitudes toward artifacts, and toward their extraction and possession, signal active and collective commitment to those very objects rather than indifference. In other words, I started out looking for evidence that nationality compromises archaeological collaboration, and ended up studying the mutually constitutive relationship between archaeological artifacts and ideas and identities within the nation-state.

PATRIMONY CAPITAL

The theme of cultural patrimony has emerged with particular prominence in the social sciences literature over the past few decades, due largely to three intersecting developments. First, archaeologists and anthropologists took notice of the demands for justice by repatriation claimants and cultural heritage activists and argued that artifacts should be protected as a particular category of cultural sovereignty. Second, landmark legal cases involving Nazi-era looted art reframed restitution and repatriation as moral acts. Concomitantly, the phenomenal growth of the global art trade in the 1990s and 2000s drew attention to the monetary value of fine art and antiquities, providing an additional line of defense to repatriation claimants, who could argue that stolen artifacts had both monetary and symbolic value. And third, sociologists began to approach cultural patrimony through the concept of nationalism, drawing on classic historical and sociological works to understand the symbolic and material significance of cultural objects in national communities. In this body of thought, cultural objects are understood as symbols that both confer legitimacy on the project of nationhood and provide particular attachments to national identities.[18] Knowledge of the nation as a real, lived entity is "kept alive by governments and communities through a range of aesthetic resources," including material objects with cultural significance, whose tactility serves as evidence of the existence of a national body.[19] But some argue that the Italian model of cultural patrimony goes beyond the constitutional imperative to protect heritage and perpetuates the worst forms of nationalism and cultural chauvinism.[20]

Critics argue that there has been a conflation of interests. On one hand, cultural patrimony can refer to cultural artifacts, and "culture" is "whatever people make and invest with significance through their creative work."[21] On the other hand, cultural patrimony can be applied to products, including objects, made by a particular group and, by virtue of that, naturally belonging to them. Because we separate issues of group identity, historical identity, and ownership imprecisely, the argument goes, "nation" stands in as a legitimate claimant even when it has little to do with the circumstances of creation of an object made hundreds or thousands of years ago. For critics of the Italian model, it boils down to this: nobody alive today had anything to do with the creation of Etruscan or Roman artifacts or any other antiquity. Further, they argue, the cultural and social contexts in which they were made no longer exist, calling into question the supposed dependence of contemporary identity on ancient objects. Those objects are instead held to be universal patrimony, belonging to all of us and reflecting in a tangible way the complex of traditions, peoples, temporalities, and institutions that made them into emblems of classical heritage. The solution to the fallacy of national cultural patrimony, in this line of thinking, is to give priority to cosmopolitan values and a framework of global culture.

"Patrimony" and "heritage" are sometimes used interchangeably but at other times are decisively differentiated. My own position is that context matters, and in the context of modern Italy, patrimony better reflects the discursive and ideational practices at play. The word is cognate with *patria* and transliterates easily from *patrimonio culturale,* a recurring phrase in Italian legal texts regarding archaeological materials and artworks. When I use the word *heritage,* it is in the broader sense of cultural practices, goods, and sites that people regard as part of their community identity but not necessarily of economic or political interest to the state. "State patrimony" and "patrimony capital," two terms that I develop throughout these pages, capture the public and private interests that characterize the contemporary period of cultural governance in Italy. Patrimony capital I find preferable to Pierre Bourdieu's term "cultural capital" because he tied it to individuals' capacities, dispositions, and knowledge of cultural forms—their personal *habitus.* Patrimony capital, on the other hand, is the value-enriching capacity of heritage objects, or their ability to generate ever more political, social, and market wealth through strategic redeployment and investment.[22]

The Open-Air Museum

The open-air museum is the staging ground for state patrimony in Italy, through the three elements of space, inventory, and expertise. In the open-air museum, space is structured by the soil, inventory comprises archaeological materials, and expertise encompasses the wide range of social actors who are enlisted as official and unofficial staff in the guise of curators, guards, and guides.

The open-air museum is distinct from the roofed and walled variety in that its primary enclosure is the ground, and the soil features centrally in the creation and management of the museum's collection. The soil is one marker of continuity among the millions of artifacts, artworks, and architectural pieces distributed across the country. It is the one classification that indexes this jumble of past civilizations and diverse linguistic and cultural groups into a single "Made in Italy" collection. In the late nineteenth century, archaeologists began to adopt uniform standards of describing and recording soil deposits. After generations of treasure hunting in which antiquarians and archaeologists tore up the earth in search of specific ancient sites, soil deposition work was recognized as an important corrective, with the soil layers providing nuanced information about past periods of occupation and human activity.[23] Sketching soil layers and their contents, and describing their color variations with standardized labels, became essential skills of professional field excavators. Through archaeological science the ground was transformed into an object of systematic study. It was the cross section of cultural, historical, and geological forces that made sherds into artifacts and rubble into "features" that matter for the polity.

In the open-air museum, one of the most powerful concepts for explaining the connection between land and culture is *patria*, or "homeland." It is a word with profound emotional and political resonance.[24] As with English, the Italian language offers several words and phrases for describing one's native land. *Paese*, for example, refers to the local place a person comes from and is generally understood in an apolitical sense.[25] *Patria*, on the other hand, is marked ideologically, and Italians who invoke it tend to do so self-consciously, in the same way that Americans who refer to their "homeland" or "fatherland" might be interpreted as making a political statement in support of strict border security or conservative patriotism. When the word *patria* is chosen over *paese*, then, it is worth paying close attention to the context. As we will see in subsequent chapters, language is important across the framework for cultural power: the Art Squad has its rhetoric, the state has its lexicon, and the tomb robbers and museum directors have their own euphemisms, metaphors, and technical terms for describing themselves in relation to the objects that make Italy a cultural power.

Riding the Matrix

At Campobello one evening, after a hard day of excavating, the director beckoned me to come sit with him.[26] Campobello, like the Vergilia field school, teaches students—most of them from US universities—the fundamentals of archaeological fieldwork. Unlike Vergilia, Campobello's staff positions are held primarily by Americans, including its director, "Mike." We were outside, in a courtyard next to the team barracks, enjoying the gradual waning of the daytime heat. We watched as the undergraduates finished eating, scraped their plates, and formed a chaotic line of dishwashing and drying. There were sixty-five of them and they made a lot of noise. "Just like Americans," he joked, "filling up space everywhere they go." I asked about relations with the locals. Pretty good, he said. Some residents resented the annual influx of students, who noticeably swelled the village population, but the hotel owner and shopkeepers appreciated the extra business the field school brought. "On the other hand," he continued, "some of the crowd at the bar resent us. There are still guys there who remember working for the dig. It was a good life for them: they worked during the dig campaign [typically four months] and collected unemployment the rest of the year. [They are] irritated by the presence of so many young Americans, who essentially usurped their position and took away a valuable income stream."

Were those guys better diggers? I asked. Other excavation teams I had studied included a complicated interplay of knowledge forms, coming from instruments and book learning, but also from lifelong experience with the landscape. I pointed out that at some dig sites, high-tech subsurface survey technologies have made local people's knowledge of the earth obsolete. Mike thought for several moments before responding:

Mike: I hope they don't. I think that we as archaeologists really should use the knowledge we get from locals. First off, those technologies are expensive, and not every field project can afford them. Second, locals do more than point you in the direction of finds. They give a history of the land, with intimate knowledge of the soil, particularly if they're farmers. For example, the idea of *terra grossa*, or fat soil. That's the condition of the soil after a human body decomposes under the surface. The soil actually does turn greasy. Farmers know this and pass along that knowledge to their kids and grandkids. By talking with them, we can get a sense for where human bodies might once have been, even if their biological traces have been consumed by the soil.

Fiona: In my field interviews last summer, I heard from several Italian archaeologists who swore that they have better knowledge of the soil than foreigners because it's "in the blood" and they know the matrices and materiality intrinsically.

Mike: I think that statement, "it's in the blood," says more about the emotional connection some Italian excavators have to the work they do here. But knowledge of excavating? That's from experience. You don't absorb that [through social osmosis]. Yes, there are Italian excavators who grew up playing with roof tiles and can spot a potsherd from a rock in an instant. I have to teach my American students how to do that—I get kids who definitely don't know these materials and basically haven't spent a lot of time digging in the earth. Some of them are very timid, very reluctant to make decisions. Some are too aggressive,

> but for the most part the problem is the opposite. They have to learn that getting into a trench is like riding a horse: you have to control the stratigraphy just as you control the horse.

I had never heard any archaeologist refer to stratigraphy this way. Interpreting, reading, deciphering, and unpacking—these terms were more likely to be used in describing archaeologists' attempt to be precise in environments beyond their control. Riding the stratigraphy as if it were a large animal was a novel idea. I knew from my own experience that archaeological excavation is a team effort. No one person controls stratigraphy. But the idea that some *do*—by special ability or secret mental access—remains popular in archaeology. One of the most dominant Italian archaeologists today is precisely this sort of figure.

DIVINATORY ARCHAEOLOGY

Andrea Carandini, a charismatic public intellectual and distinguished university professor, exemplifies a specifically divinatory engagement with the archaeological matrix. Carandini is a celebrity. He gives sold-out lectures to large crowds, ceremonially opens new museum shows and archaeological digs, and once hosted a talk show. He boasts a long list of glittering titles, including president of the Italian National Trust (Fondo Ambientale Italiano) and president of the Consiglio Superiore dei Beni Culturali, the advisory body of the Ministry of Culture. He was awarded the Order of Merit of the Italian Republic in 2006 and is regarded as one of the most powerful archaeologists of his generation, with great influence over young archaeologists' careers. His archaeological excavations in the city of Rome, published in multiple articles and books over the 1980s and 1990s, have garnered both praise and criticism.[27] In 1988 he and his excavation team made a sensational discovery: the remains of a defensive wall, dated by the archaeologists to the eighth century BCE, that could indicate a level of political power and urban sophistication achieved much earlier than in existing accounts of the history of the city. That in itself would be a remarkable finding. Carandini took the interpretation a step further. The *New York Times* reported:

> In addition, in perhaps the most contentious point associated with the discoveries, some of the archeologists working here say they have uncovered the first concrete evidence to support the legends that the foundation of Rome was a specific historical act. Most contemporary historians,

> however, dismiss as fable the tale that Romulus founded Rome in 753 B.C. and built a wall at the place where he and his twin brother, Remus, were suckled by a she-wolf in their infancy.[28]

"The foundation of Rome was a specific historical act": this interpretation amounted to a remarkable transformation of myth into fact. According to the myth, the twins were the sons of the god Mars and the mortal woman Rhea Silvia, a lineal descendant of Aeneas, who escaped the ruins of Troy after the Trojan War and settled in Italy. Their uncle Amulius, king of Alba Longa, wished to be rid of his young nephews and their mother but feared divine retribution if he killed them directly, so he ordered that the boys be exposed at birth. Indirect infanticide failed. Romulus and Remus were discovered by a nursing wolf, who allowed them to suckle, and were further nourished by a woodpecker who brought them food. Having been saved from death by the wolf and the bird, the boys were later taken in by a shepherd and his wife, who raised them to adulthood. Through a sequence of narrative twists, the brothers went on to kill King Amulius, reinstate their grandfather, Numitor, on the throne of Alba Longa, then leave to found their own city. Their dispute over the optimal location for that city led to Remus's death on the day Rome was founded, April 21, 753 BCE.

Many archaeologists regard the Romulus and Remus story as valuable chiefly because it illuminates ancient Romans' ideas about their origins. Few would go on the record as believers in the facticity of the story. Carandini challenged their position by arguing that mythographic texts—the literary sources that report the founding of the first settlement at Rome—are fundamentally reliable.[29] Building on *that* argument, it was possible and indeed logical, he said, to take the newly discovered wall as empirical evidence for the story of Romulus and Remus.[30] For historians and archaeologists skeptical of the argument, Carandini plays fast and loose with the data. But no one can deny his influence. He can "prove" the founding story because of his position and because his narrative aligns with broader cultural politics. Through his charismatic authority and mastery of artifacts, Carandini continues a long tradition of personalized cultural politics. Bringing his forceful personality into the work, he divines obscure knowledge from the earth and legitimizes the link between modern kin and ancient patria. Like the augurs consulted by the mythical brothers, Carandini interprets signs in the matrix that others cannot perceive. Divinatory knowledge is not accountable to science. It is "informal knowledge, orally transmitted, based on everyday experience (often including the accumulated experience of forebears and elders) and careful observation, which allows the observer to understand much more than can be directly seen."[31]

The "divinatory" approach, including but not limited to prophecy, conjecture, and puzzling, is a well-established style in archaeology. In Greece, Manolis Andronikos became the nation's archaeologist par excellence through his development of an experiential understanding of the past—the "sensory and somatic perception of its materiality."[32] Andronikos wrote extensively about his epistemological position:

> The time of the archaeological research is the "inhabited" time, that time that is not recorded with astronomic precision, but with cultural completion. . . . The tactile and visible image of historical time is composed of countless relics of human creation . . . in other words, the archaeologist sees and touches the content of history; this means that he perceives in a sensory manner the metaphysical truth of historical time.[33]

Advocating a poetic embrace of ancient monuments, Andronikos questioned the "cold schemata of our conceptual constructions" that barred access to the "images and voices of a human being who sees and talks to us from the depths of time."[34] Andronikos's method made archaeology relevant for ordinary Greek people and gave them direct and intimate contact with their ancestors and a basis for collective identity in the national context. Archaeological materials defied "cold" logic and offered a source of inspiration for the future.

Andronikos and Carandini were not marginalized eccentrics. They were internationally visible figures with prominent university positions. Their work was sanctioned by their respective governments. To read their interpretations, then, is to gain insight into the priorities and ideologies of national heritage institutions. That the origin story espoused by Carandini hinges on suckling is significant for framing cultural affinities in modern Italy. The milk of the wolf that kept Romulus and Remus alive metaphorically fed the Italian people in Fascist iconography, with its rich allusions to the Third Rome being the she-wolf. Milk kinship shifts the frame from elective affinity based on shared cultural meaning to sociogenetic kinship.[35] Sociogenesis, to paraphrase Norbert Elias, refers to long-range social structures that constitute a social field of relations and guide individuals' traditional habits of thought. Through "patterns of intertwining"—of people and of groups—"a social apparatus is established in which the constraints between people are permanently transformed into self-constraints." These self-constraints are a function of the hindsight and foresight instilled in a person from childhood, explained Elias, "in accordance with his integration in extensive chains of action, [which have] partly the form of conscious self-control and partly that of automatic habit."[36] Constraints and self-constraints being the backbone of the civilizing process, they shape individuals into subjects fit for the public sphere. Subjecthood, in this framework, extends beyond conscious obeisance to law or recognition of institutional symbols. It expands into the realm of unthought, unquestioned affiliations. The founding myth of Rome constitutes a particular kind of sociogenesis, that of imagined *sociogenetics*.

The matrix, in Carandini's work, performs the dual service of anchoring the wall in stratigraphic layers and originating the city's "father" in a miraculous birth story. To be Roman, then, at *any* point in history, is to share descent from the miracle of lupine lactation and to be able to justify — or simply imagine — social inclusions and exclusions based on milk kinship. It is plausible that no one, including Carandini, actually believes that Romulus and his brother were suckled by a wolf. But by asserting the historicity of the town's founding and insinuating an artifactual match with legend and myth, he suggests that all features of the myth should be taken seriously for the work of social explanation they have done and continue to do. The implication of this for state patrimony is that cultural sovereignty is extended through time as well as space, through a diachronic move that claims as "Roman" an ever-earlier origin point.

According to this logic, the soil is more than a repository of old things. It is also a creator, or more precisely an *auctor* — who "promotes, takes an initiative, who is the first to start some activity, who founds, who guarantees, and finally who is the 'author.'"[37] The soil, thus understood, takes on a mysterious quality, "the power which causes plants to grow and brings a law into existence."[38] We can add the power to bring into existence artifacts and ruins, and ancient cities so monumental and beguilingly ageless that people have at various points attributed them to otherworldly creators. If this sounds dangerously close to magic, it is because archaeological sites and artifacts have long been associated with the uncanny. Medieval monks in search of relics were cognizant that their excavations skirted the acceptable limits of the dark arts.[39] Cist graves and tomb shafts are thought by many to harbor ghosts and spirits, and archaeologists and tomb robbers alike share stories of dig site hauntings and the feeling of being watched by forces unseen.[40] Tomb robbers take care to protect themselves from curses, undergoing rituals of purification and absolution lest they disturb the ancestors' resting places. They pray to the eternal memory of other tomb robbers who died choking and gasping for air in a collapsed pit and made their own graves with the ancient ghouls below. At Vergilia and Campobello, excavators confessed to nightmares and anxiety after discovering infant and child skeletons.

Speaking metaphorically, the soil is the beginning and the end, the maker of artifacts and the repository of ruins and decay.[41] Language, symbols, and rituals balance the life/death power of the soil and ensure that the matrix remains a dynamic and constant presence in people's experience of the ancient past. If Mike is right to compare the soil to a horse, it is an untamed mustang.

Curatorial Mastery in the Open-Air Museum

Every museum relies on professional staff to conserve and interpret its collection. In the open-air museum, the "staff" is a mix of paid professionals—archaeologists like Corinna and Nino—and ordinary people, for whom expertise is based on being from a particular place. Everyday citizens comprise the ranks of unofficial docents and guides who turn archaeological rubble into historical treasure by signifying artifacts with personal and collective meaning. At the same time, they push against national narratives by recasting artifacts and ruins as products of local and regional histories. Inculcation starts young, with grade-school lessons about Italian history and art. Outside the classroom, the Gruppo Archeologico Romano (GAR) is one of several organizations that bring young people into close contact with archaeological sites and objects. GAR, a nonprofit club with chapters across the country, offers lectures on Italy's ancient history and sponsors trips to archaeological sites and museums. It redirects youthful curiosity into a formal civic obligation by teaching *i gruppi*, as GAR members are called, to safeguard the cultural patrimony of Italy. They occupy a place in society that is comparable to Scouts in the United States: earnest young people engaged in civic projects and group bonding. Relatively few *gruppi* become professional archaeologists, in the same way that few Little League players in the United States will be drafted to play for a Major League Baseball team. (There is stiff competition for employment in Italy's state archaeological service; in a typical year, there are far more applicants than there are open positions.)

The apprenticeship given to *gruppi* involves more than the transfer of professional or technical knowledge, though. It is *heritage* they are taught, a generalized notion that is one of the essential components of the global hierarchy of value.[42] Heritage differs from culture in its temporal horizon and its mechanisms of continuity. Culture transfers (or disappears) through practices, rituals, and collective consciousness. Heritage, by contrast, relies for its salience on idioms of property, wealth, and generational transfer, and it collapses individual experience of time into a generic, aspirational sense of collective eternity. Shared belief in cultural superiority is sustained by these ideas and experiences.

Nino, the trench master at Vergilia, never joined GAR. It wasn't his social scene, he explained, though as a teen he was aware of plenty of opportunities to join an excavation team or attend a summer pottery camp. Anyone growing up in Italy, he told me, gets "massive doses of archaeology" anyway. It is a normal part of life in the country. He elaborated: "The vast majority of modern Roman cities are successors of ancient Roman towns, so if you grow up here, archaeology is hardwired into the urban fabric. And then it is hardwired into us as people." *Hardwired* suggests a capacity or proclivity that is there from the start, programmed into a person's synapses. Reading Nino's words again, the circuitry links people and artifacts; archaeology is hardwired into the urban fabric, with the ghostly traces of buildings and monuments that long ago ceased to exist. Nino has the archaeologist's training and exactitude, and at the dig site he leveraged his professional credentials to command respect from the junior excavators. But as I got to know him, and particularly when we spoke privately, out of view of the undergraduate students, he let down his guard and grew more emotionally expressive. The scent of the earth and the dirt under one's fingernails, he wanted me to know, constituted real and intimate links with the national antique. This is "past mastery," or a thoroughgoing understanding of the community's history, including the negative aspects of heritage.[43] By operating primarily in, on, and of the soil, the open-air museum reassigns legitimate meaning making authority to those with intimate sensory knowledge.[44] The embodied experiences of the national antique come to matter more than what the historical record actually reveals.[45]

No museum is complete without guards, and in Italy the Art Squad provides a formal link between national patrimony and law enforcement. New recruits are rigorously trained, and selection is based on combat skills and knowledge of art history and archaeology. In a country where people mock the Carabinieri and show limited respect for the Polizia, it is noteworthy that Art Squad agents are admired. There are too few agents to be everywhere—as of 2018 there were just under three hundred, or one per thousand square kilometers. To compensate, their strategy is to make it seem as though they are invisible and unpredictable. They do this through high-profile raids ("blitzes") on tomb robbers and surveilling antiquities shops and auction catalogs, where Italian artifacts without legal paperwork are occasionally sold. The Art Squad also makes its presence evident through media broadcasts and highly choreographed repatriation events, as well as museum exhibitions and popular entertainment. Throughout the country it is easy to find such exhibitions chronicling the Art Squad's successes in recovering stolen artworks and artifacts. Graphic novels about tomb robbers and the archaeomafia are cult favorites, and the Art Squad website hosts a youth-oriented video game in which players go on patrol with a swashbuckling agent. Harnessing public fascination with artifact theft, in 2010 the Ministry of Culture partnered with the Italian environmental justice group Legambiente to sponsor a graphic art exhibition titled *Storie d'arte e di misfatti* (Stories of art and misdeeds). Prestigious graphic artists were recruited to recreate Art Squad investigations of looting and art theft. One of the exhibition's comics, *The Offering*, opens with a young child in ancient dress who gazes at the sky while cradling a small ceramic pot that is embellished with a solar emblem evocative of the red sun in the distance (fig. 2). The child then crouches to add the pot to a neat array of objects next to a solid-looking building that extends beyond the frame. The child, the pot, and the building disappear, and the middle register depicts layers of sediment accumulating over subsequent centuries. The layers grow heavier and rockier, until finally they are marked off by red-and-white police tape. In the bottom register, three Art Squad agents are in conversation. "It seems that a few meters beneath here are the remains of a prehistoric temple," says one. "It's possible," says another. "The lake is part of a vast archaeological site. Traces of ancient settlements can be found almost everywhere around here."

The lake has flooded the ancient settlement. It's worrying that the pile of backfill next to the agents suggests looters got to the site first. There is no sign of the child's offering or the other sacred gifts. Pinned to those slivers of fired earth were the supplicants' hopes and fervent prayers, vulnerable to the depredations of tomb robbers. *The Offering* is a metaphor for the tragic fragility of the country's antique legacy and for the grave responsibility of the state to protect it. "Traces of ancient settlements can be found almost everywhere"—the agent's site assessment knowingly points to the nation as a whole.

The heroism of the comic's agents is mirrored in news images of Art Squad police work. When the unit announces the successful conclusion of a raid on tomb robbers, the performative emphasis is on the sheer scale of the mission. In November 2019, for example, it was revealed that Operazione Achei (Operation Achaeans), involving some 350 federal and local law enforcement agents, shut down a "vast trafficking ring" that operated nationally and internationally.[46] Similarly, in a particularly dramatic

FIGURE 2. A comic by Sara Colaone from the *Storie d'arte e di misfatti* exhibition organized in 2010 by the Ministry of Culture and Italian environmental justice group Legambiente. *L'offerta* © 2010, drawings Sara Colaone, text Silvano Mezzavilla (by kind permission of Sara Colaone).

FIGURE 3. An agent of the Carabinieri's Art Squad (Tutela del Patrimonio Culturale) stands near an array of antiquities recovered by the Art Squad in an undercover investigation called Operazione Andromeda. July 2010. Press conference, Rome, Colosseum. Credit: Eidon Agenzia Fotografica.

staging of the Art Squad's effectiveness, the Colosseum in Rome was used as the backdrop to announce the conclusion of Operation Andromeda in July 2010. The two-year investigation netted over three hundred archaeological objects from Lazio, Puglia, and Sardinia—taken to Switzerland allegedly as part of a smuggling ring involving Giacomo Medici, who in 2004 was convicted of artifact smuggling. The "total asset value" for these objects was estimated to exceed €15 million.[47] The Operation Andromeda press conference emphasized the Art Squad's tireless, patient work to return the objects to Italian soil (*sul suolo italiano*) from which they had been "unjustly" removed, and "where they can testify to the cultural identity of the nation" (*dell'identità culturale della Nazione*).

The photo shoot featured a selection of the recovered artifacts arranged on a tiered platform on the Colosseum floor (fig. 3). The artifacts are a natural fit against the arched entryways and weathered stone of the Colosseum. The presiding Art Squad agent looks upward optimistically, reminiscent of the child supplicant in the cartoon. But this gesture is one of certainty rather than tentative hope, and the overall effect is of a country secure in its affairs—past, present, and future. It is no coincidence that cultural superiority sustains itself through these and other visible performances. Just as important as actually having cultural power is the perception and experience of being part of such a power—of *believing* that to be Italian is to have a share in the biggest, most beautiful and important and epochal body of culture that humanity has ever produced.

Securing cultural patrimony naturalizes the authority and reach of the Art Squad. When *tombaroli* are presented as enemies of the nation's heritage, it becomes expected and logical that the national government provides uniformed law enforcement agents to hunt and capture those enemies. The practices of such enforcement shape perceptions and determine outcomes. What we understand as disorder or illegality may be rooted in collective values and taboos, but it is instrumentalized and frequently subverted by state power.[48] State power has far-reaching effects on the discourse of civil society, with consequences not only for those arrested and prosecuted but for everyone else, in their imaginings of what society is and what it should be. Whether it is the airport security officer retrieving purloined artifacts from foreign visitors or the Art Squad arresting artifact traffickers, "to the degree that a society is democratic, [law enforcement] regulates every level of state power, from the humble to the grandiose."[49] If it is possible for Italians to arrive at their own creative understandings of the artifacts and ruins in their midst, outside the official strictures of national heritage, we will need to look in the shadow zones of everyday private life. We will need to look, too, at spatial and temporal relations that spill over the traditional confines of the nation-state.

ARTIFACTS AND DISTRIBUTED SOVEREIGNTY

By dissolving the traditional spatial layout of four walls and a roof, the open-air museum erases territorial boundaries between Italy and elsewhere. Italy, through its Art Squad and patrimony laws, can thereby claim artifacts and antiquities as its own even if those objects were manufactured outside the country and imported into it.[50] This was the case with the Euphronios krater, the ceramic wine-mixing bowl at the center of the Italian government's 2006 repatriation case against the Metropolitan Museum of Art in New York (fig. 4). That the krater had been made by Greek artisans in Greece was never really disputed, and Greek archaeological authorities rescinded their own country's claims on the object in the early months of the Italian government's investigation. What the Italians emphasized was the bowl's theft from a tomb in central Italy. Its being interred there for more than two thousand years made it part of

FIGURE 4. The Euphronios krater, a sixth-century BCE ceramic bowl showing scenes from Greek mythology. Thought to have been looted from Italy and illegally exported to the United States, the bowl was repatriated to Italy in January 2009. Credit: Wikimedia Commons.

Italian patrimony, even though it had no visible symbolic status in the modern era before its unveiling at the Met in 1972. It had symbolic power in Italy largely because it was stolen treasure from the national antique.

Through matricial claims making, the Art Squad's jurisdiction over archaeological materials is theoretically infinite. If the entire political territory is a museum, then all artifacts coming out of it are protected as *beni culturali*. The extensive policies, practices, and procedures that govern cultural artifacts and their circulation have profound implications for how we think about sovereignty and culture. In the late nineteenth century, Italy developed its own version of state sovereignty by turning its most valuable symbolic resource, artworks and antiquities, into a form of bureaucratic authority that could be exercised to accomplish political projects outside the realm of culture. This is *distributed sovereignty*, a term I borrow from Alfred Gell's work on distributed personhood to refer to the physical

FIGURE 5. *L'arte ritrovata* exhibition, Sale Terrene dei Musei Capitolani, Rome, 2019. Art Squad logo displayed with ancient vases recovered by the unit. Amassing antiquities in this way exemplifies the logic of accumulation in cultural power.

dispersion of state authority through material objects. That sovereignty takes material form is well established in classical theories of state power: maps, borders, and land treaties are concrete iterations of claims of sovereign territory. But territoriality is only one aspect of Italian sovereignty. Artworks and antiquities formally became sovereign attributes of the nation in 1909, and the political territory of Italy simultaneously became a cultural geography whose artifacts properly belonged to the state. In the century since then, the Italian state has effectively declared sovereignty over every artifact extracted from its territory. Conventional accounts of territorial sovereignty omit the crucial role portable objects play in constructing a distributed sovereignty that carries state power beyond cartographic boundaries. The Art Squad's jurisdiction travels with the artifacts, a subversion of traditional museological arrangements such that the "collection" expands to contain any object that traces back to Italian soil. Look again at figure 3, or at any of the innumerable displays of recovered artifacts such as those in figure 5, and note how the ancient objects stand in for modern nationhood—a metonymic play that is perfected by the absence of specific labels that would point to plural, conflicting subnational peoples and historical paths.

In his 1998 book *Art and Agency*, Gell developed a theory to explain the connection between people and objects. One of his central examples was Pol Pot's soldiers in the Cambodian civil war. The soldiers placed thousands of activated land mines across the Cambodian countryside, and those mines worked with lethal efficiency during the war and continued to kill unwitting passersby long after the war was over. The soldiers, Gell explained, were agents not only where their bodies were—where they had direct participation in immanent activity—but also where they had placed land mines. Their agency was in "many different places (and times) simultaneously."[51] The mines became components of their personhood, while the soldiers became possessors of distributed personhood. One way to write about these land mines would be to describe them as tools that turned the soldier into an elusive creator who activates the mine and is responsible for its detonation. Gell rejects that explanation. For him the mine is a component of a particular type of social identity and agency, an example of "physically detached fragments of the victim's 'distributed personhood'"—in other words, they can stand in for the person *as if being* the person.[52]

We are not accustomed to think of antiquities as parts of a person's body, much less an individual's personhood, but it is not such a stretch when we revert to the extensive discourse on state property, or the things and deeds of the body politic (*res publica*). An additional example brings the theory closer to archaeological artifacts and their circulation in the world. Gell posits a twofold definition of representing. His argument is worth quoting at length:

> The ideas of "representing" (like a picture) and "representing" (like an ambassador) are distinct, but none the less linked. An ambassador is a spatio-temporally detached fragment of his nation, who travels abroad and with whom foreigners can speak, "as if" they were speaking to his national government. Although ambassadors are real persons, they are also "fictions," like pictures, and their embassies are fictional mini-states within the state; just as pictures show us landscapes and personages who are "not really there." Although the Chinese ambassador to London does not look like China, or the Chinese government or people, he does *have to be visible,* and he does *visibly represent* China on official occasions. He does not look like China, but in London, China looks like him.[53]

When the Ministry of Culture of the Italian Republic agrees to lend objects to a museum outside Italy, the objects illustrate something about the nation's history to the museum's visitors. Simultaneously, the objects serve as ambassadors of the state to foreign audiences. Adapting Gell's theory to state-controlled archaeological materials, sovereignty lies not in the demarcated territory alone; artifacts have the attribute of sovereignty.[54]

Distributed sovereignty implies a physical connection, the way a parliamentary headquarters is part of the state by virtue of being on state territory and host to core state governance processes, and any architectonic elements that happen to fall from the parliamentary edifice are part of the state by dint of belonging properly to the building. But distributed sovereignty is something more than just instantiations of statehood spread around in time and space. It encompasses the essential notion that artifacts are *parts* of the state. Here it is helpful to think about Gell's idea of a "substantive part-whole (or part-part) relation"—the way that "smoke is a kind of 'part' of fire."[55] In this metaphor the relation between fire and smoke would be unclear if you didn't already know that smoke comprises tiny particles from combustion. Similarly, artifacts from the Italian soil became part of the matrix of Italy through scientific archaeology, and they became a part of the civic body through the state's legal framework. *Art that is of Italy* or *artifacts being of Italy* is a better approximation of the concept. The state is incomplete without them.

Once the Italian artifact is situated and given a context outside Italy, it is an index of Italianness, or of a particular milieu, to paraphrase Gell. In the social milieu of international cultural politics, Italian artifacts operate as part of the state, passing beyond the state's conventional jurisdiction and across its territorial boundaries. This idea is helpful for understanding the saga of the Venus of Cyrene, a complex geopolitical case in which the usual roles were reversed and Italy repatriated an artifact to Libya. The marble likeness of the goddess (fig. 6) was removed from Libya by Italian troops in 1913, when the country was under colonial occupation. Ninety years later, arguments about its rightful home—Italy or Libya—were framed by divergent understandings of what it means to be the country of origin. For Italy, the dispute traced back to much older discussions about Italy as a cultural "seat" (or quarry, as it has also been described) whose cultural heritage belongs to universal humanity; or Italy as an active state with territorial sovereignty and the right to control its patrimony objects as a component of self-determination. Author versus supplier, quarry versus state; these are central binaries in cultural power and distributed sovereignty.

Artifact politics are a high-stakes arena. I will return to the Venus of Cyrene, and her intimate links with the public image of Silvio Berlusconi and Muammar Qaddafi. But high-profile repatriations are only one possible process whereby artifacts extend the state. As we will see in chapter 2, fragments of Roman, Etruscan, and southern Italian blackware pottery became appendages of the state when they were classified using ethnonyms (Pelasgian, Villanovan, and so forth). The classifications

FIGURE 6. Marble statue of Venus found in Cyrene, Libya, by Italian soldiers in 1913 and taken to Italy for public display. It has featured prominently in nationalist imagery, and after a protracted repatriation battle it was restored to the government of Libya in 2008. First century BCE. © A. Dagli Orti/De Agostini Picture Library/Bridgeman Images.

linked pottery fragments with specific hyperlocal places, people, and cultures, and reestablished the soil as a de facto author of cultures whose material detritus belonged, by right, to the state.

"Every Scrap Is Ours"

Given its immense cultural wealth, one might expect the Italian government to be willing to release some of it—through sales or long-term loans to recognized cultural institutions, for example, or simply by turning a blind eye to the foreign tourists caught at airports with antique paving stones in their suitcases.[56] This presupposition is a flash point among cultural administrators in Rome. In the course of my fieldwork, I frequently heard from museum staff that the storerooms in their institutions were filled to bursting with objects and that the museum personnel lacked adequate resources to study, conserve, and display their inventory. One museum-based archaeologist, whom I interviewed in Rome, requested that I not use her real name because she feared professional reprisals for criticizing the repatriation work of the Ministry of Culture (MiBAC)[57] and the Art Squad. I'll call her Giovanna. Giovanna is a thirty-four-year-old native of Italy who completed her primary university training in Pisa. Finding no archaeology jobs in Italy after graduating, she moved to Germany and then Switzerland, where she did museum-based conservation and published papers on the Italian dig sites, attempting to remain active (an uphill battle given the culture of professional archaeology in Italy, which is structured around intimate patronage ties).

Giovanna and I met at the terrace café next to the National Gallery of Modern Art. She'd heard about my research project from a mutual friend, and when she introduced herself through a Facebook message, she told me she thought I should hear from a "true Italian archaeologist" for an alternative view of repatriation. Foreigners and outsiders to the museum system were, she felt, too easily impressed by the moral simplicity of repatriation as presented by Ministry of Culture and Art Squad officials. Shortly before our meeting, I visited an exhibition at the Castel Sant'Angelo in Rome. The exhibition showcased recently recovered artifacts and celebrated the Art Squad's repatriation successes. When I mentioned the exhibition to Giovanna, she smiled and shook her head. She said:

> What is frustrating to me, and I think this is something that many, many archaeologists here cannot accept, is the constant push to recover artifacts when, in fact, we desperately need money to conserve and preserve.

> Foreigners think that Pompeii [which is experiencing widespread deterioration] is the worst of it. I can show you ten Pompeiis right here in the city of Rome. [With repatriation,] OK, you say you want to take back the Morgantina Aphrodite or the Euphronios krater. I understand why. Such cases, they generate a lot of interest and hopefully send a message that foreign museums must stop purchasing antiquities that have a questionable provenance. But look more closely and you see that much of the recovered items, they are—what? Not so significant. I mean, perhaps significant to a specialist, but not to the public, not to the curators, and they won't be included in exhibitions or catalogs. It might be better to move our attention from repatriation to patrimony [*dal rimpatrio al patrimonio*]. I mean to say, patrimony is taking good care of what we already have.

For Giovanna, repatriation actually works against the broader investment in patrimony because it siphons off resources that would otherwise go to preserving objects and monuments that are languishing in the basements of Italian museums or are insufficiently protected out in the open.

> This is something that won't ever get me a job with MiBAC,[58] but who cares? I think that if we really care about artifacts, then sometimes the best thing is to leave them [where they are]. Again, I don't mean the masterpieces that the Met and the Getty flaunt at us. I mean the little things—the coins, ceramics, miniature sculptures, that we already have so many of. Let them remain where they are presumably cared for better than we can [care for them].

Giovanna's position was predicated on a distinction between masterpieces (her phrase in Italian was *i pezzi più preziosi*) and "the unimportant things" (*le cose insignificanti*). Her take on antiquities was informed by her professional interest in artifacts as scientific objects for study and conservation. She stressed her commitment to caring for the artifacts already unearthed and held in public collections in Italy. But if Giovanna represents, as she suggested to me, the silent majority of archaeologists working in the country, the Carabinieri Art Squad presents the official position. It is an uncompromising one. I was granted an interview with a top-ranking officer in November 2012. The meeting took place in the Palazzo Sant'Ignazio in Rome, where the Art Squad has its headquarters.

I was escorted to his office by an assistant and seated in front of the officer's impressive desk. Flanking the desk were two flags, the Italian tricolor and one bearing the Art Squad seal. Framed certificates attested to his long and successful career in the Carabinieri. He was friendly and efficient, and he punctuated his Italian with decisive hand gestures and dramatic pauses. "The Italian state owns everything [of cultural importance]. It is prohibited to sell anything. Nothing goes to foreign museums or private collections anymore." Why, I asked him, is it important to track everything? I shared a picture on my iPad, showing a recent Art Squad press conference announcing the recovery of Italian artifacts from smugglers. The event featured long tables that displayed numerous ceramic vessels and tiny bronze coins. It was an impressive display and effectively conveyed the size of the haul. But they were fairly unremarkable artifacts in the great scheme of things, unlikely to be icons of identity to the majority of Italians. Surely these little things could be given away or sold without harming the national culture? I tested a version of Giovanna's position. Why not prioritize the artifacts already in museum storage and sell or give away some portion of the rest?

What the Art Squad officer said in response captured the essence of the Italian model of cultural patrimony. "Every single scrap is Italy's," he replied. "The job of the Art Squad is to make sure that the state controls what it owns. We do this for the Italian people." The issue is not whether a workaday pot or coin is aesthetically splendid or has potential to change the course of history. The issue, he insisted, is rightful ownership. "To release the little things and pretend they are not important is to weaken the entire foundation of our heritage." The overall display of authority at the meeting was unambiguous: I was to leave the office thoroughly convinced of the scale and seriousness of the Art Squad's mission.

If the state is seen to allow even a scrap to fall through the cracks of law enforcement or tolerate private collecting, it cedes control of culture to rival cultural actors. The Ministry of Culture and the Art Squad guard against the risk that those actors might use the nation's cultural objects in ways that threaten the state's privileged position. His emphasis also contradicted Giovanna's preference for selective preservation as a sensible approach to protecting artifacts already in Italy. Working toward the same general goal as Giovanna—patrimony protection—but from a starkly different institutional perspective, the officer got to the heart of the matter: by winning back antiquities, the world's greatest cultural power is continually tested, replenished, and augmented.

THE ACCUMULATION OF PATRIMONY CAPITAL

Winning them back and piling them up—this is the simplified recipe for the logic of patrimony capital accumulation developed in Italy since the beginning of the twentieth century. Scholars from a range of disciplines have theorized logics of accumulation in different contexts of capital acquisition. In her study of big data surveillance, for example, Shoshana Zuboff describes a logic of accumulation in which technologies of information capture, processing, and sorting determine "what is measured, and what is passed over; how resources and people are allocated and organized; who is valued in what roles; what activities are undertaken—and to what purpose."[59] In short, they do not so much reflect social values and interests as impose a new social order. This new logic of accumulation "produces its own social relations and with that its conceptions and uses of authority and power."[60] In a similar vein, in their study of Italian-Chinese firm collaborations in the fashion industry, Lisa Rofel and Sylvia J. Yanagisako argue that accumulating capital to invest in the pursuit of further wealth is typically accompanied by a rearrangement of social relations to support this goal.[61] As cultural tropes and practices grow up around these rearranged relations, capital accumulation and reinvestment becomes normalized—becomes just the way things are.

Building on these and related insights, we can think in terms of a logic of accumulation of state patrimony that emphasizes enlargement, or the quantitative scale of artifactual and artistic culture. This shift was slowly underway in the nineteenth century, with Italian archaeologists' recognition that ceramics, architectonic fragments, tools, and other mundane archaeological materials had scholarly and cultural value—a departure from earlier approaches that gave priority to select items admired for their beauty and style. It was accelerated in 1909 when the country's first patrimony nationalization law declared the state the collective owner of all artworks and archaeological artifacts of a certain age. And it was given enhanced political and institutional firepower in the late 1960s and 1970s when cultural internationalism and domestic politics combined to assert Italy's right to pursue artworks and artifacts illegally extracted from its soil. The logic of accumulation absorbed and eventually replaced a *logic of acquisition* that had operated for centuries among Italian and European elites, whereby the circumstances of an object's discovery, purchase, or gift exchange were the central interest. Acquisition circumstances advertised owners' taste and social capital, placing them or their collections in a lineage of prestigious collectors. Accumulation, by contrast, makes the Italian state the only legitimate collector of its own patrimony.

Theorizing a logic of accumulation to explain the Italian Republic's state patrimony framework comes with a risk: namely that accumulation becomes structurally determined to the point that it is immune to social and political change. Indeed, accumulation cannot explain variation in the timing of particular national cultural heritage legal enactments. A certain level of patrimony accumulation was a necessary condition for the pivotal legal changes in 1909, 1939, and 2006, in other words, but is not sufficient to explain the Italian model of cultural patrimony. Accordingly, we need an explanatory framework that accounts for artifacts' multi-dimensional value in fluctuating cultural and political conditions. For this task, it is helpful to look again at the ongoing debate about why, precisely, the country manages cultural assets as it does.

When critics of the Italian model evaluate its so-called retentionist policies, they reject the argument that every artifact and artwork is significant for the Italian community's cultural identity. Cultural property lawyer Joshua Wolkoff provides a representative critique: "It is difficult for Italy to allege a strong emotional attachment to a work it never knew existed."[62] If the essence of the model was symbolic interpretation, the argument could have merit. But it is not. The essence is that the artifacts must be physically accounted for. An artifact may not symbolize a historical figure or event. It may not symbolize anything. It may be important, primarily, because it exists as a material thing in the world. Anthropologists, philosophers, and sociologists, among others, have generated a robust discussion about the sensorial and ephemeral effects of material qualities.[63] But physicality has massive *non-hermeneutic* significance in shaping social spaces and relational encounters, such that conscious interpretations are unnecessary. In this line of thought, the mediality of an object has important consequences for the nature of the response it elicits.

Literary theorist Hans Gumbrecht suggests that all human relationships with the world consist of meaning- *and* presence-based relations, and he calls for a "reconfiguration of some of the conditions of knowledge production within the humanities" that challenges the primacy of interpretation.[64] "To form an idea of what this thing may be in relation to us" is one way of understanding meaning, but it is not necessarily the most helpful when analyzing cultural objects. It is artifacts' steady presence that anchors people in daily rhythms of practice and relation and that shapes these practices and relations in ways that are overlooked because they become intuitive and unthought. We can recall Nino's experience that as a result of exposure to high doses of archaeology from infancy, archaeology is hardwired into Italians. He specified that archaeological materials, ranging in size and age, are ubiquitous in the urban fabric. Italians are surrounded by them. They fundamentally and intimately coexist, such that artifacts anchor Italians in time and space. What is at stake here for cultural power is the relationship between epistemology and ontology, or the scaffold of knowledge and the basis of existing in the world.

We can extend Nino's insight by considering presence effects in other artifactual spheres. Based on her work with the Shipibo, a Peruvian Amazonian community, anthropologist Alaka Wali identifies specific presence effects in traditional artifacts. The production and physical proximity of ceramics and textiles "enables Shipibo people to maintain close connections to their homeland environment and to their long-enduring belief system."[65] Artifactual loss from exportation or stopped domestic production alerts Shipibo men and women to the objects' value for maintaining identity and land rights. Similarly, in his archaeological investigation of prehistoric communities on Bodmin Moor (southwest Cornwall), Christopher Tilley posited a phenomenology of landscape in which stones have specific identity-forming power. The practice of setting up stones in deliberate designs had "potent structuring effects on the biographies of individuals, groups and collectivities. It provided a primary medium through which power was reproduced. . . . One of the purposes of using and visiting these monuments was to inform and sediment in the mind a sense of awe and wonder, of the significance of the place, and its ancestral connotations, the events which had taken place there and the telling of myths recounting the spirit powers inhabiting it."[66] Placing monuments in the landscape had vital significance in the "creation, reproduction and articulation of authority," in a relationship between the monument specialists and those who were guided through community life to and by the monuments.

The "oscillation between meaning and presence," as Gumbrecht would say, explains the effect of the Shipibo artifacts and the Neolithic stone monuments.[67] What presence effects give us is better analytical purchase on scale and power in human-artifactual relations. To retain and repatriate antiquities, then, is in part to retain control over the physical structures of Italian community life.

SEAT OF THE ARTS TO CULTURAL POWER

Like the belief in cultural superiority, symbolic capital had to be worked at. Italy's cultural assets are equal in meaning and historical substance to other countries' artworks and artifacts. What sets Italy apart is that it happens to have so many of the objects and historical chapters that we have decided to care about. State officials point to an impressive inventory:

nearly five thousand museums, two thousand listed archaeological zones, and fifty-five UNESCO World Heritage sites, more than any other country. (China, long in second place on the UNESCO list, tied Italy in 2020. It has a landmass thirty-two times Italy's.) So powerful is Italy's symbolic capital that 31 percent of *all* UNESCO World Heritage site inscriptions in other countries include Italy as a cultural reference point.[68] These are sites with no direct link to Italians or the formal territory of Italy. The symbolic capital of an object or building "depends on its attachment to meaningful geographies," and Italy's geography reigns supreme in symbolic meaning and cultural resonance.[69]

For Enlightenment elites, Italy's purpose—its reason for existing—was cultural refinement. Grand Tourists went there to study antiquities, sketch bucolic landscapes, and party in the seamy brothels of Naples and Rome.[70] Culturally robust yet politically weak, "Rome" belonged to everybody and to nobody in particular. Roman antiquities, like the Latin language, were part of Enlightenment Europe's lingua franca. The Romans of the eighteenth century were, crudely speaking, politically nonthreatening and backward, in a charming way that imbued the classical remnants with a ruddy authenticity yet left contemporary Italians in a disempowered position of systemic "humbling."[71]

The mass export of art and antiquities from Italy would later inflame official discourse—indeed, we will see that cries of despoliation have come in specific sociopolitical contexts in modern Italy's history—but in the eighteenth century it was taken for granted. Italy was dismissed as incapable of preserving its antique endowment. Napoleon's appropriation, in 1796, of hundreds of works from cities across the Italian peninsula reaffirmed Italy's geopolitical role. Condemning Napoleon's actions in a series of published letters, French philosopher Antoine Quatremère de Quincy defended the bond between artworks and their "homeland." The works, he said, belonged in Italy because they could be properly appreciated only in their native context. Appreciation, according to Quatremère de Quincy, was the prerogative of enlightened scholars and connoisseurs. Above all, keeping Italian artworks in Italy protected the natural order of things: "Just as careless pruning can kill a tree, unwisely removing the models of antiquity from their natural trunk would dry up the sap that the modern culture of Rome passes into all the branches of learned Europe."[72] Quatremère de Quincy's metaphor of sap points to an important underlying idea: that the antiquities belong to Rome in a natural way, like the city's seven hills or its famous pine trees. Further, alienating an antiquity from its natural setting enfeebles the entire culture by undermining the knowledge that can be drawn from it. "The decomposition of the museum of Rome," he wrote, "would be the death of its knowledge, of which unity is the primary principle." The museum of Rome had literal and figural meaning. At its broadest, it referred to an Italy-wide collection of art, monuments, and antiquities. "To divide it is to destroy it."[73]

The natural order of things was highly convenient to Quatremère de Quincy and his French, British, Austrian, and Prussian counterparts. It required that northern European elites continue to have Rome as an intact classical specimen for their own development and maturation as diplomats, officers of the state, and intellectuals. In the political thinking of nineteenth-century Europe, Italy was a backwater. By all conventional measures of development, Italy lagged behind Great Britain, France, Prussia, Austria, and Russia.[74] In 1861 Italy's national wealth was one-third that of Prussia or France and one-quarter that of Great Britain, and in 1893 per capita income in Italy was roughly a quarter of England's and a third of France's.[75] High infant mortality rates (220 per thousand) and low life expectancy due to disease, malnutrition, and hard physical labor presented significant obstacles to economic growth and civic stability.[76] These demographic and epidemiological challenges sustained a widespread belief that Italy was stuck. Buttressing this myth was a second one, namely that of Italy as a geographical and cultural *idea* rather than a political unit.

The territory we now think of as Italy was a dual entity: "Rome" was a prestigious cultural destination disconnected from the modern polities and organizational structures of "Italy."[77] This perception radically distanced contemporary Italians from the achievements of historical artworks and artifacts. Nineteenth-century Italians were neither authors of nor heirs to their past, but rather historical placeholders whose role was to serve as pliant shepherds, *ciceroni*, and hoteliers to cosmopolitan connoisseurs and collectors. Against the backwater thesis, however, a complex process of cultural reappropriation was under way as Italian scholars and state officials turned rural archaeology into an asset. Building the national antique into a source of cultural power has involved a concerted effort of law, scholarship, state bureaucracy, and citizens' buy-in—even if some of those citizens have always refused to play by the rules.

Back at Vergilia, what Corinna knew well, and what I would come to understand in the following months, was that the national antique is held together by a tenuous assemblage of interests among citizens, cultural professionals, and state bureaucrats. All these people have something to say about Italy's cultural patrimony and its future, but they often disagree about whose patrimony it is, what it means, and how much money to spend to stave off ruin and decay. But decay is also a permanent feature of historic conservation in the city of Rome, being the outcome of material entropy and bureaucrats' decisions. And thieving, smuggling, localism, legal skepticism, and graft are not, it turns out, aberrations in an otherwise smooth-running system of national patrimony.[78] These things *are* the system, and they are vital to understanding the national antique and the belief in cultural superiority.

Intimacy and Embarrassment inside the National Antique

To construct themselves as morally acceptable participants in the open-air museum, tomb robbers mobilize two core narratives. The first is populist: antiquities belong to the people, and the people should have a say in how such objects are interpreted, evaluated, and displayed. Within this narrative, keeping objects to study or admire and giving them as gifts to friends and loved ones are the markers of proper populist engagement with antiquities. The second is preservationist. Tomb robbers see themselves as performing an invaluable service by unearthing long-hidden objects and taking care of them *outside the museum system*. Maligning museums as catering primarily to foreign tourists, Italian tomb robbers justify their digging activities as being in solidarity with their neighbors and kin. When Italian politicians boast that Italy has half or more of the world's cultural treasures, tomb robbers write themselves in as heroes who safeguard those encrusted prizes. They do this, in part, by committing the very crimes the Art Squad relies on to justify its expansive powers, and by supplying local stories, claims, and props that keep Italians emotionally and pragmatically invested in a construct—the open-air museum—that would otherwise seem abstract and impersonal.

Tomb robbers are one reason Italy is said to be systemically dysfunctional. This dysfunction is held to be a societal fault—rooted in the culture—rather than a bureaucratic one. Successive government dissolutions, political scandals, and economic failures from the twentieth-century annals of Italy are routinely trotted out as proof of the country's inability to manage its affairs. In the cultural realm, Italy's embarrassment of riches is literally embarrassing when its treasures crumble from neglect. The sorry case of the ancient city of Pompeii has become a favorite scapegoat for the foreign press. When large portions of a two-thousand-year-old house fell to the ground in 2010, media coverage focused on the ineptitude of local cultural officials. One British newspaper wrote:

> Collapses at the ancient site of Pompeii underline what experts have been warning for years: Italy's priceless cultural heritage is slowly but surely disintegrating and the famous archeological site's decay is a metaphor for the nation.
>
> With chunks falling off Rome's Colosseum and the seemingly inexorable decline and fall of Venice, the world looks on anxiously to see if the rot can be stopped. Few countries have a greater wealth of cultural and archaeological marvels than Italy, but experts warn that few nations are as complacent about them.[79]

"The site's decay is a metaphor for the nation." The text presents the physical changes at Pompeii as a perfect example of professional ineptitude, with the implication that political corruption—a perennial accusation against the Italian state—is at the heart of the matter. *Rot, decline,* and *complacency*: this is code for a struggling state, and even though it is language that its own citizens mobilize when frustration with bureaucracy boils over, they feel self-conscious when it is applied to Italians by foreigners. Having a large number of artistic treasures is a luxury; it requires constant investment to maintain. Even as Italians recognize the state's inability to pay for the entirety of this luxury, and disagree about how to address the shortfall, foreign ridicule forges a sense of collective pride and defensiveness.

Corruption and dysfunction are components of the identities and relations that flourish in zones of intimacy, outside the gaze of external observers. It is this framework of intimacy that familiarizes Italians with bases of power and teaches them strategies of coping and evasion. The concept helps explain why Corinna could grumble to Nino about the ineffectiveness of the Carabinieri but why he silenced that line of complaint when the non-Italian observer (me) started asking questions. The national antique is a prominent discursive thread of public culture, and cultural intimates are fluent in this discourse even if they deviate from it in practice. The production of identities meant to be public "will create, of necessity, a special terrain of things, relations, and activities that cannot themselves be public but are essential aspects of whatever reality and value public things might possess."[80] Here, that special terrain is populated by people figuring out how to live in a country sworn to patrimony protection but where artifacts and ruins are seen as both blessing and curse.

I never did find the Vergilia tomb robbers. It remains unclear whether they got away because they were insiders with a lucky break or outsiders who meticulously planned the heist. The tomb robbers I talked to swore they would never steal artifacts from an archaeologist's locked cabinet. That's the behavior of common thieves, they said, of the lowliest of *tombaroli*. Honorable diggers do their own prospecting and digging. Honorable diggers understand the lay of the land, and if they violate the archaeologists' protocols, it's because they have their own method, one that combines traditional knowledge of the soil with respect for a local history that gets short shrift in official, national cultural projects. It is easy to read their explanations as farce: all that symbolic distancing and double-jointed twisting of reality when a thief is still a thief. Yet those of us on the "good" side—the law-abiding, fare-paying visitors to the open-air museum—are also guilty of a certain willful blindness when we distance ourselves from tomb robbing. In Italy tomb robbing is both an actual criminal act and a mode of thought in which artifacts are primarily valued for their capital potential through extraction from the ground.

✷ CHAPTER 2 ✷

The American Price

In 1911 the British writer Saki published a short story that skewered the Italian model. Henri Deplis is a traveling salesman from Luxembourg who has the luck to inherit money from a distant relative. He is in northern Italy when he receives the news, and while the inheritance is no fortune, it is enough for him to delay his return home and indulge his appetite for fine things. He splurges on good wine and other treats, but the biggest extravagance is a purchase from the municipality's most revered artist. Signor Andreas Pincini is a master tattooist, and the work he creates on Deplis's body is a showstopper. Covering his client's back "from the collar-bone down to the waistline," Pincini's tattoo is a stunning picture of the fall of Icarus. Immediately proclaimed to be Pincini's finest work, it is also his last; the artist dies shortly afterward, before Deplis can pay him. This is when Deplis's troubles begin.

Pincini's widow demands full payment from Deplis, but at this point his legacy has been greatly spent down. When Deplis meekly suggests paying a fraction of the sum originally agreed, the insulted widow cancels the bill of sale and goes to the municipal authorities with a stunning offer: she will donate the Icarus tattoo, her late husband's last major work, to the town as an enlisted artistic treasure. The authorities promptly accept. To his horror, Deplis realizes that the artwork on his skin now has legal standing above and beyond his person, and he is no longer a free man. Deplis cannot bathe in the public bathhouse because it might damage the *Fall of Icarus*. He cannot display the tattoo without permission from the municipal authorities. When he attempts to cross the border into France, the Italian border guards stop him, invoking "the stringent law that forbids the export of Italian works of art." Diplomatic efforts between the Luxembourg and Italian governments having failed, Henri Deplis, commercial traveler, and the *Fall of Icarus* (by the late Pincini, Andreas) are declared property of Bergamo and thus a protected cultural asset of the Italian nation. After years of miserable enchainment to Icarus, trapped in Italy and unable to return home, Deplis is finally released when an acid attack at an anarchist convention in Genoa dissolves the tattoo and Deplis is no longer of artistic interest to the country.

The sad plight of Henri Deplis is fiction, of course, from Saki's short story "The Background."[1] But the cultural anxieties embedded in the story are real. Saki wrote his story in 1911, two years after the passage of Italy's cultural patrimony law. The contemporary political satire is clear: while Deplis is a fool for spending his inheritance on a tattoo, the Italian government is ridiculous for zealously enforcing the law and for giving an artwork priority over the rights of a human being. In Saki's telling, Deplis's attacker is sentenced to seven years in prison for defacing a national art treasure, not for maliciously wounding Deplis. Saki places Deplis's body at the heart of his story, and the dilemma of the body's autonomy confronts the logic of state patrimony. Deplis's body can be understood as a metaphor for the public itself, that complex social entity whose political and cultural dispositions do not always align. Saki (the pen name used by H. H. Munro) was British, and his protagonist is from Luxembourg. The Italian innovation he derided is now the status quo. Italian policymakers and intellectuals were completing a centuries-long process of converting art appreciation into cultural power. Italian artworks and antiquities had long been regarded as a substantive asset with material, economic, and territorial value. Nationalizing those prized cultural objects into state-owned assets constituted a novel conjunction of the corporeal and symbolic elements of culture.[2]

Saki does not specify his motive in "The Background," but it may have been connected with a law passed by the Italian government in June 1909: Decreto legislativo 364/1909, "Sui Beni d'Interesse Storico-Artistico" ("Pertaining to Goods of Historic and Artistic Interest"). It had far-reaching consequences. Henceforth all "immovable and movable objects" made fifty years ago or earlier, "in the ground and above it, having a historical, archaeological, and artistic interest to the nation," were considered to be the permanent property of the Italian state. Passing the law was a bruising political battle. Antiquities collectors and dealers, and others with entrenched interests in the art market, lobbied against it and warned that nationalizing the country's artistic stock would harm the interests of ordinary Italians. The art market, they argued, was an essential platform for conveying Italian diplomacy abroad. Not only did foreign elites' interest in Italian art and history confer legitimacy on the country; they were also seen to have a *right* to possess Roman antiquities, being equal heirs to the classical tradition. Defenders of the art market, in sum, argued that it was good for Italy's political and economic dealings to sell its antiquities and that it was not within Italy's authority to restrict the circulation of goods that were of universal interest.

Why did the law pass in spite of powerful and very vocal opposition, and what compromises were made to protect the art trade? How was the labor of artifact extraction absorbed into the new cultural heritage framework? These questions are the focus of the current chapter, which traces the development of earlier models that laid the groundwork for the symbolic transfer of cultural wealth to the nation-state in 1909. I will answer them with evidence from political speeches, export petitions, newspaper articles, unpublished personal letters, and other primary source materials. We will see that the 1909 law passed, in part, because it managed to preserve the *form* of a world republic of antiquities while shifting the basis of its authority from foreign elites to the Italian state. Over a forty-year period, the unified Italian government initiated a series of reforms in the museum, archaeological, and market sectors, culminating in the legal shift that ensnared the fictional Henri Deplis. In writing the story of a nation's rise to power, it is tempting to focus on the obvious political players: the armies, monarchs, religious institutions, and acts of God that give dramatic color to social change. The art market is typically omitted from narratives of state formation or is, at best, a bit player. That approach would be a mistake for the study of Italy, however, where the art market presented a number of early challenges to nation-state sovereignty. Establishing a national archaeological patrimony, and declaring state authority over it, required that private collectors—particularly foreign ones—be redefined as a single opponent and rebranded as an existential threat to the country. It required, too, that artworks and antiquities be recast as having collective value—a symbolic worth that transcended any particular collector or dynastic family.

The World Order of Antiquities and Pre-unification Patrimony Capital

For centuries, humanists across Europe recognized Italy as the heartland of Roman civilization. Manuscripts and reprints of ancient texts circulated among educated readers, followed later by antiquities. Popes, cardinals, wealthy merchants, and eventually princes and aristocrats from other European kingdoms paid high prices for discovered works and commissioned excavators to find and retrieve new ones. Collections of fine art, Martha Feldman explains, were part of a system of "a world order in which ranks cascaded downward in the great chain of being from God to sovereign or ruling class to the various classes and orders below" (2007, 6). Exchange and admiration were structured by entrenched economic and political interests, and elites were not prepared to relinquish control over Italy's ancient treasures.

This was the order of things: being Europe's "seat of the arts" meant providing the material supports for the great chain of being. Antiquities and artworks conveyed dynastic messages that enhanced the collector's position in the agonistic field of elite social relations. Paintings, tapestries, and sculptures were curated and displayed in specific configurations intended to signal their owners' acculturation, taste, and power. Marble portrait busts of Roman emperors and members of the imperial family, for example, preferably set up in manorial gardens or urban courtyards, served as status symbols by connecting the owners' families with the antique and suggesting that "they descended from Caesar himself."[3]

Antiquities in a private palace were doing something else important: they were advertising the owners' access to extensive resources. Acquiring marble statues and portrait busts required manpower and machinery to exhume and move them, skilled artisans to make necessary repairs, masons to create appropriately ornate bases for statues, carvers to chisel base inscriptions, and in some palaces a *letterato* with sufficient knowledge of art history to explain the works' history and meaning to visitors. Crucially, elite collecting depended on diggers who carried artifacts out of the ground and into the palaces. Despite numerous legislative initiatives to combat this activity, deliberate violations were rampant. Some influential patrons "made use of (and assured impunity for) diggers who, using strong-arm tactics, carried out undisturbed whatever they had been ordered to do"—occasionally even threatening to kill the officials in charge of monitoring excavation activities.[4] Antiquities, then, were produced by networks of people, tools, and institutions, and by their very presence in a palace they nodded graciously to the hidden labor of extraction that was at the owner's command.

The Grand Tour expanded the field of antiquities collecting from an exclusive network of European elites to a sprawling touristic and commercial trade. From the late seventeenth century, wealthy Britons toured the main cultural sites of Italy, in some cases spending years on an itinerary of cathedrals, salons, Roman ruins, *palazzi*, and gardens. Along the way, Grand Tourists purchased artworks and antiquities that they would take back to Britain and display in private residences. A vast industry grew up to support their collecting, with *ciceroni*, or expert guides, serving as liaisons between Grand Tourists and local artisans and excavators. For the right price, *ciceroni* could broker a staged discovery at an archaeological site, letting the wealthy visitor feign pleasure at finding his own ancient treasure. With the recovery of foreign tourism after the Napoleonic invasion and then the rise of mass tourism, *ciceroni* were supplemented by shops in Rome and Naples that maintained a supply of affordable ancient coins, cameos, ceramics, and statuettes. Just as staged excavations indulged the fantasy of discovery, so did selecting an antiquity from an urban shop. Augusto Castellani, a Rome-based jeweler and antiquities dealer, decorated the interior of his shop to look like an Etruscan tomb and encouraged his visitors to imagine they were plumbing the distant past. In these ritualized and highly structured commercial transactions, the buyer was encouraged to participate in an adventure. *Ciceroni* and dealers supplied them with a story about how they acquired the object. Along with the provenance, or ownership history, of the artifact, the discovery story functioned as an embellishment to the original work and increased its social and market value.

Attempts to protect the church's interests in classical art and archaeology accelerated in the early nineteenth century, after the restoration to Italy of artworks and antiquities that Napoleon had plundered in 1796. Abbot Carlo Fea (1753–1836), commissioner of antiquities and excavations for the Papal States, introduced a series of measures, including excavation licenses and regulatory oversight, meant to improve the methods of digging for artifacts. Despite formal rules protecting classical sites from despoliation, deliberate destruction, and excessive digging, authorities had few resources to enforce those rules, and the rules were easily circumvented by procedural loopholes and routine bribery. Wealthy landowners often employed local peasants and tenants to dig for artifacts on their land, with valuable finds going to the landowners' own collections or being sold through the international art market. Archaeological materials were regarded as *potential* antiquities, meaning they could attain the status of coveted, collectible artistic and historic objects that marked them as salable items. By law and by convention, antiquities were eligible to be sold for profit or displayed in the home for private enjoyment, as the owner saw fit. As Ronald Ridley (2009) shows, Fea doubted the basic logic of that view. Antiquities were not market goods, Fea argued, or trophies for the aggrandizement of individual collectors. They were public goods belonging to the church. From at least the Middle Ages, Fea pointed out, popes had a sacred duty to protect the patrimony of Rome and therefore to act as stewards of antiquity for the benefit of the public.

Hundreds of rules and procedures had come and gone through the years, all with the broad intention of keeping artistic treasures in the domain of the Papal States. Fea's contribution was to rationalize the patchwork of cultural patrimony laws and organize them into a centralized system of enforcement mechanisms. This system was approved by Pope Pius VII. It is remembered today for placing Italy's artworks and antiquities into a "framework of industry" in which they had economic and pedagogical value for the public.[5] The state now had a legal obligation to block the exploitation of ancient monuments for private gain; modern civic values required it. But the pope's 1802 chirograph went even further. It insisted that excavators follow scientific procedures and introduced permits and site inspections to ensure that digging was carried out with sensitivity to the historic substrate. It challenged private, land-based ownership claims to antiquities, and turned antiquity itself into a policy object for the state.

More fundamentally, the chirograph provided important groundwork for contemporary cultural politics by turning a claim founded in ecclesiastical tradition into a secular legal principle. This move planted the seeds of nationalization by suggesting that antiquities had a meaning and purpose not just for the church but also for the general public. One hundred years later that idea would be invoked as an important precedent by the unified national government when it declared itself the presumed permanent owner of all artworks and antiquities. In this environment, private collectors and connoisseurs were increasingly at odds with the state's patrimony project. When the 1820 Edict of Cardinal Pacca succeeded the chirograph, the situation for private claimants was even more dire. The edict implemented several new procedures for asserting state control over the sale and export of cultural goods.[6] Its administrative regimens, including systematic cataloging of all known cultural assets, anticipated modern systems of cultural inventories.[7] What it did not do was offer a blueprint for "national" patrimony. Even as nationalist sentiment entered Italian intellectual life, the state remained a conservative domain.[8] The sale and export of antiquities was too lucrative to disband. The pontifical government imposed a 20 percent value-added tax on ancient art leaving the Papal States, and excavation permits generated an underground economy in bribes and favors. The patrimony ambitions of Carlo Fea were, in his lifetime, tempered by the interlocking interests of transnational elites and Papal State tradition.[9] Had he lived another twenty years, he would have seen the world order of antiquities reshaped by the rise of nationalism and the fall of an antiquities king.

SCANDAL AND THE REMAKING OF THE ART MARKET

To his contemporaries, Giovanni Pietro Campana was the epitome of cultural power. He was born in 1808 in Rome to a family that was wealthy, well connected, and artistically sophisticated. His father was a passionate coin collector, and his grandfather had excavated at famous ancient sites including Ostia, Rome, and Castelnuovo. Campana inherited land and artworks, and he built his public image around the allure of antiques. In his twenties he began selling antiquities found on his family property near Frascati and used the proceeds to purchase more valuable objects. Over time, he amassed one of Europe's most impressive private collections (fig. 7). At its peak, the Campana museum held about fifteen thousand pieces representing two thousand years of artistic practice, making it one of the largest and most diverse of all nineteenth-century collections. In 1849, in recognition of Campana's financial and cultural influence, Ferdinand II, king of the Two Sicilies, conferred on him the title Marchese di Cavelli. Two years later he married Emily Rowles, a British aristocrat whose family had close ties to Napoleon III. Campana's rise seemed unstoppable.[10]

At age twenty-five, Campana was appointed director of the Monte di Pietà bank in Rome. The structure of the bank explains how and why Campana fell, so it is important to take a moment to peer inside its operations. The Monte di Pietà (Mount of Compassion) traces its origins to fifteenth-century institutions in Perugia and Orvieto that, with pontifical approval, lent money to the poor. Instead of charging interest, which would have violated church teachings against usury, the Monte allowed borrowers to pledge collateral in the form of "salable goods reliably appraised at double the loan amount and entrusted to faithful custodians" during the life of the loan.[11] Over the years, thefts and mismanagement had prompted internal reforms and stricter punishments for embezzlement. Campana nevertheless found loopholes in bank policy and took some 900,000 scudi for his own purchases and needs. When Campana was arrested for financial crimes in 1857, his art collection became a flash point.

One of the accusations against Campana was that the collateral he put up for the Monte de Pietà loans was worth significantly less than the amount of money he had taken. Campana's defense rested in large part on burnishing his reputation and proving that the value of his artworks was equal to or higher than the money taken. In petitioning Pope Pius IX for clemency, Campana confessed to having a "noble but exces-

FIGURE 7. A portion of the enormous collection of antiquities assembled by Giampietro Campana, the Marchese di Cavelli. Campana was the most powerful antiquities dealer in mid-nineteenth-century Italy. He was arrested for embezzlement of public funds in November 1857 and sentenced to twenty years in prison (commuted to exile). His collection was sequestered by the Papal States, and many major works from it were sold to foreign governments and royal families. By Unknown (Campana?)-Anne Viola Siebert, Geschichte(n) in Ton. Römische Architekturterrakotten, Schnell und Steiner, Regensburg 2011, ISBN 978-3-7954-2579-1 (Museum Kestnerianum 16), Wikimedia Commons.

sively ardent passion" for archaeological exploration and for "the precious monuments of ancient Italian civilization that preceded the glories of eternal Rome."[12] His collecting passion, he explained, was motivated by his dream of creating a museum—"a gigantic museum," according to his courtroom testimony. He compared his collecting habit with his "services to the state and to the public."[13] Britain had its British Museum, France had the Louvre, and now Campana, it seemed, was intent on giving Rome an equally grand museum. In March 1858, four months after Campana's arrest, the defendant's administrator shrewdly suggested that Campana's galleries be opened to the public. The response was swift and affirmative. Visitors were satisfied that the artworks and artifacts were more than sufficient to satisfy Campana's debt, triggering a wave of public sympathy that strengthened the defense. Campana was eventually found guilty and sentenced to twenty years in prison, but he was pardoned in exchange for surrendering his property and titles and leaving Rome permanently.

Over the next two years, Campana's artworks and antiquities were sold to the Victoria and Albert Museum in London, the State Hermitage Museum in St. Petersburg, and the Louvre, which acquired about twelve thousand items. Rome's archaeologists and artists, and the Italian public, were despondent. Papal authorities had sold the Campana collection for more than his alleged debt, and now they would lose the cherished works (Pianazza 1983). With breathtaking disregard for Italian public opinion, Edmond Taigny, one of the art experts sent to Rome to inspect the collection for the Louvre, surmised that while the Roman people would regret the loss of the Campana works, in the end they would prefer to see them go to France because of the Louvre's superior hospitality. The only portion of Campana's collection to remain in Italy was a set of four hundred coins, which was purchased by the Capitoline Museum in 1873. The breakup and sale of the Campana collection traumatized the public. Adding insult to injury, major pieces went to France, whose invasion of Italy was within living memory. The Campana scandal galvanized Italian intellectuals and government officials, and the episode served as a cautionary tale in later legislative debates.

Extracting Patrimony Capital

Campana was in many ways a product of his time. Midcentury, the city of Rome and its environs were largely rural. The primary industry was agriculture, and landownership was concentrated in the hands of a tiny elite (less than 5 percent of the population). Most residents were poor and survived on subsistence wages as agricultural workers on private estates. Produce, wine, and animal products for domestic and outside consumption were major sources of wealth, and archaeological artifacts were among the goods extracted from estates. Title to the land conferred ownership of any artifacts found within it. When Campana sold antiquities from his estate at Frascati, the law was on his side. Antiquities were commercial objects available for private procurement by market regulations. The landowning elite was also responsible for local governance, and it ensured favorable trade conditions for antiquities. Campana, Augusto Castellani, and other wealthy families relied on antiquities for symbolic and economic capital. The process for exporting antiquities illustrates just how entrenched were their social, cultural, and monetary obligations and favors. By comparison with the contemporary Italian model, antiquities exports in Campana's time were a fairly lax affair, governed by personal ties and individual judgment calls about the value of a given artifact.

Requests to export antiquities and artworks from Rome were directed to the Ministry of Commerce, Fine Arts, Industry, Agriculture, and Public Works. There was a constant outward flow of historic artworks and antiquities. To keep track of what was leaving and (ostensibly) what had been blocked from export, the ministry relied on a multi-step extraction petition. Starting with a list of requested items, the extraction petition sustained an exchange of obsequies and requests channeled through multiple letters. To initiate the process, the petitioner was required to submit a description of the desired objects. Petitions were handwritten, with ministry letterhead occasionally used but mostly blank sheets embellished with diplomatic seals and signatures. Government officials sometimes inspected the objects to determine their historical value, but there were no standard criteria to guide the evaluation. Petitioners—the owners of the objects or the owners' representatives—wrote to the minister himself asking for permission to export, sell, or alter the antiquities and artworks in question. A ministry employee was asked to make a recommendation, and the minister often accepted the recommendation without further scrutiny or an in-person inspection.

The following petition illustrates how the process worked. It is presented here with my translations of the original papers (written in French and Italian), and my paraphrased summary of other texts involved in the exchange. The petition begins with an official request from the senior Belgian diplomat in Rome to Pier Domenico Costantini Baldini, the minister of commerce.

> Rome, December 19, 1862
>
> To His Excellency Monsieur le Baron Costantini Baldini,
> Minister of Fine Arts, Commerce, and Public Works
>
> I am preparing to send back to my Government shortly, about 75 vases and utensils of Etruscan and Greek art of different sizes. I have, as a result, the honor of begging Your Excellency to give me the authorization necessary that the items might be taken out of the Papal States.[14] [My translation from the French]

The Belgian office then sent a second letter, this time an invitation to view the objects at the Villa Strozzi, in Rome. It was correct form to ask His Excellency the Minister for permission to export and then, separately, to initiate the practical work of inspecting the artifacts and preparing them for export. The Villa Strozzi was a distinguished sixteenth-century residence near the Baths of Diocletian, acquired in 1619 by Leone Strozzi, a prosperous Florentine merchant. The villa had long been associated with classical art and erudition, being a noted display space for Roman sculptures and a *Wunderkammer* of ancient coins, cameos, and gems.[15] When the Belgian ambassador to the Holy See rented the villa in 1861, it had hosted numerous conferences of ecclesiastical scholars and foreign dignitaries. It would later serve as the first location of the École française de Rome. For petitioning the Ministry of Commerce, it was a suitably impressive location. The inspection apparently took place on December 23, 1862, and was led by one of Baldini's staff members. The next day that staffer sent Baldini a note recommending a course of action:

> I have recently been to the Villa Strozzi to inspect there the 75 ceramic vases of Etruscan manufacture, which his Honor the Minister of the Belgians has asked Your Excellency's permission to extract [*estrarre*] from Rome.
>
> None of these vessels, most of which are black and without painting, is of such merit for scholarship or art that they occasion any remarks. For this reason Your Excellency can without further consideration approve the petition.
>
> Yours with profound respect,
> Your loyal servant [handwriting indecipherable].
> [My translation][16]

This exchange offers the salient features of how the government managed cultural patrimony. The employee who went to the Villa Strozzi to inspect the artifacts may have known something about Etruscan ceramic wares or very little. Expertise in specific types of objects was not a requirement for the position. We do not know what was said during the inspection, but we can image it was similar to the *palazzo* visits of the early modern Roman courts, with a gracious reception and erudite exchange of compliments about the surrounding artworks and furnishings—except that in 1862 the Belgian diplomats had to demonstrate that the antiquities they wanted were not so fine or singular that their export would be a perceptible loss to the Papal States' collection of antiquities. In my review of the archival records of the Ministry of Commerce, I found that most petitions were approved outright or with minor amendments (such as insisting on a higher export fee than had been proposed).

The extraction petitions in the Ministry of Commerce archives are handwritten on expensive paper and embellished with elaborate ligatures and stamps. They use formal language by bestowing the highest honorific titles and passing on compliments and obsequies ("Your loyal servant"). In reminding their recipients of previous encounters and petitions sought, they establish interactional continuity between the petitioner and the ministry, which in turn suggests a favorable record of acquiring antiquities. Export petitions, then, should be regarded as continuing the early modern tradition of patronage letters, a "corpus of patterned discourse" that was vital to the performance of social networks.[17] Personal ties and favor seeking were now subsumed in the complex operations of the Papal States and its ministries. But it remained important to invoke personal ties—to flatter, esteem, and politely remind the minister of his importance, not just in a government office but in the world republic of antiquities. In the extraction petition, then, we have another example of concrete interactions involving people and artifacts, with artifacts serving to link Italians and non-Italians in vast networks of obligations and favors. The ruling culture of Europe's elites was (ancient) Rome, and the (modern) Roman bureaucrat could fantasize himself a ruler *of* that culture.

Guardianship laws were ineffective to stanch the outward flow of Italian cultural treasures; they left too many loopholes and encouraged systemic ambiguity in which individual ministry staffers could be swayed or bought outright. The intent of the laws had been to allow the export of duplicate or superfluous objects from the Papal States, but in reality the main beneficiaries of the system were foreign elites. The world republic of antiquities served as a parallel system of patrimony capital. On one hand, there was the Papal States' framework of cultural policy management—the set of laws that Fea worked assiduously to implement and that Italian scholars supported by protecting archaeological sites from foreign and amateur diggers. But the framework was young and lacked sufficient support to give it teeth. The elite system of exchange had been in place for centuries and operated with its own set of norms and agreed practices. It transcended national legal regimes and operated autonomously. Transnational elites, who styled themselves heirs to a humanistic tradition that predated national boundaries, were the self-appointed guardians of Western classicism and its artifacts. They were the owners and rightful developers of patrimony capital.

When we arrive at 1909 and the angry denunciations of the national patrimony law, it is important to hold in mind the long-term social and economic relationships that the law upended. It is a familiar argument in the literature on nationalism that countries like Italy implemented cultural heritage laws as part of a collective determination to protect art and antiquities for the national community at large. By looking at the politics of patrimony capital, however, we can see that some Italians—notably those with economic and social investments in the trade—rejected that idea and maintained that the status quo was optimal for protecting the country's historic legacy. Protection and valorization were, to them, one and the same. Extraction petitions were not just a way of doing business; they were a way of conducting one's social life. Nationalizing antiquities was one stop on a winding and disjointed path of changing ideas about the relation between contemporary Italy and the region's long history.

THE JEWELRY MAGNATE

So far, I have referred fairly generically to "elites," in the sense of wealthy individuals buying and selling art and antiquities. At this point I want to emphasize that there was no single, elite position on the question of Italian heritage (however defined). Political cohesion among elites after unification, during the 1870s, 1880s, and 1890s, was limited.[18] And within elite circles, there were diverse perspectives on the idea of a collective national culture. Local and family relations were still the primary source of identity for most Italians. To illustrate elite complexity, I have chosen one strand from the ball of tangled nineteenth-century interests in Italy's antiquities. Over the course of nearly a century, the Castellani family—Fortunato Pio Castellani and his sons, Augusto and Alessandro—put together one of the largest private collections of antiquities in Italy, totaling some six thousand pieces (rivaling even Campana's collection). The Castellani family firm built an international reputation for its high-quality replicas of ancient Italic jewelry and tapped into the fashion for ancient styles that swept the country after unification (fig. 8). Castellani senior started his own collection by purchasing ancient jewelry and other works in precious metals.[19] After Alessandro joined the fight for unification and was forced to seek exile in France, Augusto took over the family's collecting and dealing operations in Italy.[20]

Augusto built an antiquities empire. Through his brother's connections to the French court, Augusto was much sought after as a broker for aristocratic French and Italian collectors of antiquities. He specialized in ready-made collections of Etruscan urns, Greek vases, Roman intaglios, and women's jewelry. His foreign clients no longer needed to wait years to amass a collection or scour the length of Italy in search of objects. For an agreed price, Augusto Castellani would ship an antiquities collection, complete and prepared for display, to his clients in Paris, London, Munich, Amsterdam, Vienna, Geneva, and Moscow. To help them brush up on antiquities (and thus make the collections feel like their own), clients were given crib sheets with brief explanations of object type, age, material, history, and meaning for every object in the collection. In this way the objects' meanings were commodified and transcribed from their Italian findspot to the private home or palace where they were sent.

Improbably, at the peak of his career Augusto Castellani, the inveterate private collector whose homes and horses and fabled dinners were paid for by antiquities sales, became an advocate for state ownership of antiquities. Elected honorary director of the Capitoline Museums in 1873, Augusto was tasked with stocking the Capitoline galleries with Roman and Etruscan objects. It was at his urging that the museum purchased the Campana coin collection. He threw himself energetically into the work, and spoke passionately about the importance of protecting Italy's artworks and artifacts for the glorification of the nation. He paid cash for artifacts found by Lazio's peasants, who trekked to Rome proffering statuettes, bronze helmets, and painted vases they had found.[21] Castellani was working amid sweeping legal and administrative changes. All archaeological and public monuments in Rome were now public property, and new viewing spaces were required to share that largesse with the Roman people. In addition to Castellani's Capitoline Museums, the Villa Giulia Museum of Etruscan Art was inaugurated in 1889, and another major museum, the Museo Nazionale Romano, followed in 1890. There remained conflicting ideas about local, national, private, and public audiences.[22] Public museums were not consistently nationalistic in their strategies of acquisition, display, and interpretation. The Uffizi Gallery in Florence was inaugurated as a state museum in 1861, and it espoused a universal vision of Italian artworks, while the Archaeological Museum of Naples, which also opened as a state museum in 1861, situated antiquities in a regional history.[23] But from this point onward, there was a central framework for managing antiquities collections as public assets.

When dynastic family collections were absorbed into the state museum system, the political power of the family was also transferred.[24] The family names stayed attached to the collections, drawing attention to the state's authority over the artworks and, symbolically, over the families themselves. Elite families also produced distinctive subcollections that highlighted local narratives, traditions, and histories.[25] As objects from cities across Italy made their way to the state museums in Rome, the state was also demonstrating its substantive connections with those cities. What kind of sovereignty was this? It was the new nation-state demonstrating to its own subjects that it had sufficient authority to amalgamate

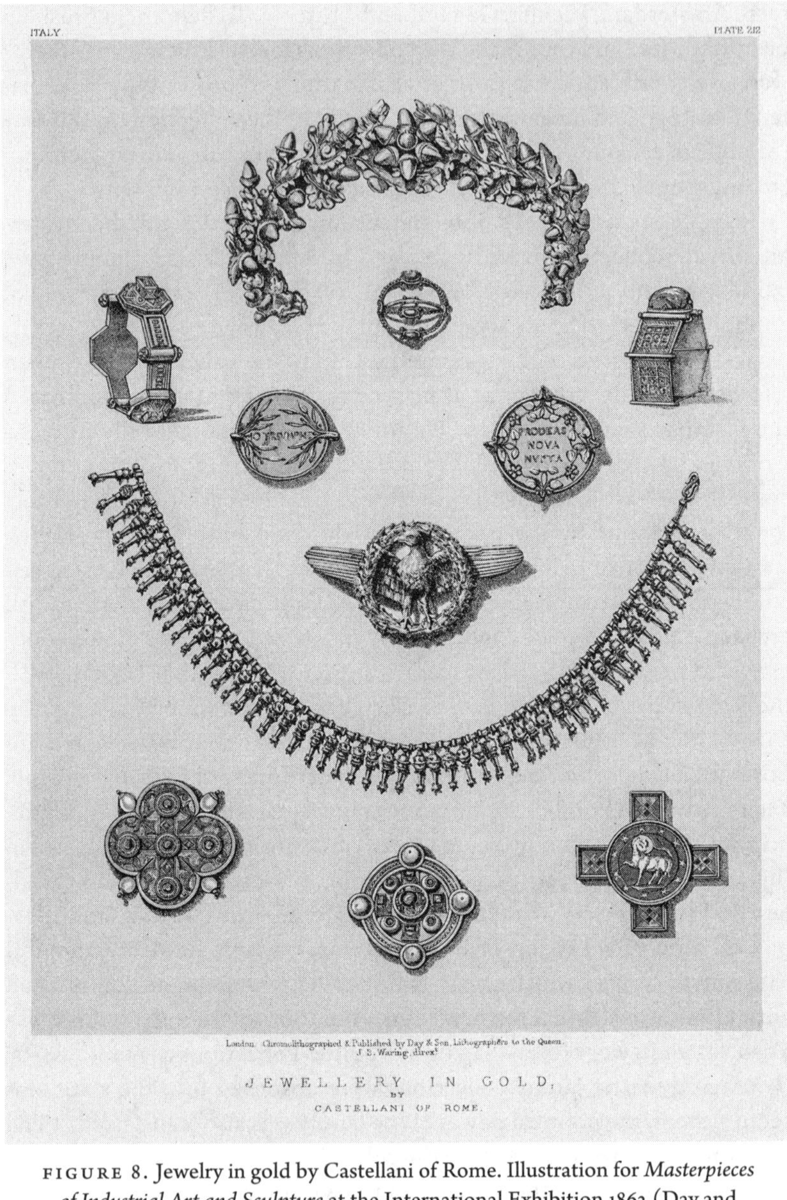

FIGURE 8. Jewelry in gold by Castellani of Rome. Illustration for *Masterpieces of Industrial Art and Sculpture* at the International Exhibition 1862 (Day and Son, 1863). The Castellani family firm specialized in high-quality replicas of ancient Italic jewelry, part of an Etruscan and Roman revival that swept Italy in the 1870s–80s. Augusto Castellani went on to play a major role in the founding of the national museum system, contributing antiquities from his own collection. Private Collection © Look and Learn/Bridgeman Images.

regional artistic centers into a single national artistic center. The Castellani family's antiquities career, then, mirrors broader shifts in the antiquities sphere. It is noteworthy that near the end of his life, Fortunato Pio expressed regret about his role in exporting so many cultural treasures from Italy. He left a substantial portion of his estate to hire artisans to reproduce some of them (Moretti Sgubini 2000). The world republic could no longer assume that "global" humanism was the rightful claimant to antiquities. Italy's dynastic collectors, too, were facing a new way of thinking about national patrimony and its material components.

Archaeological Expertise and the National Matrix

The first archaeological administration act, passed in 1875, clarified the state's right to issue excavation permits and adjudicate artifact claims, confirmed professional archaeology as the preeminent authority over artifacts and classical ruins, and solidified the growing consensus that excavation required specific expertise and regimes of knowledge. The act established a formal organizational structure for national and local archaeological offices. It was the product of some four decades of development within the discipline and, more broadly, among the antiquarians, excavators, art historians, and museum professionals who engaged with Italy's ancient sites and material culture. The overall achievement of their work was to change the structure of archaeological space. First, it reserved for the state and its archaeologists the prerogative of excavating anywhere that historically protected materials were found. This included the right to dig on private land, with compensation arranged for the landowner. Second, it meant that every object within it was potentially an artifact deserving professional examination and protection. Third, archaeologizing the country turned the seat of the arts into an active space in which Italy had a superior position over foreigners. Organized around these developments, this section charts how the open-air museum, with its theoretically infinite accumulation of artifacts, was born.

ORSI THE ENFORCER

Paolo Orsi, inspector of archaeological works for the region of Calabria, was "the heroic figure of a new age of state-sponsored, scientific archaeological research in the Italian South."[26] He earned notoriety and respect for strictly enforcing Italian control of Italian archaeological sites. It was because of his work that the central role of the state in archaeological work became politically legitimized through organizational systems and procedures, and gave Italy authority over artifacts and excavation sites, superior to the claims made by non-Italian scholars and collectors. This effort culminated in his dispute with American excavators at the site of Croton, which had been founded as a Greek colony in the eighth century BCE. Croton and its environs had not yet been methodically excavated, and it was a plum site for rival archaeology teams. When a wealthy American digger and his team turned up in the summer of 1887, they paid a local landowner for his personal permission to dig on the land near Croton. In doing so they followed established archaeological practice, which held that permits were a matter of local negotiation and (often informal) administration. In their effort to bypass Orsi's office, they triggered a standoff that ended with their humiliating defeat and sulky retreat to North America.

Orsi insisted that the American excavators' agreement with the local landowner was invalid. The team was operating *senza regolare licenza*[27] (without a regular operating license), rendering their activities illegal. Orsi permitted a limited excavation over two months at a site near Croton, then had them removed. The team protested, and one of its leaders later vented his frustration:

> The laws regulating archaeological investigations and excavations in Italy should be changed. Firstly, they are too restrictive and unenlightened, and, secondly, each province has preserved its antiquated laws, so that there is no uniformity throughout the land. Owing to the confusion and uncertainty reigning in this question, there are endless law-suits and violations of the laws: such an amount of red-tape officialism [*sic*] is required as effectually to discourage scientific work in many cases, and, notwithstanding the most benevolent of intentions, the letter of the law is made to kill the spirit.[28]

By enforcing the letter of the law, Orsi did two things. First, he asserted the Italian state's right to protect and manage its own archaeological objects. In Orsi's day there was widespread despair among foreign scholars (and some domestic ones) over the Italian government's perceived inability to systematically study and protect its archaeological artifacts and sites. Orsi explicitly addressed this issue when he wrote about his confrontation at Croton: "As soon as I was appointed director of the archaeological superintendence at Calabria, I took it upon my honor to demonstrate how Italy, too, could muster its own resources, even if on a more modest scale, to meet the just desires of the scientific world."[29]

Orsi's second impact was to expand the definition of unlawful excavations. He, like many archaeological superintendents, already faced the problem of local residents' digging for objects without official permission and selling their finds to private collectors.[30] The American archaeologists at Croton could differentiate their own efforts with those of the local tomb robbers on grounds that as archaeologists they worked in the interest of science. Orsi rejected this argument and, while not going so far as to call permitless archaeologists "looters," he subjected them to the same bureaucratic procedures and punishments. The idea that scientists had a special claim to the land, one that transcended state policies and procedures, was no longer taken for granted. At Orsi's behest, Italian archaeological officials were empowered to make decisions about who could access archaeological sites and the artifacts within them.[31] The raw material required to produce patrimony capital, in other words, was being transformed into a state resource.

POOR MAN'S SILVER

While Orsi was doing battle with American archaeologists over excavation access, the field of Italian archaeology as a whole was developing new platforms for intellectual self-assertion. Italian-language antiquities journals in the late nineteenth century drew a broader readership among Italians and gave them a voice in controversies over objects' meaning and worth. New object typologies, especially in the study of pottery, supported novel theories of preclassical migratory patterns and settlements in Italy. Those theories enjoyed mass popularity in local myths and festivals that celebrated ancient lineages. These developments were part of the rise of professional archaeology, a movement that was unfolding in different permutations across Europe.[32] Scientific excavation focused on the principle of stratigraphy, the careful recording of different levels of settlement. Stratigraphy gave every artifact a context, or provenance, linked with a specific place in the earth. Metaphorically, artifacts without provenance were lacking their biography. It was this final development in professionalized archaeology that bridged classical antiquity and the modern nation-state. Archaeological materials were no longer free-floating specimens of ancient Rome. They were now anchored in particular findspots in the soil of Italy, and precisely mapped the distribution and density of the country's cultural treasures in the earth and on it.

Bucchero, an unglazed, unpainted pottery that is normally black or gray, is a noteworthy example of this transition. The pottery is found primarily in the regions of Tuscany, Umbria, Emilia-Romagna, and Lazio. Modern excavations date the oldest bucchero vases to the second quarter of the seventh century BCE.[33] The first European specialists to write about it found bucchero unimpressive. When Henry Walters, a prominent nineteenth-century English antiquarian and ceramics expert, described bucchero as the "national pottery of Etruria," it was not a compliment.[34] In his two-volume *History of Ancient Pottery*, he wrote dismissively, "There are here [among bucchero vessels] no signs of inventive genius. The technique is purely native, but all is founded on foreign models. . . . In short, they reproduce for us what is wanting in our knowledge of early Greek metal ware."[35] Walters insisted that Etruscans would have made metalware if they'd had the requisite technological knowledge and apparatus, but because they lacked that knowledge they had to make do with baked clay. Bucchero was the "poor man's silver"—or in this case the poor nation's silver.[36] He was not alone in this opinion. When George Dennis, the British consul in Rome, traveled to Vulci to see the excavations there, he reported seeing peasants deliberately trampling a "variety of small vases in black clay" (possibly bucchero wares).[37] Bucchero was snubbed by collectors, seldom published, and generally regarded as rubbish. Dennis's comments, it should be noted, echo denunciations of *tombaroli* for deliberately destroying mundane artifacts in order to find salable objects. At Vulci, however, it was the excavation leaders who authorized the destruction of bucchero as part of a "rubble clearance" to make it easier to find prized burial goods.

From the point of view of Walters and others working in the Kunstgeschichte tradition, the problem with bucchero was that it lacked iconographic embellishments on a par with Greek red- and black-figure vessels.[38] Nineteenth-century scholars distinguished between ceramic fragments useful for "pictorial" study and those better suited for "plastic" analysis.[39] Pictorial study concentrated on figures painted on or incised into the surfaces of ceramic objects, the classic example being fifth-century BCE Greek vases with mythological scenes. Plastic study focused on the shapes, wall thickness, and composite materials of ceramic wares. The division between pictorial and plastic was politically charged. Top scholars promoted themselves as experts in the former, placing painted vases and other ceramics along with marble sculptures in a lineage of objets d'art.[40] Plastic analysis was left to those engaged in the technical tasks of archaeological digs—deemed second-rate manual work by classical historians and art historians.[41]

While Greek objects were considered masterpieces, native Italian ceramics were seen as inferior because of their date and style.[42] Samuel Birch promulgated this view in his highly influential *History of Ancient*

Pottery, originally published in 1857 and the first comprehensive study of ancient ceramics. Birch summarized the issue as follows:

> In the application of form in art, the Greeks have excelled all nations, either past or present. The beauty and simplicity of the shapes of their vases have caused them to be taken as models for various kinds of earthenware [but even] the cleverest imitations of nature, and the most elegant conceits of floral ornaments, whether exhibited in the efforts of Oriental or European potters, appear coarse and vulgar when contrasted with the chaste simplicity of the Greek forms.[43]

Birch's analysis aligned with the historical positivism of his generation of scholars. "Earthenware" supposedly offered a window onto the civilization and intelligence of the nations of the past. The ancient Greeks were the exemplum of civilizational development because they had mastered form. Other ancient peoples were rendered inferior, despite the cleverness of their efforts to imitate the Greeks, because they never quite managed to match Greek object-forms. This meant that the Greek-influenced potters of southern Italy and Sicily, too, were mere imitators, and their third-century BCE efforts represented "the last stage to which Greek painting could ever have reached."[44]

By Walters's time, however, archaeologists' appraisal of the usefulness and scientific function of pottery fragments was undergoing change. The legendary German archaeologist Alexander Conze, who rose to prominence in the 1870s through his digs at Samothrace, argued that proper excavation must take into account the "full study of the 'physiognomy' of each site, without regard to the artistic value of excavated fragments."[45] Artistic adornment was deemed irrelevant to the technical work of scientific archaeology. With the creation of labels such as geometric, Orientalizing, bucchero, and red-slip, pot fragments were fully enlisted in the scientific project of classifying artifacts as a means of accurately recording past events. This same system allowed pot fragments to be inscribed in the discursive work of nationhood.

While Birch, Walters, Conze, and other English, German, and French scholars debated the significance of Italy's ancient ceramics to the general development of Western culture, Italian thinkers were articulating their own typologies along national lines. Among excavators, Antonio Zannoni broke new ground by using pottery fragments to differentiate among Etruscan peoples and trace discrete lines of cultural development.[46] Zannoni spoke of the Etruscans as an ancient "nationality" that predated the Roman invaders.[47] As intellectually interesting (and socially fashionable) as the Etruscans were in the eyes of Zannoni and his contemporaries, their real significance lay in their historical inheritance. The Etruscans, Zannoni argued, had supplanted the Iron Age cultures known as the Pelasgian and the Umbrian. These groups were held to be Italy's autochthonous people, settled on Italian soil since time immemorial. Such ideas must be read against the Etruscomania that captivated Italians in the 1860s and 1870s. Etruscan decorative motifs had been popular in northern Europe since the late eighteenth century, but Italian nationhood gave Etruscan material objects a new meaning within Italy and among Italians. As putative heirs to Italy's earliest period of habitation (or the autochthonous peoples themselves, as some Italian thinkers continued to insist[48]), the Etruscans opened up the country's immense antiquity and woke the nation from its "epochal sleep."[49]

Pottery was a link with the mythical past. The system of archaeological classification legitimized pottery fragments as a serious subject of study. Their link with ancient history and their verifiable antiquity made the fragments themselves worthy of state protection—without concern for whether they approximated ancient Greek aesthetics. Late nineteenth-century archaeologists relied on qualitative assessments of topography and artifact deposits to identify and define a "site," and they classified their findings according to their proximity to significant structures within the site.[50] Site names emphasized cultural groups, which were in turn being used as signifiers of "authentic" or autochthonous presence. The landscape of archaeological activity in nineteenth-century Italy absorbed historical myth and folklore into Linnaean object classifications and soil stratigraphy. The fantasy of autochthony, for example, or of the facticity of Romulus and Remus, persisted because of, rather than in spite of, formal schemes of quantification and taxonomies of labels. Traditional local beliefs that archaeological ruins were haunted by the ancestors, or that statues were kin, could not be corrected by rational science; but nor did artifactual politics require that change. A new matrix of meaning was at hand, and it combined the firmament of universal classicism with the gritty and familiar soil. Orsi's legacy reveals the complexity of archaeological epistemology in this period. The scientized soil and the sacralized soil could contain both bucchero taxonomy and Etruscomania's fantasy of autochthony. This flexibility in archaeological method enriched the logic of accumulation by giving the stockpile of state patrimony an expanded variety of valorization techniques.

SCAVI ABUSIVI AND THE DIRTY WORK OF DIGGING

With legitimate excavation monopolized by professional archaeologists, people digging for artifacts outside the ambit of official archaeology were proscribed. Their work was recast as *scavi abusivi*—"unlawful excavations." No longer mere diggers, they were folded into collective anxiety about banditry and its mix of thieving and raiding. Brigands were unnerving because of their knack for disappearing into the rural population through concealment and disguise, sometimes aided by peasants, and reemerging when law enforcement agents least expected them. Coalitions between brigands and rural peasants constituted a significant political challenge to state and local authorities in Napoleonic Italy, and brigands consistently and explicitly defied state authority. During this period, "brigandage" came to describe any form of collective resistance and lawlessness, and its invocation in judicial language allowed the authorities to place accused brigands outside due process of the law.[51] Brigands were tried in military or other extrajudicial courts where punishments were harsher.[52] Public disorder served as a pretext for arresting and prosecuting individuals seen to be engaged in collective political activity. What banditry and tomb robbing share is that both activities are situationally defined and largely—but not always—embedded in rural societies. They worry and infuriate state officials because they refuse to conform to social rules and legal norms. *Tombaroli* were not *briganti*, but they were tarred by the same brush of social disorder and rural illegality.

What made tomb robbers so dangerous? Working in their pits and shafts, they transformed the material and symbolic basis of the young nation's cultural knowledge. That knowledge resisted the encroachment of national and global articulations of identity.

Lay diggers took on the stigmatized status of tomb robbers with the entrenchment of scientific archaeology in the nineteenth century, as important intellectual and praxis developments occurred in universities and in the academy system in Rome.[53] As we have seen, this included new ideas about excavation methods and new practices of interpreting archaeological materials, an important strand of which regarded artifacts as essential to contemporary national identities. Instead of excavating solely to find artifacts, archaeologists argued that their goal should be to make careful records and try to understand the relation of artifacts to each other through their position in a legible and systematic substrate. The key was to build archaeology into a discipline that affirmed nationhood but that also retained the prestige associated with having material culture of universal significance. To make this possible, antiquarians, amateur diggers, and tomb robbers were recast as predators of the nation's body.

"American Prices" and the New Regime of Cultural Power

In Campana's and Castellani's collecting days, demand for Italian antiquities came primarily from European elites. This changed in the third quarter of the nineteenth century with the increased interest of American millionaires in Italian art. Before the 1860s, cultural prestige among Americans was largely articulated at the local level.[54] Gilded Age elites, however, fashioned themselves as cultural consumers and patrons of international stature. Homegrown works were no longer sufficient. For the new breed of American super-collectors, prestige was conferred through the idiom of universal culture, and Italian art and antiquities were the coin of the realm. As Carol Helstosky explains:

> For the nineteenth-century art collector, Italy was a land rich in art and antiquities, possessing more than enough art for prospective buyers. According to American collector James Jackson Jarves, art was literally embedded in Italy's soil. One need only dig in the dirt to discover an Etruscan tomb or the fragment of a column: "Italy is foremost in its harvests of antiquity, because her soil is the richest to work."[55]

Antiquities dealers scoured the country for rare and unique items. The more adventurous buyers went along for the journey, and could indulge in the fantasy of finding their own artifacts by purchasing access to an archaeological site, which would have been carefully planted with objects ahead of time by a paid guide. But for millionaire buyers too busy to make the trip, a rapidly professionalizing class of dealers and middlemen stood ready to procure and pack antiquities and ship them to New York, Baltimore, and Philadelphia.[56] The dominance of American buyers—and the fear that they would deprive Italy of its greatest artistic treasures—generated a new term of opprobrium: the "American price" (*prezzo americano*). The term became the rallying cry of cultural nationalists and eventually tipped the balance of power in favor of state ownership of all antiquities.

"GROUNDING OUR NATIONAL SPIRIT"

We have seen that at least since Carlo Fea's time, there were isolated calls for state-mandated control of the circulation of antiquities. Those calls failed against powerful interests.[57] Artworks and antiquities were market goods first and public goods second. Even after national unification, if the national government wished to keep an artwork or antiquity from being sold abroad, it had to bid against collectors on the open market. More often than not the government could not raise the necessary funds and watched helplessly as the work was sold off to the highest bidder. Florence, one of the cities hardest hit by the American price, experimented with policies designed to invest conservation powers in civic officials rather than private philanthropists. In 1903 a new local law gave Florence's city administrators the funds and authority to conserve and protect designated historic monuments. Now those monuments could not be sold abroad no matter the price.

The gradual acceptance of antiquities as cultural goods *first*—and market goods never—emerged from a constellation of popular ideas about nationhood and Italian culture: nostalgia for traditional practices and myths; renewed appreciation for classical motifs in furnishings, architecture, and literature; and a new appraisal of artistic and natural beauty as a vehicle of national identity.[58] This last idea found a powerful advocate in Luigi Rava, who served as minister of agriculture (1903–5) and minister of public education (1906–9). In 1905 Rava successfully pushed for a law to protect the pine forest at Ravenna as a cultural treasure with national interest. The forest was a favorite subject for Italian painters and was poetically invoked in Boccaccio's *Decameron* (5.8). Landscapes, like artworks, were potential state property because of their capacity to express national culture. The parliamentary debate that surrounded passage of this law established a discourse and framework for state management of cultural goods. It set the stage for the 1909 law. For that effort, Rava teamed up with Corrado Ricci, the art historian and director of the Museo Nazionale di Ravenna, and Giovanni Rosadi, a Florentine member of the Chamber of Deputies. The three of them set to work persuading lawmakers to dismantle the antiquities trade. But first they had to surmount a major obstacle in the form of property rights.

Existing patrimony stewardship laws prohibited people from inflicting specific harms (razing, defacing, exporting) on designated objects and vested responsibility for guardianship in local authorities. What such laws generally did not do was grant ownership of historically significant objects to public authorities. Italian owners of private collections could give objects away or sell them to foreigners without penalty. Cherished as they were by their collectors, antiquities and artworks served as a convenient source of cash when funds ran short or unusual expenses arose. But that strategy, liquidating a collection piece to raise funds, was severely constrained by new patrimony restrictions after unification. Cash-poor dynastic families found themselves unable to sell artworks that were deemed national treasures, even if those works had been in their family collections before unification. They resented the new restrictions and organized to block further incursions into what they regarded as their private financial matters.

Rosadi and Rava tapped the power of the press to win popular support for their plan. Italian newspapers published impassioned editorials in favor of central government control over the excavation and circulation of antiquities. Influential editors at both the *Corriere della Sera* and the *Giornale d'Italia* supported the idea of a national policy of art. An editorial by journalist Alberto Bergamini in the left-leaning *Giornale d'Italia* set forth the main arguments. Bergamini was a high-profile journalist and a vocal advocate of government supports for national unity. In his view, artistic goods were essential to the national spirit, and the completion of unification depended on stronger, public sector control of those goods:

> On the forty-third birthday of the Italian nation, the heritage of four or five civilizations is both glorious and a major responsibility. . . . The possession of so many famous monuments . . . infects us now, more than ever, with the biting urge to pay most careful attention to our works of art, to protect them from the snares of time and men, to entrust to the people of Italy the protection of the monuments of Italy [*la tutela dei monumenti*], and to commemorate the great historical traditions that accompany our conception of these works. [We say yes]: to reinvigorate the people of Italy and render them a more profound Italian national consciousness, the Italian government needs a policy on art. While for some people [in the world] art remains a luxury [*un lusso*], in Italy art is the grounding of our national spirit and radiates perennially for thirty centuries.[59]

Bergamini's argument presented a direct challenge to private property interests. Guardianship of cultural patrimony, he maintained, would stimulate the collective consciousness of Italians, and the unified government was precisely the organ to organize the effort. His final sentence was a rebuke to private and foreign claims on Italian art. They considered art to be a luxury good for the privileged and wealthy few. For Bergamini, art was the common ground in which society was rooted; it was the very basis of the national spirit and belonged to everyone.

Claiming Italian art for the Italian people was a direct challenge to the art market. The once-lauded world republic of antiquities was recast as a corrupt and grubby enterprise:

> The fiercest enemies of the national artistic heritage are the art dealers. They are running [around] the city and the countryside to find these objects, they are profiting off economic hardship or ignorance of the owners to buy them and concoct the most audacious fraud to export them to people even more clever. [These dealers] are the accomplices of the art criminals, the thieves of art objects.[60]

The speaker, Carlo Ferraris, the deputy from Casale Monferrato, was urging his fellow deputies to regulate the art trade by limiting private ownership of artworks and directing the state to assume full responsibility for artistic patrimony. To carry out that directive, the state had to play an active role in setting objects' values and prices, not just in caring for them in museums or taxing their export. By referring to art dealers as the fiercest enemies of Italy's artistic heritage, he dramatically recasted what had been a respectable and influential profession. Antiquarians and art dealers became political actors, not just market ones, and they were unfavorably placed against the patriotic values of the unified kingdom of Italy.[61]

Consider an incident involving J. Pierpont Morgan, one of the richest men in America in the late nineteenth century. Morgan was a high-profile buyer of important artworks, and his collection included celebrated pieces by Dürer, Leonardo da Vinci, Michelangelo, Rembrandt, Rubens, and Picasso. In 1903 Morgan purchased a cope, or liturgical vestment, that had apparently (unknown to him) been stolen from the cathedral in Ascoli. The cope, made sometime in the thirteenth century, presents a series of figures embroidered in silk and gold thread, encircling and arrayed along both its sides.[62] It was presented by Pope Nicholas IV, whose family came from the area. A replica in the Metropolitan Museum of Art shows the sophisticated level of precision and artistry in its execution (fig. 9).

The Ascoli cope went missing from the cathedral in 1902 while the building was undergoing restoration. There was no trace of it until summer 1904, when it was put on display in the South Kensington Museum in London. Corrado Ricci happened to visit the museum. In his letter to the *Giornale d'Italia,* which reported the incident, Ricci noted that the cope was presented with the following label: "Cope embroidered with the Virgin and Child, English manufacture. Second half of the thirteenth century. On loan from J. Pierpont Morgan." Acting together, the Ministry of Foreign Affairs and the Ministry of Public Education wrote to Morgan asking that he return the cope to Italy immediately. Morgan angrily denied accusations that he had purchased a stolen work, arguing that he had

FIGURE 9. Early twentieth-century watercolor reconstruction of the thirteenth-century Ascoli Cope purchased by J. Pierpont Morgan from an Italian priest who was later sent to prison for art theft. The episode galvanized Italian elected officials to crack down on private sales of Italian artworks. Department of Medieval Art, Metropolitan Museum of Art. Gift of J. Pierpont Morgan.

bought the cope in Paris from a party who had "the right to sell it." The Italian authorities conducted a criminal investigation and made arrests in Italy and England, tracing the theft to cathedral staff and clergy in Ascoli. After one of the suspects committed suicide in his cell, Morgan agreed to return the cope through negotiations between the Italian embassy and the US government in Washington, DC. Morgan continued to insist he had done nothing wrong.

Rava specifically mentioned Morgan's case in his 1909 speech to the Chamber of Deputies. "We all know the story of the cope of Ascoli," he said, which had been smuggled out of the country by "the accomplices of corrupt collectors and conniving art thieves." Rava was arguing that the art market was a peculiar trade meriting special attention and regulation by the state. "From the moment that we establish our control over the circulation [of artworks] by limiting private ownership of artworks," he argued, "from the moment that we recognize in the state the directive to care for our artistic patrimony, . . . it seems to me necessary to consider the commercial aspects." In other words, the government's ability to protect and conserve art and antiquities was predicated on its power to set their values and prices. Market regulation and material *tutela*, or custodianship, were tightly linked. This was why Rava proposed that the commerce in art and antiquities be drastically restricted, with exports permitted only through a special license issued by the Ministry of Public Education and approved by the High Council of Antiquities and Fine Arts. With this proposal, he confronted a gap in the existing export system and explicitly linked running the state with monitoring the antiquities market. Rava and his allies recognized, however, that tighter export regulations would not be enough to stop the sale of protected cultural objects to private foreign buyers.

Transactions involving foreign buyers had long been described as a loss to Italy. In the course of the 1909 legislative debate, the loss took on new and dramatic dimensions as the permanent depletion of a national resource. "The quarry has no more marble left to give," remarked Rosadi in his remarks to the Chamber: *La cava non dava più marmo*.[63] With this analogy, art and antiquities were shifted to the column of natural resources, in relation to which the government had an acknowledged role. The language was intentional. Rosadi, Rava, and their allies sought to emphasize the art market as a one-way commercial chain leading outside Italy, with little or no compensation to the Italian people. The system had been set up so that antiquities were market commodities, with ownership predicated on buying power. There was no mistaking who the winners were, as Luigi Rava emphasized in his remarks:

Now here we have to recognize: it has come to fashion—outside of every honest provision to the contrary—the American price [*il prezzo americano*]. Every time that they offer the state an object of art to acquire, or a private collector finds something in an excavation, . . . in our soil, the Italian market, the experts, the artists, the archaeologists, those who have dedicated much study and much love to this material, fix a price; the price is what is highest at the time.

But before proposing the sale, we come up against the American price, and it is so fabulously, inconceivably high that we must defend ourselves against this exaggeration, and against the skillful maneuvering of sellers, antiquarians, agents, etc. . . . We should take into account that the antiquities market prices are fixed by exporters or sellers, and that given their desire to create museums and galleries quickly in far-away America, they create ownership possibilities through fabulous prices.[64]

Rava frames the international art market as a national struggle between Italy and the United States. The devious maneuvers of wealthy buyers and their agents, designed to create ownership possibilities, were the nemesis of honest Italian efforts to value and manage artworks. Rava had a pricing solution to a pricing problem. He proposed as a fix that the state should assert itself as having primary authority over establishing prices, directed at the Italian market (in his words) rather than the American market. This, he said, would send a clear message to the "acquisitive Americans as they tally their lists." Rava was still situating art and antiquities in the market system, albeit proposing much more state control over that system. The next speaker, however, took the discussion in a different direction, which would have significant effects on the substance and reach of cultural power in Italy.

Giovanni Rosadi refuted the notion that the task of the chamber was to design a better pricing system for art and antiquities. Those items were not to be priced at all, he suggested, because they were not supposed to leave the country in the first place.

Why are we spending our time trying to evaluate the export price while by law, the thing should not go abroad? It cannot go because article 9 regulates the prohibition of export in just this kind of case. An object cannot be exported if the government is forced to pay a price that would obtain only outside the country, perhaps beyond the ocean, in America. The price objectively set by the government is intended for the confines of the kingdom. Where are those prices promised by the ministry?[65]

Rosadi argued that the pricing logic of the Italian government was the outcome of a well-intentioned but ultimately naive understanding of the art market. The original intention had been to give the government an advantage in negotiating purchases of artworks from Italian collectors and family estates, negotiations that assumed both parties had an interest in keeping the artworks in Italy. But the government was now on the losing end of a bidding war with wealthy foreign buyers. Rosadi wanted to reinscribe artworks into the cultural economy, in which they were valued not in monetary units but for their social value.

The theme of art as a unifying social element was echoed throughout Rosadi's speech to the Chamber of Deputies in May 1909. He differentiated artworks from ethereal cultural experiences such as poems and dreams and asserted they were hard, essential components of society. Artworks were the great class equalizer: "It is for art and in the name of art that the salt miner from the smoking entrails of the earth and the astronomer descending from the stars, shining in joy, meet the same pleasures and comfort of the same pains."[66] Art has a social function, he concluded; it *is* a social benefit, and by assuming strong protective measures, the state would be benefiting society more broadly. Rosadi introduced the law by explaining that the nation had a particular interest in artistic works and antiquities, specifically those things that were considered to have a singular value (*un valore particolare*) and were held in private collections. Notwithstanding their private ownership, Rosadi asserted, the nation's interests overlapped with those of the private sphere. "Although it is the work of a particular person, who can in turn transfer it to another person, the work expresses the intellectual life of society and summarizes the various and indefinable elements of social life. [As such] the work is not the product solely of the artist's brain; rather it comes from those various and indefinable elements that are not his own but those of everyone [in society], because everyone, some more and some less, contributed to forming those elements."[67]

Rosadi's vision was striking. Breaking with the long tradition that understood artworks as the unique creation of the maker, Rosadi was adamant that artworks came out of society—not that they constituted a *reflection* of society, but that they were produced by shared ideas and forms that all people in society contributed to. As a result of this relationship between art and society, the nature of public and private would need to be distinguished. For Rosadi, the practical implication of this relationship was that the state was duty-bound to protect the nation's interest in important artistic and historical things by assuming responsibility for conservation, market controls, and export limits. This requirement also justified the state's right to enter as a third party into art transactions between private individuals and to have priority in purchasing the work, if necessary, to maintain the nation's cultural interests. The right to preemptive action—intervening in the sale of a work of art before its title could be transferred—amounted to an ambitious vision of cultural heritage as public property. It was justified on the grounds that the state's hands-off approach to the art market had resulted in the outflow of countless artistic treasures.

The 1909 debate involved a far-reaching reassessment of the centralized management of artistic goods in Italy. It codified the principle of inalienability, that specific term chosen because it signaled the fundamental connection between the artistic thing and the social group. It stressed that movable *and* immovable works were equally inalienable. Size and portability were no longer indicators that objects were available to private buyers. Previous cultural protection laws had stressed that municipal bodies had custodial obligations to artworks and monuments. The 1909 law made it plain that the Italian state had primary responsibility for the nation's artistic interests, and that along with this responsibility came the right to regulate the art market. That right to intervene was made possible by extending the concept of public property into a previously private sphere of commerce, thereby reformulating the entire set of relationships among artists, artworks, buyers, the public, and the state.

✷ CHAPTER 3 ✷

Distributing Sovereignty

FROM FASCISM TO THE ART SQUAD

In February 1909—a few months before passage of the watershed legislation we encountered in chapter 2—Filippo Tommaso Marinetti, poet, performer, and cultural entrepreneur, pronounced antiquity dead. His sensational *Futurist Manifesto* called on Italians to sever all ties with the country's past.[1] Ancient ruins, he argued, were a degenerative social disease, and the cure—the "sole hygiene"—was modern warfare.[2] Born in 1876 in Alexandria, Egypt, to prosperous Italian parents, Marinetti was a dashing figure with a penchant for silk cravats and fiery invective.[3] Equally at home in elite Parisian and Milanese society, he wrote poems in French and Italian and set his sights on literary greatness. Addicted to the adrenaline rush of motorsports, Marinetti was behind the wheel of his fast car when he swerved to avoid crashing into a pair of bicyclists and landed headfirst in a muddy ditch. Concussed but intact, he walked away from the accident with a dazzling vision: a truly modern Italy, freed from the shackles of ancient ruins. For the first time, Marinetti saw clearly that it was not only foreigners who regarded Italy as an ossified landscape of ghost worship. Italians themselves, he averred, were blinded to the possibilities of a brilliant future by the haze of mystical antiquity. Futurism was Marinetti's solution to this collective myopia. Attacking establishment intellectuals for pushing the "poison" of nostalgia and deluding themselves with their mania for antiquity, he argued that his modernist agenda for Italy could be fulfilled only with the total overthrow of the country's classical past.[4]

> It is in Italy that we are issuing this manifesto of ruinous and incendiary violence, by which we today are founding Futurism, because we want to deliver Italy from its gangrene of professors, archaeologists, tourist guides and antiquaries.

> Italy has been too long the great second-hand market. We want to get rid of the innumerable museums which cover it with innumerable cemeteries.
>
> Museums: cemeteries! . . . Do you want to poison yourselves? Do you want to rot? What can you find in an old picture except the painful contortions of the artist trying to break uncrossable barriers which obstruct the full expression of his dream? To admire an old picture is to pour our sensibility into a funeral urn instead of casting it forward with violent spurts of creation and action.
>
> . . . We will have none of it, we, the young, strong and living *Futurists*![5]

The resort to violence was not new. Marinetti wrote at a time when it was fashionable to link destruction with spiritual and ideological renewal.[6] What was novel was his rejection of the entirety of Italian art. Earlier thinkers had struggled with the place of art and antiquity in modern Italy, but they did agree that Italy's cultural past constituted a shared patrimony and that the unified nation needed it. Marinetti wanted to overthrow that history completely, and he was calling for a revolution that was at once artistic and political.[7] "We Futurists have as our sole political program the pride, the energy, and the expansion of the nation," he wrote in his first political statement. "We want a national representative body, which, freed from mummies, released from all pacifist cowardice, will be ready to thwart any affront, to answer any insult."[8] Italy did not need cultural patrimony. Antiquity had to be eliminated because its ruins and inert inscriptions obscured Italy's best vision of itself as a hawkish global power capable of conquest and sovereignty. The *Manifesto* was immensely popular.[9] It would serve as the founding document for the Futurists and inspire a generation of artists and intellectuals across Europe. It also inspired a young journalist named Benito Mussolini, who shared the movement's enthusiasm for machines, speed, and war but spurned its hatred of the antique and instead developed a highly selective program of classical revitalization.

As the door shut on the unregulated art market, a new chapter in the history of cultural power opened: a struggle to affix meaning to Italy's ancient heritage. This story begins as parody and ends in tragedy as clashing ideas about history, modernity, and the nation propelled a violent fantasy of imperial destiny embodied in Mussolini.[10] The essential themes of this story were incipient a full decade before the Fascist party takeover. While the Chamber of Deputies attempted to assert state authority over art and antiquities, a growing chorus of artists and intellectuals criticized the government's obsession with the past as the cause of Italy's social and economic stagnation.[11] But during the Fascist period, the government turned the economic vulnerability of the nation's cultural patrimony into a powerful asset. This historical moment saw the convergence of art, money, and politics into a new iteration of national patrimony (*patrimonio nazionale*). It amalgamated clashing ideas about public, private, and state cultural interests into "the unique (if not contradictory) space of a historical past and a political present."[12]

This chapter is structured around two significant 9s—1939 and 1969—from Mussolini and the Fascist articulation of Italian heritage, through the creation of the elite Carabinieri Art Squad at the end of the 1960s. I argue that national heritage was structured and administered in specific ways that developed cultural sovereignty—or aesthetic and ritual self-determination—into distributed sovereignty, a material- and object-oriented style of claims making by the Italian state. This style of claims making is temporally ambiguous and links people and events of the remote past with contemporary social units as though their continuity is taken for granted. It is also territorially fluid, exceeding the geographic boundaries of the nation-state and supporting the invocation of artifacts as flexible signifiers of geographic indebtedness. Distributed sovereignty took its modern form in the Fascist years. Politically, the Chamber of Fascists passed successive legislative measures that greatly increased the state's authority over cultural property, extended the definition of state patrimony to include ever more diverse object types and time periods, and granted itself the right to confiscate artworks and artifacts from Italian Jews and other "foreign" persons in order to keep those objects for the "Italian people." In this specific version of the logic of accumulation, the state required artifacts to justify colonial occupation, displaying them in exhibitions and shows, and using their abundance as proof of imperial destiny. Symbolically, artifactual power was concentrated in the body of the dictator, who used image, discourse, and physical action to develop his authority as maker and creator of a new Rome. Even after Mussolini's death and the forced (but far from complete) removal of Fascist symbols from the public sphere, antiquities retained his mark. In a cultural theory of distributed sovereignty, one based in artifacts and images and their meanings, the objects convey the real presence of the author.

Mussolini built the case for Fascism on a list of grievances. He argued that corrupt, decadent leadership under the Piedmontese, effeminate public culture, and the erosion of traditional values had weakened Italy and prevented the country from reclaiming its historical place of greatness. The nation's vulnerability, he insisted, was manifest in the despoliation of the classical landscape, with its marble temples and monuments built by the Caesars. The fear of losing antiquities that punctuated the 1909 parliamentary debate had become a bigger concern—the survival of the young nation. Resisting vulnerability and redeeming national preeminence demanded a reformulation of sovereignty, and antiquities became the ideal platform for disseminating and conveying that power.

Mussolini and the Lictorial Generation

In September 1911 Italy declared war on the Ottoman Empire, and six weeks later it annexed the territories of Tripolitania and Cyrenaica in North Africa. Italian dominion over those territories was eventually recognized by European powers in the Treaty of Lausanne of July 1923. The period of occupation was marked by violent control of local populations, exploitation of natural resources, and the systematic degradation of native Libyans in favor of the Italian rulers. Against this backdrop, the Italian state enlisted antiquities in the project of colonialism. The Venus of Cyrene, a beautifully preserved Roman copy of a Greek statue, was discovered in the Libyan settlement of Cyrene by Italian troops in 1913, some two years after the annexation. The sensational find was shipped to Rome and displayed in the Octagonal Hall of the Baths of Diocletian (Museo Nazionale delle Terme), where it remained for ninety years. The statue became an emblem of Italy's new empire, appearing in official images from postage stamps to public art exhibitions. The statue's antiquity suggested long-term Roman presence in North Africa, while the form of the statue itself fit comfortably within popular understanding of what the art of ancient Italy looked like. It had the supreme symbolic advantage of establishing historical remoteness, in the sense of creating the appearance of long-term sociocultural presence of Romans in Libya, and of fostering cultural familiarity because Italian audiences could assimilate the Venus into a generic visual vocabulary of the Roman antique.

In antiquities, ruins, and the material fabric of classical Rome, Mussolini saw the building blocks—literal and figurative—for a redeemed, Fascist nation. "Concerns about prestige and form weighed heaviest in Italy," Ruth Ben-Ghiat argues, "where reclamation [of land and civilizational legacy] represented above all a chance to reverse the nation's perceived subaltern status with respect to other foreign powers and to all things modern."[13] The regime emphasized the capacity of culture to bring order to society, focused on a populist idea that ties of solidarity arose through public rallies and spectacles that showcased shared symbols and standardized aesthetic forms. In 1922 Mussolini wrote, "Rome is our point of departure and reference; it is our symbol, or if you want, our myth. We dream of a Roman Italy that is wise and strong, disciplined and imperialist. Much of what was the immortal spirit of Rome is reborn in Fascism. . . . Not only were the Romans soldiers, but also excellent builders who could challenge, as they did challenge, time."[14] Fascism would "glorify the nation" by sacralizing Roman history as national myth. The aesthetic forms of classical Rome, combined with machine-age ideas about bodily discipline and conformity, constituted a powerful expressive platform for the Fascist regime. This is the language of *romanità*, the Fascist admiration of antiquity as expressed through militant idioms and performance. The word *fascismo* derived from the Latin *fascis* (English "fasces"), a bundle of rods tied together and topped with an ax blade, carried in formal processions by attendants called lictors to symbolize the authority of the high magistrates.[15]

In May 1936 the regime declared victory against Ethiopia ("Abyssinia"), and Mussolini proclaimed to his public "the reappearance, after fifteen centuries, of empire on the fated hills of Rome."[16] The image of a legendary victory in Egypt was exploited to "create a strong consensus about the imperial status in Italy. . . . What made such propaganda especially important overseas for both liberal and Fascist Italy was the aura of prestige that the State emanated toward the public, and outward to the ensemble of great powers."[17] Cartographic tablets on the Via dell'Impero in the heart of Rome proclaimed a new Italian geography, tracing the borders of the ancient empire to the contemporary African conquests of Il Duce. Using white for Italian-occupied land ("ROMA") and black shading for the lands outside, the lapidary maps emphasized the civilizing mission of the colonial rulers.[18] The display space par excellence for the new propaganda was the colonial exhibition, above all the Fiera Campionaria di Tripoli (National Exhibition of Tripoli), the first of which Mussolini initiated in 1927. Principally, the Fiera Campionaria informed visitors about the colony of Libya, using props and stagecraft to recreate the "traditional" living quarters and marketplaces of local people. In publicity materials connected with the colonial exhibitions, artworks and artifacts suggested a long-term historical link between Italy and Libya (fig. 10). But this is not a friendly gesture, nor was Libya seen as a cultural equal.[19] The Venus of Cyrene and other Roman antiquities advertised Italy's ongoing generosity toward the supposedly inferior North African country, and the bridging device was cultural as well as economic. Elsewhere the Venus statue is paired in Fascist iconography with a twin-prop airplane, contrasting Libya's "stunted" economic and technological growth with Italy's forward movement. As we will see in chapter 5, when Silvio Berlusconi returned the sculpture to Libyan leader Muammar Qaddafi, the

FIGURE 10. Postage stamp commemorating the 1934 Second International Colonial Exhibition in Naples. The stamp features the marble Venus of Cyrene, which was taken to Italy from Libya during the Italian occupation. After years of diplomatic negotiation, the statue was repatriated in 2008. De Agostini Picture Library/Bridgeman Images.

Venus itself became the embodiment of Italian vulnerability to the colonial Other.

ROMANITÀ AND THE BODY OF IL DUCE

Mussolini's body stood at the center of Fascist symbology. His authority "derived directly from his body."[20] Italy was Mussolini and Mussolini was Italy. This elision was so pervasive that even Mussolini loyalists worried that Fascism was *too* dependent on the dictator's physical vigor and charisma and that without him there would be insufficient ideological or programmatic capacity to sustain the movement. His strength and virility helped make Italy's imperial claims plausible and intoxicating, and the Italian public came to know his features intimately through photography, film, and live spectacle. He incorporated specific gestures, postures, dress, and manly acts of vigor to promote the Fascist ideal of self-discipline. Drawing on a pastiche of actual and imagined classical practices, Mussolini offered a militant performance of Romanness. Among the most visible was the *passo romano*, the goose-step march that was a staple of Fascist parades and other public spectacles. In *Scritti e discorsi* he explained the importance of the *passo*:

> Our march . . . imposes individual control on everyone [and] impresses on everyone order and discipline. Because we want in fact to initiate a solid national discipline, because we think that without this discipline Italy cannot become the Mediterranean and world nation of which we dream. And those who reproach us for marching like the Germans should realize that it is not us who are copying from them but the Germans who copy and have copied from the Romans. Thus it is us who return to our origins, to our Roman, Latin, and Mediterranean style.[21]

Note the way Mussolini asserts cultural authority over the *passo*. It is the Germans who are the imitators, deriving *their* marching style from a practice that is manifestly Roman. The version of ancient Rome being summoned here is in sharp contrast to that of Ferraris, Rava, or Rosadi, the architects of the 1909 national patrimony law. Mussolini's Rome is not a source of contemplative ruins or idioms and objects whose chief purpose is beauty. Fascist *romanità* emphasized Rome as *imperium*, with its professional and ruthlessly efficient army that once occupied much of Europe and North Africa. Here and in other writings, Mussolini blurs time in referring to "us" Italians as "Romans." This was not an invocation of civic identity. He initially loathed the city of Rome and remained ambivalent about it. Rather, Il Duce resurrected the collective signifier of imperial Rome to label his compatriots *new* Romans and "the energy of the young lictorial generations who are enthusiastic about . . . the authentic military spirit."[22]

This appropriation of a specific aspect of classical Rome, and its didactic role in generating a Fascist social order premised on conformity and bodily subordination, was to have long-term interpretive implications for Italian patrimony. Mussolini made Caesarian modernity possible by proclaiming shared meaning in the material remnants of antiquity and then defining that meaning through his robustness and martial masculinity. To show his endorsement of the Fascist revitalization of the city of Rome—a project that involved demolishing impoverished neighborhoods—he put his back into the effort. In 1931, to initiate construction on the Via dell'Impero design, he delivered the symbolic first blow. This plan entailed massive displacements—of people (four hundred Romans were removed from their homes) and building rubble (forty thousand cubic meters). On this occasion, as at other official demolitions and construction launches from 1929 to 1936, Mussolini was said to have proclaimed, "Let the pickax speak!"[23] Blunt edges and hard blows were to do the talking, not words. By displaying impatience with negotiation and talk, the dictator deployed a Fascist performative trope: We have waited long enough; we have listened to the beguiling speech acts of the politicians; we will take back the country through the grueling but honest physical work of clearance and redemption. The image of Mussolini wielding a pickax—in film, painting, and photography—was an effective style of claims making. Its close association with the fasces was unmistakable. Demolition disciplined the urban terrain, purged the city of "old Rome" infrastructure, and signaled the regime's authoritarian command of the broader civic landscape.

Pickax imagery also celebrated Mussolini as the nation's premier archaeologist. The March 3, 1935, edition of the *Domenica del Corriere,* a popular weekly magazine, celebrated this aspect of his authority. The cover presents a colored ink drawing of Mussolini, in military officer's costume, standing on a shingled rooftop in the foreground (fig. 11). Readers familiar with urban Rome would have immediately recognized the setting: with the monument of Victor Emmanuel II in the left background and Trajan's Column to the right, the action is situated just off the ancient Roman Forum. These were highly significant monuments in Fascist symbology. Mussolini holds a pickax with both hands, swinging it over his head as he shifts his weight to the back before striking forward. The tiled roof is already crumbling, and the force of Mussolini's blow suggests it is unlikely to last long. The tiles are clearly out of place: rotting, peeling, and discolored, they are an eyesore against the clean orderliness of the classicizing backdrop. Two young men dressed in workers' clothes crouch near the dictator's back foot. Their faces are obscured, affirming their secondary role. They stand for the workmen who will take over the demolition after the dictator leaves, and they also stand for the gains of this project to the generic Italian man or woman.

The dictator's plan is explained in the picture's caption: "Il Duce strikes the first blow of the pickax to liberate the area destined for the Mole Littoria which, within four years, at the front of the glorious monumentality of the city, will symbolize the power of Fascist Italy."[24] He is *liberating* the ancient forum from the decrepitude of the urban slums. That these slums contained buildings one thousand years old, and were themselves important markers of the city's medieval period, was of no interest to the Fascist regime. Fascist historiography selected past people, events, and sites that aligned with a teleological vision of past and future. In doing so

LA DOMENICA DEL CORRIERE

Si pubblica a Milano ogni settimana

Supplemento illustrato del "Corriere della Sera"

Uffici del giornale
Via Solferino, 28 - Milano

Anno XXXVII — N. 9 | 3 Marzo 1935 - Anno XIII | Centesimi 30 la copia

Il Duce vibra il primo colpo di piccone per liberare l'area destinata alla Mole Littoria che, fra quattro anni, di fronte alle glorie monumentali dell'Urbe, simboleggerà la potenza dell'Italia fascista. (Disegno di A. Beltrame)

FIGURE 11. Mussolini striking the first blow of the pickax in the Fascist regime's effort to "liberate" the ancient Roman Forum from the modern slums. Cover image of the *Domenica del Corriere*, March 3, 1935. Bridgeman Images.

it also made archaeological stratigraphy a spectacle of masculine power. What is startling about the scene is precisely how *un*-archaeological it is. Mussolini carries out a demolition job. The slow and methodical clearing of soil to study past levels of inhabitation is here replaced with a highly visible—because literally on the skyline—presentation of obliterating unwanted historical material. Professional archaeologists of the era used trowels and brushes and were photographed in pith helmets and jodhpurs or, back in their offices and departments, in the suits and ties of academics. While fieldwork campaigns retained terminological vestiges of nineteenth-century colonial treasure hunts, archaeologists themselves did not normally pose in military dress. They also did not undertake the grueling physical labor of clearing topsoil or removing modern structures. That work would have been assigned to hired laborers.

By appearing in military dress with a pickax, Mussolini carves out a unique visual niche. Coarse, muscular, and possessed of primal physical power, he gestures toward the tomb robber. He, like the *tombarolo,* demonstrates his loyalty to the patria by rescuing antiquities from interpretive corruption *outside* the normal processes of state administration. In this guise, Mussolini was adamantly not a deskbound academic who studies artifacts within the strictures of science. The demolition of the Roman slums was a symbolic blow against the degeneracy of Italian manhood and the sloth of the liberal city. Fascism's ahistorical conception of history was expressed in spatial terms, thereby leaving a permanent imprint on the fabric of the nation's past. For Mussolini, as for *tombaroli* today, Italy was both an idea and a physical space to be shaped by stratigraphy and extractive mastery.

1939: The Fascist Expansion of State Cultural Power

With the dictator's pickax metonymically invoking archaeological discovery, Fascist lawmakers were busy designing an administrative structure that would greatly expand the curatorial, market, and interpretive authority of the state. Fascist cultural policy was characterized by a repressive, racialized ideology that redefined Italian nationality as based on skin color and blood rather than shared language and history.[25] Classical Rome was now the birthright of a select, racially pure Italian community whose mission was to bring social "harmony" by subjugating the individual will to the collective spirit. Rituals, symbols, and ordered spaces were central to this vision.

The Fascist government dramatically reorganized the administration of material patrimony. The most important legislation was the Decreto legislativo 1089/1939, "Guardianship of Items of Artistic and Historic Interest" ("Tutela delle Cose di Interesse Artistico e Storico"). The law was named for Giuseppe Bottai, the minister of national education and primary sponsor of the legislation. Bottai was an avowed anti-Semite and proponent of "Aryan" supremacy. The previous year, in remarks prefatory to his legislative push, he had claimed that the 1909 law was too passive in its approach to protecting patrimony. To realize the full economic potential of Italian artworks and antiquities, he called for a more stringently enforced form of guardianship (*tutela manovrata*) that would exploit the art market and thus promote the visibility of patrimony. The Bottai law proposed changes to the organization of regional patrimony offices, looser art market regulations, and greatly expanded seizure authority. Three weeks after its passage, in May 1939, Italy and Germany signed the Pact of Steel, a military and political agreement articulating mutual support on the path to global war.

PATRIMONY AND FASCIST IMPERIALISM

To understand the full force of the 1939 law and its support by Fascist leaders, we can start by looking at the bureaucratic arrangements. Legal responsibility for state management of artworks and antiquities initially lay with the lower house of the national government, the Chamber of Deputies, and it was incumbent on this elected body to evaluate and change the legal infrastructure as necessary. But by January 1939 the Chamber of Deputies had been replaced with the Chamber of Fascists and Corporations (Camera dei Fasci e delle Corporazioni), a renaming that reflected Fascist support for corporatism—the oversight of economic and social functions by corporate interests.[26] The chamber's members were appointed rather than elected and were called national councillors instead of deputies. Elected deputies had represented geographic districts, but councillors represented specific branches of trade and industry. Councillor Alberto Calza Bini, an architect and painter, represented the building construction industry. He proposed to restructure the superintendencies because, according to him, the old system had failed. The pre-Fascist system included twenty-eight superintendencies across the national territory. Each one was responsible for excavations as well as monuments, galleries, and artworks. It was too much for any single superintendent to handle, he complained, since it was unrealistic and redundant to expect every unit to employ specialists in every period or material category of cultural patrimony. As an alternative, Calza Bini advocated replacing the regional offices with superintendencies that focused on specific material and disciplinary subjects such as ethnography and paleontology, subjects not mentioned by the 1909 law. These subjects were, as it happened, epistemologically significant for Fascist theories of Italy's history and civilizational progress.

In response, several officials voiced concern that the organizational change would erode the salience of local cultures by turning symbols and aesthetic traditions into a weak imitation of Italian culture. There was also concern that the so-called primitive civilizations favored by ethnography and paleontology would dilute the value of the fine arts. Addressing these anxieties, Biagio Pace, president of the Legislative Commission for National Education, explained the higher mission of artistic culture and ethnography for Italy's place as a powerful nation:

> As for the superintendencies without territorial jurisdiction, they have been designed to respond to a need of high culture. Italy, which lives in the reality of the Empire, must have an organization of ethnographic studies, destined not only to maintain a primacy of studies and collections, but also to document one of the most formidable elements of our imperial law: the actions of Italian adventurers [*viaggiatori*] of the 1800s. The precious Italian collections . . . not only have an intrinsic material value, but are the titles of our right to the Empire, because they document the fervor and individual passion of these explorers in the darkest periods, even before unification.[27]

The nineteenth-century explorers he invoked were irredentists who championed the reoccupation of lands they considered historically "Italian": parts of France, Albania, Libya, Ethiopia, and Dalmatia. The phrase "titles of our right to the Empire" (*i titoli del nostro diritto all'Impero*) cued a discourse popular among supporters of Italian colonial expansion.[28] This discourse held that the material remains of past cultural groups, from classical antiquity through the Renaissance and early modern period, justified Italy's occupation of lands settled by Italian ancestors. The cultural materials of the Italian territory were the cornerstone of the imperial claims of Fascist Italy.

The 1939 law had three major effects. The first was the erosion of scholarly autonomy, specifically in archaeology and anthropology. Because the legitimacy of Fascist imperial Italy required solid evidence of prior occupation by Italic peoples, Italy must form "a fierce array of scholars of imperial ethnography" and support research "dedicated to the enhancement of this scientific and political heritage."[29] Archaeology became a political minefield of interests, and ideological loyalty *as well as* conformity to new methods and classifications were de facto requirements for funding and employment. Further, the sector of state cultural management was ordered to reengage with Egyptology, a subject area in which Italian scholars were once highly regarded. It was imperative that Italian Egyptology regain its place of superiority, according to Pace, in light of the country's colonial holdings in North Africa.[30]

Second, the law overhauled the art market once again. "Today's provisions account for—even excessively catering to, at times—the needs of the antiquarian market for artworks," announced Bottai in his opening remarks, "which has important repercussions for the field of trade and currencies." The 1909 law maligned the market, he said, and was misguided in its attempt to restrict art exports. Tourism and market demand were in fact valid forms of artistic appreciation. If preserving the artistic and historical national heritage of the country was to be an urgent priority for the state, a "collecting spirit" must be nurtured.[31] The list of object types eligible for sale was expanded. It was a paradoxical provision for a national patrimony law, and its inconsistency was soon exploited. In mid-1937, Adolf Hitler transmitted a request to obtain the Discobolus Lancellotti, a Roman marble copy of a fifth-century bronze original by the Greek sculptor Myron. Bottai denied the request, citing the 1909 law and arguing that the sculpture was a protected item of national patrimony and could not be sold. After repeated petitions from Germany, in June 1938 Mussolini ordered Bottai to approve the transfer of the Discobolus to Germany. This transaction set a precedent, and with the passage of his law the following year, scores of masterpieces were removed from Italy to Germany. Nazi collectors including Hermann Göring strong-armed advantageous art purchases out of Italian cultural authorities and resorted to nontraditional market transactions including tax-free gifts. Bottai objected to the duty-free art allowance Mussolini gave to the Germans, and at this point he had lost control over the market that he had helped deregulate. In November 1941 Bottai allowed thirty-four crates filled with artwork and antiquities to be shipped to Germany at Göring's personal request (Coccolo 2016).

Finally, Bottai's law expanded the list of things eligible for protection, thereby extending the state's authority over private cultural property. Whereas the old law limited the state's interventionist power to cases of "great danger for the conservation of works," the Bottai law would allow the state to appropriate "for public use" (*per pubblica utilità*) any areas and buildings that the ministry determined to be of essential interest. The state could do this if it felt it was necessary to protect a monument from urban development, for example, or to add artificial light to enhance public enjoyment. Under the Bottai law, it could also remove cultural patrimony from Jewish owners. Successive legislative reforms in 1938 restricted the type and amount of property Jewish citizens could own (*RDL* 1928/1939 and 1728/1938). After November 1938 all Jewish-owned property was subject to seizure by Italian authorities. As Jewish citizens attempted to flee the country with their property, the Ministry of National Education grappled with the massive outflow of art. In March 1939 it issued circular 43 to prevent Italian Jews from taking art and antiquities out of Italy. Customs officials deliberately overestimated the value of works so they could not be exported. The following year, the Directorate General of Public Security banned all trade in Jewish-owned artworks and antiquities. Seizure of art and antiquities from Jewish citizens became so rampant that further reforms were required to prevent works from disappearing into Fascist officials' private collections. Jewish property seizure, fueled by Mussolini's paranoid distrust of an international Jewish conspiracy, both imperiled Jewish citizens and enriched the state patrimony.[32]

THE LONG SHADOW OF 1939

The Bottai law remained essentially intact until 1999. It survived postwar anti-Fascism and was praised by scholars for its "bold and progressive ideas" about national heritage and the state's obligation to protect it. Their praise came with full awareness of the law's origins and deep entanglements with Fascist ideology.[33] An attempt was made to separate Fascist ideas from Fascist institutional reforms, as though the ideological element was an unfortunate ancillary component of the Bottai law. But the debates in the Chamber of Fascists were thoroughly informed by interests in colonial expansion, nationalist exclusions, and racial reordering through scientific research in paleontology and ethnography. Further, the rules and regulations were enforceable by a repressive regime willing to use its power to imprison and censure violators. The dissolution of regional jurisdictions in the superintendency system has been cited approvingly as a farsighted move to strengthen national cultural policy by prioritizing disciplinary expertise over local identity. But this is a superficial rereading of intent. The members of the Chamber of Fascists meant to weaken local authority, strengthen national authority, and concentrate expert energy in research and conservation projects supportive of colonial expansion. Fascist politics focused on an exclusive categorizing of national identity, divided along lines that blurred "race" and culture by pointing to artifacts as substantive evidence of such divisions.

Taken together, the organizational changes brought by the 1939 Bottai law constituted a significant development in the cultural sovereignty of the state. In 1909 the state's official interest was in fine arts and things of beauty whose full meaning drew from its link to the Italian soil. Cultural power was solidified by controlling the circulation of art and artifacts and preserving them in place. Once an object left the country, unless theft was suspected, it was beyond the reach of the state. The "open-air museum," in sum, was synonymous with the bounded political geography of Italy. With the 1939 law, cultural sovereignty was no longer limited to territorial jurisdiction. Now it was a national self-determination anchored in objects with plausible cultural affiliation, even if those objects were embedded in soil outside Italy. Roman antiquities were a beachhead—the strategic landing points for the Fascist colonial expedition. Jurisdiction metaphorically extended to any instantiation of *romanità* in material form. The expansion of the types of objects to be protected—adding fossils, ethnographic materials, and paleontological materials to the state's list—gave Italy more things to claim as its own. This justified seizure across borders, into Africa and the so-called unredeemed territories. It also strengthened state intervention into domestic affairs, an authority still exercised by Italian law enforcement. State authority extended to wherever its claimed artifacts were physically present, and those artifacts became the basis for new capital projects.

The Personalized Politics of Patrimony

Mussolini's image, we have seen, was ubiquitous. He was posed in a range of situations, activities, and costumes. Like divine figures from classical mythology, he had multiple aspects or components of his character and ability—Mussolini the harvester, Mussolini the excavator, Mussolini the father. His iconography deployed objects to signal these aspects: the pickax, fasces, and black shirt were among the most popular. Mussolini "was everywhere with his name as well as his effigy, in gestures as well as in words—and more than Kemal in Turkey and even more than Lenin in Moscow."[34] Bars of soap, postage stamps, belt buckles, bathing suits, hatbands, children's schoolbooks, and kitchen calendars are a few of the many items that bore his image. His presence was made palpable by materializing his image in diverse forms. The presence effects of the dictator were not confined to official reprints or monuments, of course; they flowed through tactile encounters with mundane objects.[35] His ubiquity enhanced his divinity, suggesting the ability to appear simultaneously in different places and to permeate society through multiple media and manifestations. It was not just his image that was distributed, it was his authority and, by extension, the nation he commanded.

The prolific and diverse materialization of Mussolini's authority was part of a broader politics of embodied knowledge of the patria. Through his patronage of artwork and archaeological digs and his avid assembling of antiquities exhibitions for political propaganda, it was not just his regime but also his *person* that was associated with Roman artifacts.[36] His person became fused with the material substance of the artifacts and the very act of their creation. To explain what this kind of authority did and how it developed, I examine two contrasting figures: *Homo faber,* whom I draw from the work of Hannah Arendt, and *Homo autotelus,* from Walter Benjamin and one of his most influential theorists, Susan Buck-Morss. *Homo faber,* man the maker, has the power to craft material experience, while *Homo autotelus,* self-created man, points to the power to determine the boundaries of possible experience.

HOMO AUTOTELUS AND *HOMO FABER*

Homo autotelus is the myth of man being "creator ex nihilo of his own work of art."[37] In Buck-Morss's analysis, *Homo autotelus* is "one of the most persistent myths in the whole history . . . of Western political thought."[38] Grounded in the fantasy of autogenesis, *Homo autotelus*'s ability to make himself dispenses with women as necessary contributors to creation and, transferred to Mussolini, jettisons the effeminate trappings of culture. Indeed, *Homo autotelus* gives no credit to anyone for his accomplishments. Nothing about him is derivative. For Buck-Morss the fantasy is highly gendered, but gender alone is insufficient to understand the power of Mussolini's vision of himself as creator of a new and better modern Italy. His endowment to his people was cultural patrimony, which he was entitled to bequeath both because he was the fictive father of the nation and because sovereign power was vested in him. This model of sovereignty was of primacy, indivisibility, and self-sufficiency. Fascist Italy was reliant only on itself—on its loyal, industrious, and vigorous population. And Il Duce—the self-sufficient leader—captured those ideal qualities of state in his own fantasy of remaking the nation as a sculptor shapes a block of marble.

At issue here are two understandings of culture and power: power through the manufacture of culture, and power through the capacity to create the possibility of culture. In her 1958 essay "Culture and Politics," Hannah Arendt examines states' anxieties about the power of culture and the ways they have attempted to control it. The essay centers on *Homo faber*, roughly translated as "man the maker," whose power extends from the ability to make images from raw materials.[39] Comparing ancient Greece and Rome—a favored move in Arendt's work, reflecting her conviction that premodernity offered the clearest historical backdrop for rethinking modernity—she finds that the Greeks made a stronger effort to circumscribe the influence of *Homo faber*. In Athens, artists were excluded from the political realm. While at first blush this arrangement sounds sinister, Arendt sees in it the potential for liberation. Excluding *Homo faber* from political life allowed artists and artisans to work free from ideological constraint, creating paintings, sculptures, and plays without fear of electoral censure or vendetta. The *polis*, or public sphere of activity and work, did not control culture, but it *limited* the "love of wisdom and love of beauty." Arendt leaves open the precise meaning of this idea, which she takes from Thucydides, but what was central for her was that "the political limited the cultural."[40] On the other hand, culture was not a priority in Roman society, she says, since its leaders did not regard artistic labor as equal to the contributions and gravitas of politics. As such, they "did not take culture seriously until it was ready to become an object of care for them, and thus a part of the *res publica* [public matters]."[41] We see two models, then, for culture and politics in ancient states: the Roman model of "care," which adumbrates the *custodial* model of modern heritage work, and the Greek model of free but limited artistic expression.

Imbued with the dazzling skills of image making and imagination, *Homo faber* represents the sovereign power of the artist. The dilemma this presents for states is the potential usurpation of the function to create reality. Arendt suggests that this dilemma is perennial, persisting wherever culture and politics exist. The ancient states contended with it by controlling *Homo faber* as a thing of public interest or accomplishment (the *res publica* Arendt refers to). In Fascist Italy, the state's solution was for its leader to *become* the *Homo faber*—in other words, to assume fictive authorship through physical acts (the man of action) and bureaucratic processes (the men of classifications and stratigraphic levels). The sovereign power of *Homo faber* was transferred from the dictator to the artifacts he "created." As *rector*, to borrow Reed's terminology, Mussolini was both the person at the top of the chain of relations and a "representation of the world that accounts for where authorized action comes from": "The accoutrements of rule that 'stand for' him (ministers, materials used in rituals, the grand mansion in which he lives, his uncle-qua-guardian, the papers he has signed) have more to say about what you do, when you do it, and who you do it to and for, than does the emperor himself, qua human person."[42]

Antiquities, as representations of Mussolini and the regime he created, expanded the grounds on which the Italian state could claim authorship and hence colonial "re"occupation. Reformulated as such, what counts as "Italian" and "patrimony" includes any archaeological materials that have historical, aesthetic, stylistic, linguistic, or material precedents in "Rome." The tightly packed stratigraphy of the soil has now become the first link in a chain of cultural power that stretches across any of the lands once inhabited by Latin speakers. Like the emperors before him, Mussolini was a man of action (*Homo faber*) and the author of miraculous creation (*Homo autotelus*). In the artifactual domain, he could both carve marble out of the rocky confines of the earth and create a horizon of imagery to conduct its transformation into sculpted masterpieces. Buck-Morss writes, "The fact that one can *imagine* something that *is* not, is extrapolated in the fantasy that one can (re)create the world according to plan.... It is the fairy-tale promise that wishes are granted—without the fairy tale's wisdom that the consequences can be disastrous."[43] It was into the realm of fairy-tale wish fulfillment that antiquities distributed the authority of the dictator. Indeed, patrimony itself was turned into a dangerous parody of history—a form of wish fulfillment predicated on the Italian people's "unfailing faith in the destiny of the Fatherland."[44]

In April 1945 Mussolini was captured by Italian Resistance fighters and shot, along with his mistress and several aides. Their corpses were hung from meat hooks in the Piazzale Loreto in Milan, but only after angry crowds had been allowed to beat, kick, mutilate, shoot, and desecrate their corpses. In a strange and ironic twist, Mussolini's chance at political resurrection was granted through a daring act of tomb robbery—the very sort of action harshly punished by the 1939 law the dictator had personally approved. On Easter Day in April 1946, his body was dug up from an unmarked grave in the Musocco cemetery in Milan. Over the course of a hundred days, the Italian press breathlessly followed the ensuing manhunt. The culprits were tracked down and arrested, and Mussolini's remains were recovered from the convent of Sant'Angelo in Milan, stuffed into a small trunk. State officials condemned the theft of the corpse; by contrast, Fascist sympathizers praised it as a heroic defense of Mussolini's legacy. Domenico Leccisi, the twenty-six-year-old ringleader of the tomb robbers and an ardent Fascist, became a cult hero and was eventually hailed as the founder of the neo-Fascist Italian Social Movement.[45] Tomb robbers, whether disinterring Il Duce's body or long-hidden artifacts, confirmed the Futurists' fears that Italians will never escape their obsession with the dead past. We have come full circle with Marinetti and his manifesto.

Celebrated and condemned by turn, the Mussolini grave robbers' ambiguous status in Italian political memory points to several features they shared with *tombaroli*. First, both sets of actors claim to be defending a pure and honest Italy that is vulnerable to the depravities of state corruption and foreign meddling. Second, they do so through artifactual relics, whose material tactility is mobilized to justify their cause as historically legitimate. Third, they are not classic grave robbers in the sense of disturbing the dead and committing a religious taboo. Historical proximity—simultaneously immanent and remote—minimizes that stigma. In life, Mussolini had turned the political order upside down by becoming the intimate embodiment of the Fascist state. His death left the state without its *Homo autotelus*, its visionary builder and inspiration for the national community. Mussolini made Roman antiquities indissolubly Fascist, and it was the set of meanings read through his body that promised a resurrection of civilization for the Italian people. If the relics were to survive the bloody regime transition, they needed to transcend the script written for them by the Fascist state. Bottai, once the architect of the Fascist state's patrimony laws but now a repentant former Fascist, understood what the dictator's death meant for Italy. "No longer is the state man writ large," he argued. "Man is now the state writ small."[46] Rebuilding Italy demanded rethinking the relationship between the state and the national community of Italian women, children, and men. All those artifacts, those bits and pieces of earlier eras, had some kind of role to play. Italy had lost the war, civil society was fragile, and Italians struggled to make sense of what their history meant for the country's future.

Losing the War, Rebuilding Cultural Power

Defeated, humiliated, and depleted, Italians faced a long road to recovery after 1945. The collapse of the Fascist regime caused chaos at all levels of the state, with the economy, military, and civil service in disarray. Immediately after the armistice with the Allies, the Badoglio administration moved to purge the government of Fascist sympathizers and punish Fascist crimes.[47] The first wave of postwar political reform focused on individuals in positions of power. While sharing superficial features with German denazification, Italian defascization differed in significant aspects. The Allied governments blamed Germany for the war and recognized that long-term democratic peace in central Europe would require dismantling the Third Reich and rebuilding the country from the ground up. Postwar reform in Germany was a massive effort at reeducation, "born of a deep distrust of German culture but also of a pragmatic hope for the future."[48] The Allies believed that German reform at all levels—economic, cultural, social, and political—was vital to stability in Europe and to global peace. Germany, not Italy, had instigated two disastrous world wars in quick succession. Germany, not Italy, was seen as the bulwark against the encroachment of Communism from the East to the West. In the future of Germany, in other words, lay the future of the world. The stakes were different in Italy. Allied interest in defascization centered on political stabilization. Whether Italian culture was salvageable was less important to the Allies than the expediency of keeping Italian Communists from seizing power. The United States needed Italy to be a stable democracy, and so pragmatism trumped ideology: as Victoria Belco writes, "Not all remnants of the Fascist *ventennio* (or of pre-Fascist Italy) were abandoned. . . . Some Fascist era (and some pre-Fascist era) institutions and organizations still worked in whole or in part."[49] State administrative functions were subject to ad hoc revision. Some policies and procedures were retained because they made sense, and because regional and local administrators were desperately trying to patch together a functioning civic sphere after the horrors of civil war and German reprisals.

REHABILITATING ROME

Italian intellectuals and politicians grappled with how to disentangle classical Rome from Mussolini's legacy. In Germany the question of what would now be acceptable public iconography was forcefully answered in 1949, when all Nazi symbols and celebrations, including the Hitler salute, were banned from public settings. No law of comparable reach was passed in Italy. The 1953 Scelba Law included provisions to block political organizing by Fascists and Communists but did not explicitly prohibit symbols. Purging Italy of Fascist monuments was impractical because there were so many of them, and because the party's ideology had been grafted onto the country's massive ancient patrimony. The Roman Forum was an essential space in Fascist spectacle. Should it be razed? Emperors' portraits reminded the public of Mussolini's imperial aspirations. Should they be removed from displays? What about the millions of fasces and she-wolves embedded in the everyday fabric of public life, including manhole covers and mailboxes?[50] Answers to these questions focused on dismantling *Roma Mussolinea*, or Mussolini's variant of *romanità*. Historians and archaeologists sought to wash their hands of Fascist archaeology and the stain of collaboration. They rejected *romanità* as ahistorical and unscholarly and advocated a return to inscriptions, historical texts, and scientific archaeology that would recover the true legacy of Rome. As Amedeo Maiuri, an influential archaeologist made famous by his excavations at Pompeii and Herculaneum, put it, "While we are led back from the difficulties of those trials undergone and those still to undergo, not to Imperial Rome, a phenomenon more universal than Italian and instruction more for others than for ourselves, but to the Latium and Republican Rome, to a Rome which must newly re-conquer, more in terms of spirit than of institutions, the unity of the homeland."[51]

The emphasis here is on Latium, as the center of the peninsula was known in antiquity, and the Republic, two terms that resonated with *virtus*, *humanitas*, and the honest simplicity of cherished figures from history (Brutus) and historical myth (Romulus). Note that Maiuri preserves the possibility of a legitimate role for imperial materials in postwar Italy. Rebuilding ("those trials undergone and those still to undergo") is in its first phase to be inward-facing, and a matter of reunifying the homeland. That is the domain of Latium. Empire, however, retains its universal significance and capacity for instruction in civilization. The task of classical studies was no longer to find evidence for Italian modernity, or to celebrate the achievements of the Caesars. The task was to go back further, "to examine what might have been the virtues of the Latin people before Grace illuminated them, in order to make them worthy" of the Roman legacy.[52]

Fascist leaders had failed to live up to the martial ideals of *romanità*. In this view, ancient Rome *had* been correctly reactivated for the modern Italian empire—the flaw, such as it was, was in Italians' defeatism, in their waiting for war's ignominious conclusion instead of defending their two-thousand-year-old civilization. Without reaffirming the warlike qualities of Rome, the country would revert to enfeebling cultural practices and complete the backward slide into "a small and servile country, becoming again a people of hotel owners, museum custodians, [and] shoeshiners."[53] Still others sought to limit the significance of Fascism in their historical accounts of Italy. Benedetto Croce argued that while Nazism represented "a terrible crisis that brooded through centuries of German history," Italian Fascism was an aberration, an "intrusion foreign to the centuries-old Italian history."[54] This position aligned with the myth of the *brava gente*, or Italians as fundamentally good people who had been victimized by Nazism and misled by corrupt Fascist leadership at home.[55]

REPATRIATION AND REDEMPTION

Scholarly disavowal of *romanità* cleansed antiquities of their Fascist connotations and defused their contentiousness. Doing so made possible a second redemption: that of the state itself, by participating in acts of art repatriation. By 1945 the Nazis had stolen an estimated one-fifth of all the artworks in Europe: some two million paintings, sculptures, manuscripts, and sketches, among other works, taken from synagogues, churches, museums, and private family collections across the Continent. The Nazis took thousands of works from Italy, through quasi-legal—and sometimes explicitly illegal—gift giving among high-ranking Fascists and Nazis. Italy's efforts to recover lost works began shortly after the war, spearheaded by Rodolfo Siviero (fig. 12). Siviero, a secret agent and art historian who was appointed minister plenipotentiary to the Allied military government in Germany, urged European governments to act in concert to recover works from German repositories. He cast Italy as a victim of Nazi plunder and asserted the Italian people's right to reclaim their patrimony. It was Siviero who established the technique of combining military-police extrajudicial powers with art historical expertise, such that the analytical skills of art historians became the pretext for revocation actions by police.[56] Siviero's work created an administrative blueprint for later multilevel art policing.

In the 1947 Paris Peace Treaty, Italy had to dissolve its colonial claims to Eritrea, Libya, and Ethiopia, cede territorial holdings in Albania and Yugoslavia, and return all cultural property that Italian forces had taken from those areas: "All objects of artistic, historical, scientific, educational or religious character (including all deeds, manuscripts, documents and bibliographical material)" were to be returned by Italy to their originating territories.[57] Italy returned hundreds of items of cultural property, initially minor objects and, later, monuments including the famous Axum obelisk.[58] In the role of returner, Italy downplayed its own malfeasance and exercised divergent understandings of its responsibilities toward the source country. The Axum obelisk, for example, remained in Rome for another sixty years because the Italian government refused to pay for its transport to Ethiopia, pointing to an ambiguity in the text of the agreement. The obelisk was returned to Axum in 2005, after decades of political wrangling. In the end, Italy paid for its dismantling, shipment, and restoration.[59]

Reluctant to return the cultural objects it had taken, but clamorous to repatriate objects taken from its own territory, the Italian state adroitly

FIGURE 12. Rodolfo Siviero (*left*), head of the Italian commission for the recovery of artworks, examines one of thirty-six paintings returned from Germany, where they were taken during the retreat of German Occupation troops. This particular set of returned masterpieces was dubbed "Group Hitler" because many of them were given to the Nazi leader by Mussolini. Getty Images/Bettmann. Editorial #514959684.

adapted to postwar cultural internationalism and its conjoined principles of territorial provenance and the cultural sovereignty of minority groups. The motif of national vulnerability was activated once again, this time symbolically placing Italy in the company of Allied countries that had also endured Nazi art plunder. The country was asserting more than its right to possess and practice cultural patrimony; it was claiming the right to defend itself from perceived threats to that patrimony. Cultural internationalism could have been the end of distributed sovereignty, with its implied rejection of colonial teleology. The 1947 and 1956 peace treaties had, after all, denied the cultural property claims of the Fascist government. Instead, cultural internationalism set the stage for distributed sovereignty's second act. Territorial sovereignty and cultural sovereignty were fused together: the recognition of the collective identity of the Italian people and the state's authority over its territory "was implied in the recognition of cultural autonomy and sovereignty over cultural re-

FIGURE 13. Italian Police with an Etruscan sculpture at an exhibition, 1955. Photo by Touring Club Italiano/Marka/Universal Images Group. Getty Images.

sources."[60] Siviero and his allies championed a new formulation of an old cause: "la difesa delle opere d'arte," literally the defense of artworks (fig. 13). If the country was ever to redeem itself and become a great power, it would start with its leadership in the arena of international cultural governance. As we will see, the language of defense and threat would have powerful resonance as Italy built itself into a cultural power in the 1960s and 1970s.

Modernity and Cultural Power in Crisis

Before the war, Italy was primarily rural and poor. After it, the country underwent rapid industrialization and urban growth. The economic miracle brought higher standards of living for most Italians but also anxiety about its broader consequences. As rural dwellers poured into cities for better-paying jobs, urban life took on a new vitality and contentiousness. The complex of images and practices known as Italian culture was questioned and reconfigured.[61] Family life itself was perceived to be under intense pressure. Many people worried that moral standards had worsened and culture was eroding.[62] There were growing concerns that the forces of modernity threatened Italy's landscape and cultural treasures. Adding to those forces, from the mid-1960s onward, was a considerable increase in tourism. Foreign visits to Italy plummeted during the war but began to recover as newly prosperous Italians made more leisure trips within the country: it was an era of cheap *pensioni* and beachside resorts, and it brought Italians into contact with patrimony sites and objects that many had never seen in person.[63] They were followed by foreign tourists, whose numbers were so great that the country's cultural infrastructure reached breaking point trying to accommodate the crowds. Lawmakers pronounced that Italy was "under siege" (*presa d'assalto*)—a phrase that can connote an attack or foreign takeover. What everyone knew was that foreigners were spending money on more than hotels and meals: antiquities, fake or authentically old, were favored souvenirs. With *presa d'assalto*, the nod toward the *prezzo americano* was hard to miss.

Italian lawmakers faced a dilemma. Powerless to stop urbanization, and desiring economic growth, they also wanted to preserve the landscape and cultural assets that made the country a desirable destination. Two attempts were made to do this—to develop a form of preventive conservation that would permanently protect the landscape and its historic assets from industrial development.[64] Neither succeeded. Instead, the holistic effort at cultural heritage protection was pared back to a narrowly tailored war against the art and antiquities trade. This final section of the chapter explains the international and domestic political forces that led to this, and how the crackdown on the antiquities trade provided political cover for expanded cultural security powers.

CULTURAL INTERNATIONALISM AND THE CONVENTION ERA

As Italy was working to redeem itself on the international stage, cultural policy emerged as a redemptive platform for interstate negotiation and cooperation. "World-making through the valorization of collective cultural achievements" became a priority among states.[65] A new form of Utopian "one-worldism" was articulated through the exchange of art, education, culture, and scientific knowledge. The organizing body for this mission was the United Nations Educational, Scientific and Cultural Organization, or UNESCO, a special agency of the United Nations founded in 1945. Through its conventions and policy recommendations, cultural heritage was rearticulated as a legal right of states and the human communities within them.[66] It also reframed culture as property.[67] Each state would have its own heritage to cherish and protect, and foreign states would respect the boundaries of heritage protections, but the international community retained an interest in multiple heritages. To be a legitimate state actor in the arena of international cultural politics in the Convention era required a delicate balance between accepting that other states had an interest in one's culture and at the same time agreeing not to interfere in member states' own cultural projects.[68] The principle of sovereignty emergent in Convention projects can be summarized in the classic formulation *par in parem non habet imperium*: no state has authority over another state with equal sovereign standing. Operationalizing this vision required multiple treaties, statements, and conventions over two decades.

Monumental universality moved heritage from "an initial preoccupation with art and museums . . . toward technical expertise, preservation, and conservation science."[69] The new technocratic expertise suggested a realm of unruly sites and artifacts that required management. Heritage became something to be ordered, and to be ordered along lines of state authority. The core idea was that archaeological materials, in some cases spanning five thousand years, could be classified and categorized in ways that aligned with modern states' political and territorial interests. Through the Committee for Safeguarding the Monuments of Nubia, for example, European states contributed to the recovery of ancient structures in the Nubian Desert of southern Egypt, an area threatened with extensive flooding by the Aswan Dam. Joining the mission to protect two ancient temples at Abu Simbel, Italy reoriented heritage from postwar reconciliation to a "heroic quest to save antiquity."[70] As with every heroic quest, this one was populated by romantics and strongmen alike.[71] The language of safeguarding became associated with state intervention. Italy's Abu Simbel mission was an early instance of the state's deploying cultural capital to spread its influence in the politics and economies of the Mediterranean and the Maghreb after the war.

There was a shared conviction that "global peace and security could also be achieved by promoting international collaboration in the cultural arena."[72] The concept of security once occupied a specific place in the discourse of global cultural heritage governance. It referred to rules of military engagement that would protect cultural sites and monuments from wanton destruction during times of war.[73] After World War II, the keywords for heritage protection in Italy—*protezione* (protection) and *tutela* (custodianship)—emphasized active *difesa* (defense) over passive *protezione*. The 1954 Hague Convention for the Protection of Cultural Property in the Event of Armed Conflict promoted the universal importance of culture, yet it also articulated a system of member states' own cultural property, with transnational obligations for its protection.[74] The Hague Convention obliged member countries to refrain from deliberately damaging or destroying the cultural property of others during times of war.[75] Significantly, it also required member states to take steps to identify and protect their own artworks, artifacts, and culturally significant sites and buildings during peacetime: "The High Contracting Parties further undertake to prohibit, prevent and, if necessary, put a stop to any form of theft, pillage or misappropriation of, and any acts of vandalism directed against, cultural property."[76]

How this obligation should be discharged was ultimately the decision of each country. The Convention did not require a specific approach, but it did make some suggestions. Article 7 instructed member countries to introduce regulations to make their own armed forces available during peacetime to "ensure observance of the present Convention" (article 7.1). It also recommended creating special units of the armed forces to protect cultural heritage: "The High Contracting Parties undertake to plan or establish in peacetime, within their armed forces, services or specialist personnel whose purpose will be to secure respect for cultural property and to co-operate with the civilian authorities responsible for safeguarding it" (article 7.2).[77] But the Convention also stressed that maintaining the security of cultural property should be kept functionally distinct from military actions: "The guarding of cultural property [in the event of armed conflict] by armed custodians specially empowered to do so, or the presence, in the vicinity of such cultural property, of police forces normally responsible for the maintenance of public order shall not be deemed to be used for military purposes" (chapter II, article 8.4).

The Hague Convention framed cultural internationalism as a moral effort at monumental universality, but subsequent UNESCO conventions redirected the mission to member states' internal affairs. Major UNESCO conventions were passed in 1970 (Convention on the Illicit Import, Export and Transfer of Cultural Property) and 1972 (Convention on the Protection of the World Cultural and Natural Heritage).[78]

The World Heritage List of cultural sites was created through the 1972 Convention: each member state shall create a list of "properties forming part of the cultural heritage and natural heritage . . . which it considers as having outstanding universal value."[79] From the egalitarian notion of inventories, the list became a competitive ranking, with member states making the case for listing their own properties. Italy has done exceptionally well. As of 2020 it has fifty-five World Heritage sites and accounts for about 5 percent of all World Heritage site listings. Italy is successful in the World Heritage arena in part because it assembled an efficient and professionalized bureaucracy for completing UNESCO documentation and putting together persuasive cases. But it is also true that Italy has the sort of sites that the World Heritage List was made for. Put differently, it was always, already a "world heritage" country. In her study of World Heritage List site descriptions, sociologist Victoria Reyes (2014) found that nearly one-third of all World Heritage sites *outside* Italy, France, Greece, and Spain specified Italy as an important source of influence. Sites considered to have "outstanding universal value" are those inspired or influenced by Italy, and to a lesser extent by Spain and France. Such is the power and salience of Italian patrimony that other countries consciously make connections to it to bolster the prestige and resonance of their own. With a further recommendation by UNESCO in 1976, heritage was reformulated as a basic element of a people's identity. In this framework it not only made sense that states would seek to repatriate artifacts, but that they were expected to do so. Heritage was a state asset that *required* armed protection from looting and smuggling.

Tomb Robbers and the Scandal at Tarquinia

In late September 1963, cinemas across Italy screened a newsreel that alerted audiences to a dire situation: a sustained attack on Tarquinia, a small town thirty kilometers north of Rome and one of the richest archaeological areas in the country. Viewers would have known already that, as Italians, they enjoyed a collective claim on a glittering cultural patrimony. In print media since the opening decades of national unity, and later in film and radio, audiences were invited to celebrate the glory of that legacy. Heavily publicized events, including the opening of state museums, Mussolini's restoration of the Roman Forum, the return of artworks to Italy from Germany after World War II, and the breathtaking discovery of Etruscan tombs at Cerveteri in the 1950s sent a clear message: the country's cultural treasures made Italy special and thus were an

FIGURE 14. *Sensazionale a Tarquinia* (1963) film screen shot from the opening sequence: "Scandal at Tarquinia: How many tombs pillaged?"

important source of social cohesion for Italians. All that past glory and national pride was on the line, then, when the film *Sensazionale a Tarquinia: In quanti rubano nelle tombe?* (Scandal at Tarquinia: How many tombs pillaged?) announced that tomb robbers were steadily destroying the nation's cultural patrimony through a large-scale, organized effort to steal antiquities and sell them through clandestine networks (fig. 14).

In the eight-minute film, a young reporter describes the thefts as a matter of great national urgency, of "affliction, desolation, and powerlessness," as he traverses the Lazio countryside looking for answers and apportioning blame. He interviews a local man, Luigi Perticarari, described as the chief of Tarquinia's tomb-robbing trade. Perticarari admits that he violates the law by digging up Etruscan tombs but defends his actions: "These authorities . . . that blame me for damaging the national patrimony, they should know that I've spent my life practically always in tombs, among vases and potsherds, and I've even found painted tombs but I obviously didn't know what to do with them so I've given them back, I've marked them [*l'ho restituita, l'ho segnalata*]." The reporter is not impressed. "Did you hear that?" he asks the audience. "He speaks as though he is the benefactor. As though it is *his* to give back." The interview continues. "Excuse me," the reporter asks, "but is what you already took not enough?" Perticarari fumes:

> Well, what bothers me is that there are many people who come excavate [at Tarquinia], like the king of Sweden.... I don't pretend to be as important as the king of Sweden, God forbid, I'm just a poor bricklayer. However, at least I descend from, we here in Tarquinia, and so in Lazio, descend from the Etruscan race [*discendemo dalla razza etrusca*],[80] if I'm not mistaken, right? So why does the king of Sweden come here to excavate, in Tarquinia, Cerveteri, and other places? He has rights and we don't. Why is this?

Perticarari, the authentic local, is labeled a criminal, a *tombarolo,* the lowest of the low, because he excavates tombs that are his by right. The king of Sweden, who has no natal connection to the region, does the same thing and is painted as a hero by Italian cultural officials. Why, Perticarari wants to know, does the government propound a national culture, then persecute an actual national for having the audacity to claim that culture for himself?

Perticarari has posed a reasonable question. If the logic of national culture is that artifacts, tombs, and the other material stuff of the nation's history belong to the Italian people, then it stands to reason that he has a right to antiquities that no foreigner, even a king, can match. The Swedish monarch, Perticarari wants us to know, and foreign elites like him are the real beneficiaries of the state's cultural politics. Before viewers are allowed to internalize this logic, however—before they can align themselves with Perticarari and see things from his point of view—the reporter announces a surprise. It's nighttime now, and the camera crew has serendipitously encountered a trio of masked men. It is a rare opportunity to watch the tomb robbers at work. Like bandits, the masked men move stealthily across a field under cover of darkness, carrying pickaxes and shimmying into tomb shafts. In one tomb they find Etruscan vases, statuettes, and jewelry. "Who buys this stuff?" the reporter asks them. "Antiquarians in other places," one of them responds, "in Rome, in Florence..." His voice trails off. He doesn't know, won't say, or doesn't care what happens to the artifacts after that. It is the tomb robbers' indifference to the common good that is emphasized. The music rises in a dramatic crescendo and the lights dim. "Who will stop the *tombaroli*?" the narrator asks. "What will happen to Italy's patrimony if nobody controls them?"

Scandal at Tarquinia leaves no doubt about the tomb robbers' malice; they are motivated by a greed and self-interest so pernicious that it negates whatever plausible aspirations to archaeological expertise or local affinity they proffer. But the tomb robbers are not the only bad guys in this story. The state, too, is indicted for having betrayed the nation through its incompetence and corruption. The authorities in Rome have abrogated their responsibility to the collective patrimony, and the archaeologists are outnumbered or simply nowhere to be found. The scandal, then, is not that tomb robbers are making a killing. The real scandal is that the clandestine excavations in the heartland of ancient Etruria are directly exposing the state's weak control over the nation's cultural treasures.

CLEANING HOUSE

The film was an embarrassment. It made government officials look lost and overwhelmed. It portrayed Italy as neglectful of its treasures, and it made the tomb robbers look invincible. The Ministry of Culture was regarded as a dumping ground for inept civil servants.[81] Its budget was insufficient to give cultural administrators effective decision-making authority. Art and archaeology were not given adequate resources. Nationally, cultural heritage management was divided among sixty archaeological superintendents and nine autonomous institutions of major cultural importance, including the Central Institute for Restoration and the National Prints Cabinet. Reporting lines were inconsistent. Some superintendents were responsible for museums and galleries as well as archaeological sites, while others specialized in one or the other. Graft, bloat, and redundancy had been central complaints during the 1909 and 1939 legislative debates, and in 1964 they resurfaced. "The vastness of the superintendents' territories," one elected official grumbled, "makes for an untenable situation."[82]

Calls for stronger measures came from across the political spectrum. Jole Giugni Lattari, a member of the Movimento Sociale Italiano, argued that the protection of cultural goods was a nonpolitical issue that should engender support from everyone. "Our artistic patrimony is perhaps our greatest national asset," she said, "and it is one of the few points on which we can speak without politics: diverse groups, in fact, have declared their agreement with the necessity of safeguarding Italy's historic sites and bringing into law and order the private initiatives that have constantly caused such damage to art, archaeology, and landscape."[83] Lattari condemned industrial development and unauthorized exploitation of the landscape. With inadequate state oversight, private companies built commercial real estate and manufacturing facilities on land containing archaeological sites and historic structures. To stop that, she proposed to require that privately held monuments and antiquities—those owned by churches, for example, or by ordinary citizens—be registered with the Ministry of Culture and subjected to unannounced inspections of their display and curation circumstances. Momentum accelerated for these and similar reforms. Roberto Lucifredi, a senior Christian Democrat, stressed that the loss of Italy's historic landscape rendered art and artifacts meaningless.[84] It was senseless, he said, to think of the country as containing a historic landscape discrete from an artistic heritage that could be parceled out for separate administration. The landscape and the heritage were continuous; *they were one*. Whatever historic interest they held was seamlessly bound up with contemporary life and local identities.

True to form, the government responded by forming a new committee. Francesco Franceschini, a teacher from Venice and a prominent Christian Democrat, was selected to head it. The committee comprised sixteen members of Parliament and eleven experts in art history, archaeology, law, and library science. They were charged with revising the administrative framework and funding mechanisms for cultural heritage protection. After a thorough three-year study period (1964–67), the Franceschini Commission produced nine recommendations for urgent action.[85] These included creating a systematic inventory of the country's cultural heritage; eliminating unacceptable treatments of/incursions into cultural heritage sites and objects; increasing funds for conservation and study; increasing funds for living artists; and raising public awareness of the value of cultural heritage through a national campaign. It also encouraged the creation of a security service to protect cultural heritage: "For the execution of its [assigned] actions, the superintendents [of archaeology] will avail themselves of a security service of administrative autonomy, with the powers necessary to carry out their prescribed functions."[86] The Franceschini report reiterated the economic, social, and cultural value of *beni culturali*, or "cultural assets." The change in terminology from *cose d'arte*—works of art—to *beni culturali* signaled another key change in the way Italian officials talked about material culture. The criteria for being of "interest" to the nation were rethought. Now, materiality—the essential fact of an object's *being*, as distinct from its aesthetic qualities—counted toward the codification and protection of national culture. Emphasis on the relation between cultural objects and the soil matrix was renewed, along with a more comprehensive understanding of what sorts of things counted toward national cultural heritage.[87]

The report declared that the cultural heritage of the Italian nation consisted of any good that "constituted material testimony to the value of civilization," thereby extending beyond the traditional focus on artistic interest and insisting on a broadly historicist interpretation of shared culture. Defining national culture as comprehensively as possible expanded the content of the country's patrimony and provided state actors with new lines of argument about territory, historical origins, and cultural inclusion. By and large, the report did not have the intended effect. Real estate firms lobbied against restrictions on new building projects. There was insufficient support among Parliamentary members for the funding requests. And the year after the report's release, political unrest diverted government priorities once again. Neither the Franceschini Commission nor its successors, the Papaldo I (1968) and II (1970) Commissions, resulted in the sort of comprehensive policy and practice changes being called for. Instead, the government made piecemeal progress on a handful of the Franceschini recommendations. The inventory was started. Historic buildings were reserved for administrative functions. And, notably, the designated security service was promised and delivered. The earliest known appearance in print of the term *il tombarolo* occurs around this time, in a 1965 newspaper article about five men accused of stealing objects from an archaeological site in Tarquinia.[88] This is not a random appearance but coincides with the government's evolving strategy for state patrimony. Blaming tomb robbers for cultural loss and setting up a military-police unit to combat their supposed attacks on patrimony was easier than addressing the deeper, more politically sensitive, problems imperiling the open-air museum.

Birth of the Art Squad

The Italian Art Squad was founded in May 1969 as the Nucleo Tutela Patrimonio Artistico (NTPA). The unit reported to the Ministry of Education but operated as a unit of the Carabinieri.[89] It started with just three employees but quickly garnered positive press. During the Fourteenth UNESCO General Conference in Paris in October and November 1970, Italian officials presented the NTPA model to the general assembly and expounded on its merits. Other national governments were encouraged to take similar steps. The discussion assumed that recourse to military-police power was the best way to support archaeological finds and other cultural materials. Scholars have suggested that the Art Squad's creation was caused by a massive increase in tomb robbing in the 1960s.[90] The Art Squad has offered a similar version of its own origins: "The 1960s, while marked by an important economic recovery, were also, on the contrary, characterized by an intensification of clandestine exports of culturally significant items stolen or illegally excavated, for enriching museums and private collections all over the world."[91] These claims are difficult to corroborate because reliable, comparable numbers do not exist. What we have are estimates from the government, archaeologists, and nonspecialist observers of looters' pits and the remnants of ancient tombs. Tomb robbing was always a feature of Italian social life, and it is not certain that the 1960s brought a significant quantitative difference in the practice.

The formation of the Art Squad was not required by international convention, nor is it a given that recourse to police power was popular with the public. It should be assessed against a long tradition of authoritarian solutions to public order "problems."[92] This mistrust was exacerbated by the Fascist regime, which relied on a secret police (the OVRA) to terrorize the public.[93] Postwar defascization removed surface-level signs of Fascism from law enforcement, including symbols and ideological discourse. Beneath this, however, "much of the cultural, professional and jurisdictional discourse remained relatively unchanged."[94] Well into the 1970s mistrust of state law enforcement persisted.[95] A critical history of Italian cultural power, then, must consider that the birth of the Art Squad came from a politics of patrimony capital as competitive state-building. The Italian government's framing of tomb robbing changed in this period from petty crime to a problem of public order. The antiquities market took on its own character outside the art market, becoming the "dark side" of art buying and presumptively guilty of theft. This way of talking about the trade in antiquities updated the "loss anxiety" about Italian national culture. It involved inciting alarm about the nation's cultural materials ("our heritage is disappearing" or "the foreign museums are taking everything"), and pointing to the Carabinieri as the best solution and the only effective one.[96]

From its origins as a small state office, the Art Squad has grown to be the most visible manifestation of the state's control of national art objects. The Ministry for Internal Affairs designated the NTPA as a Special Force of the Carabinieri in 1992, at which point its functions and duties were formalized under the name Comando Carabinieri Tutela Patrimonio Artistico (TPA). By the end of 1994, the Carabinieri TPA had 145 staff members. Just four years later, the unit size had nearly doubled, and the TPA, now known as the Tutela Patrimonio Culturale (TPC, or Art Squad), became the largest law enforcement agency in the world specializing in the protection and recovery of national culture. By 2018 there were 300 agents spread across the Italian peninsula. The force's activities and functions continue to diversify: "performance of specialized investigative activities aimed at identifying the perpetrators of crimes against cultural heritage, and recovering illicit stolen assets; monitoring of terrestrial and marine archaeological sites, as well as significant landscapes and UNESCO World Heritage sites; control of commercial activities such as fairs and markets where the sale of cultural goods takes place, as well as auction house catalogs and e-commerce sites; verification of anticrime security measures in museums, libraries and archives; management of the Database of Illicitly Stolen Cultural Heritage, where all the information relating to crimes involving cultural heritage in Italy and that of foreign states ask to enter for searches; other activities."[97]

The unit claims that its agents have recovered over half a million items of "national cultural treasure," totaling hundreds of millions of euros. The Art Squad's headquarters are in central Rome, though the unit presents itself as a force with no single head but with a capillary presence—spread thin but everywhere, even in the parts of the country described as *prive di strade*—a term that translates literally as "deprived of roads" but that can be invoked to justify state inaction with the excuse of impenetrability. The text comes from the Art Squad–funded film *Gli anni del Drago* (The years of the dragon) (2009), one of several media productions made available to the public through schools, museums, tourist offices, and television as a public relations strategy. The Art Squad's arrangement of power is highly effective in creating an all-pervasive positionality. Rather than weakening the central node, capillary structures strengthen centralized power by making it invisible.[98] Power penetrates every crevice of Italy; uniformed and plainclothes officers patrol Italy from the sky and under the sea, giving them "ample presence everywhere."[99] This policing model is symbolized by the Art Squad's crest, which features a dragon looming over the ancient Pantheon in central Rome. The dragon's tail snakes around the piazza in front of the building, as if to demonstrate its reach in public life.

In press conferences broadcast from majestic ruins or dazzling museum interiors, uniformed agents stand guard over recovered objects, gently adjusting the treasures with white gloves, admiring the paintings, or simply standing at attention, grim and dutiful (fig. 2). Bringing its claims of heritage expertise to war zones and natural disaster areas in the Middle East and Africa in the 2010s enhances the prestige of the unit. Such is its influence that several other countries have created their own versions of the TPC. In 2018 the United Kingdom announced the formation of the Cultural Property Protection Unit, headed by a Gulf War veteran and staffed by armed services personnel with training in art history, archaeology, and conservation.[100] And in 2019 the United States followed suit with a joint initiative of the Smithsonian Culture Rescue Initiative and the US Army Civil Affairs and Psychological Operations Command.[101] Through its extensive reach, the Art Squad exercises distributed sovereignty in several important ways. In the following chapter we will examine how looters make their own contributions to sovereignty, and why their persistence provides continual justification for the Art Squad's existence.

CHAPTER 4

Tomb Robbers and Cultural Power from Below

In his 1992 memoir, retired tomb robber Gismondo Tagliaferri explained his essential rules for being a successful *tombarolo*. Published under the title *Tombaroli si nasce* (Tomb robbers are born [not made]), the rules are as follows:

1. A proper looter must have extensive knowledge of the countryside.
2. He must have a high tolerance for rain and cold.[1]
3. He must be ready to sacrifice [comfort and safety].
4. He must be discreet, speaking little of what he does.
5. He must never excavate a tomb without a partner to keep watch, for police and for natural hazards.
6. When he finds something interesting, he must take it home on foot.
7. The proper tomb robber must have nerves of steel.[2]

Every one of these rules is important, Tagliaferri asserts. The Ministry of Culture has its rules for excavation and conservation, and tomb robbers have theirs. Expert knowledge of the terrain is pointless if a person has a big mouth. Even the most discreet digger, on the other hand, inured to the hardships of cold and damp, will fail if he goes it alone or strikes out for unknown topography. But the most important rule, according to Gismondo Tagliaferri, master looter of Vulci, is the seventh. If a tomb robber does not have nerves of steel, as soon as his colleagues shout, "Run, run, the police are coming!" he will die of fear inside the tomb.[3] Nicknamed the Red Cricket (Grillo Rosso) by his dig team, Tagliaferri frequently found his own nerves tested during his four decades of tomb robbing. For him the thrill was worth the risk. He made astonishing discoveries in some of the richest Etruscan tombs in Italy, following in the footsteps of looters two millennia before him. It was not money but love of adventure that motivated him, he writes, and a sense of historical destiny: "Every era has its tomb robbers."[4]

Tomb robbing has been described as the principal enemy of Italy's archaeological patrimony.[5] In a 2015 scholarly book about the Art Squad, tomb robbers are described as ruthless scavengers who are "willing to destroy ancient tombs, scattering human remains across the countryside while helping themselves to the jewels of the deceased" and "feeding the voracious black market that devours them."[6] What they have inflicted is a "mass depredation" without parallel in the Western world.[7] Part self-styled folk hero passionate about culture and history, part thief with a stunning indifference to artifacts and historical practice, the tomb robber is a complex social construct. This chapter draws on interviews with current and former tomb robbers to explore this complexity. I make no assumptions about tomb robbers' criminality or innocence.[8] Instead, I want to explore the possibility that state cultural power is informed by tomb robbing—perhaps even *depends on* it.[9] For all its harms (and there are many),[10] tomb robbing provides a foil to the Art Squad, and it feeds the allure and mystery of the artifact. I am not suggesting that archaeologists and the Art Squad support tomb robbing. They insist they do not. My argument is about long-term patterns of institutional power that rely on particular arrangements of social activity, including deviant behavior. These are patterns that no single person, department, or office can undo, no matter how strong their convictions. Tomb robbers are habitual social actors operating along well-worn grooves of cultural engagement.[11] Tagliaferri's rules constitute a code of honor for the heroic unauthorized digger—a code existing outside the control of the state and running parallel to civil society.

In the Den of Antiquity

"My main memory," says Michele, a native of Lazio now in his sixties, "is of being the first one in the tomb. [Because I was the smallest] I was often the first one inside, crawling through the shaft." Were you ever afraid? I asked. This was, after all, the stuff of childhood nightmares: airless, subterranean chambers containing skeletons and spiders. The adults who took him on tomb raids were too big to shimmy through the narrow tunnels that they punched through the earth with the *spillone*, a long metal pole.[12] They stayed aboveground, holding the rope that was Michele's only way out. Michele was ten, and down below he was on his own with the body parts and grave goods. Michele had to summon his courage and make a series of calculations. How sturdy were the walls? Where would he find shelter if the shaft began to crumble? Most important, were there any valuable artifacts? Answering my question, he continued:

> At first I was scared, but then it was really amazing because it was my job to look through the objects there and decide if they were worth my father's time or [if it was] better to move on [to another tomb]. I quickly learned what was valuable and what wasn't.

Michele's eyes lit up as he recounted his tomb-robbing days. He was raised near Cerveteri, an ancient Etruscan town with hundreds of elaborate tombs. His boyhood raids took place in the early to mid-1970s. At the time of our interview, Michele had moved on; he taught history at a university in the United States. He called himself a reformed tomb robber. We met through friends who knew about my research project and about Michele's colorful past. Over drinks at an upscale urban bistro and in a follow-up phone conversation, Michele shared childhood memories of tomb robbing in central Italy, acknowledging sheepishly that looting is illegal now and "probably was then" (it was). But it didn't feel like looting, he told me. Everybody was doing it. Several small groups of men from his town went out and looked for tombs. It was a normal part of life, a form of masculine bonding similar to hunting:

> [Digging tombs] could be really physically intense. I felt sometimes dizzy with excitement—like I was high or something. You have to picture it: four or five Italian males with big shovels, showing off our strength, getting dirty, with our hands bleeding from the digging because we wouldn't wear gloves. The older guys would be smoking cigarettes, and I can still remember how my clothes smelled the next morning: that mix of, sort of, dirt, perspiration, cigarette smoke. . . . That is when a memory really means something to you, when you feel and smell and taste it.

The "high" that Michele remembers from tomb robbing was echoed by forty-three-year-old Rafal, a resident of Rome:

> It is the best feeling in the world, to be in the fresh air, smelling the fresh dirt on a cool evening after a hot day. I can tell you, absolutely certainly, how it is in the dirt here and how that is maybe different in the dirt elsewhere [rubs his fingertips]. Because when I am an old man, in my bed,

> not able to walk, forgetting my own name, what I will remember is that feeling, of being in the land, with my friends, the rocks, the dirt, the little pieces of pottery making my pockets heavy.

Community ties, group identity, rural esprit, and obsession with artifacts: these were themes that recurred throughout my interviews with current and former unauthorized excavators. The interviews took place in shops, bars, and cafés because my Institutional Review Board (IRB) forbade me to meet with tomb robbers in private places. They were worried about my safety. Among other restrictions (discussed at length in the methodological appendix), I was not allowed to record both first and last names in case my field notes were subpoenaed, to use snowball sampling (a common strategy for increasing an interview sample size), or to accompany my subjects to a crime scene (in this case a looted archaeological site or a private residence containing stolen artifacts). The restrictions were well intentioned and ethically solid, designed to support my research while protecting informants from potential legal prosecution and community opprobrium.[13] But the restrictions also reveal something interesting about the power of archetypes. Before meeting anyone who engaged in illicit digging, I was given a set of research parameters that reinforced a particular way of thinking about such people. Ironically, the IRB's view of things aligned with the very categories I was attempting to engage with critically: the Italian government offers a similar way of disaggregating varieties of illicit diggers, separating "occasional" lawbreakers from systematic "raiders": "Clandestine excavations are defined as occasional when they are the work of local farmers or land owners whose land is involved in building works, or take place sporadically by individuals in digs; in these cases, the person who has found the relic decides to keep it for himself or resell it rather than deliver it to the competent authorities."[14]

According to the same official, making distinctions among types of unauthorized diggers has implications for the social organization of crime. "Tomb raiders" are described as pillagers who frequently work in organized groups and use heavy machinery in their digs. They are said to operate local "collection centers" controlled by one or more individuals, who in turn report to a local "collector" in the area. The collector is generally a seasoned professional well versed in the rules of the black market, who knows exactly the best time to place the relic on the market. He is therefore also the reference person for export and sale abroad.[15]

The categories and criminal networks described by the state, and implicitly validated by my IRB, reveal the real source of the state's anxiety:

that all types of informal digging represent a threat to the unity of patrimony. Another interview subject set me straight on these distinctions after I insulted him to his face. The mistake was mine, and the insult was inadvertent. "Domenico," a lifelong resident of the city of Rome, used to hunt for artifacts with his uncle in Viterbo. Before I fully understood the sensitivity around terminology, I asked Domenico how much money his (now deceased) uncle had made as a *tombarolo*—using that specific word. He answered sternly:

> Excuse me, but you are foreign so you do not understand everything about how it works here. When you ask me if my uncle sold the artifacts [*i reperti*] you insult him. He was a collector. He admired his objects. You are asking about the *tombaroli*. They sell [artifacts] for money. That is the main distinction. My uncle was not a *tombarolo*. He never sold anything.

What Domenico objected to most vociferously was my suggestion that his uncle (and, by association, Domenico) was in it for the money. According to Domenico, he was motivated to dig by love of history. Rafal, too, was visibly wounded when I asked whether he destroyed tombs to smuggle out artifacts. He replied, "We were always careful. We showed respect. It was for fun, maybe to collect a few things. [Some of] those guys were much worse, they used drills, backhoes, you name it." In highlighting his care and precision, Rafal was insisting on a clear distinction between his activities and those of the truly criminal *tombaroli*. He was also distancing himself from the violators ("those guys") of the imagined national community.

These and other comments present us with a complicated set of ideas about what Italian cultural power means at home, among ordinary Italians. My informants situated their tomb robbing in a rich folkloric narrative that transcends the state's operation of *beni culturali*, or legally protected goods of cultural and historic interest to the national community. Honest tomb robbers, they insisted, act from a love of artifacts and a curiosity about their own local past. Culturally acceptable tomb robbers adhere to particular rules and master the art of being *sottile*, which literally means "subtle" and here encompasses a broader set of virtues including class-conscious demonstrations of expertise, agility in the physical work of digging, and discretion. Discretion, Lilith Mahmud recounts in her study of women Freemasons in Italy, can be thought of as "a set of embodied practices that simultaneously conceal and reveal valued knowledge." Correct deployment of such practices was essential to her subjects' successful navigation of the pull between secrecy and having "nothing to hide."[16] The concept is very similar to being *sottile* in tomb robbing, in that the trick to mastery is not feigned ignorance and eternal silence, but rather knowing which truths to reveal and which to conceal, when and to whom.

"The Great Raid"

When Michele admitted that his father's tomb digging was "probably" illegal in the early 1970s, he said it with a wink. He knew full well that it was. That's what made it thrilling. La Grande Razzia, "the Great Raid," is what Fabio Isman (2009) calls the period from 1970 to the mid-2000s, when, he says, more than 1.5 million antiquities were illegally excavated and exported from Italy. This raid was a vast enterprise, he argues, involving some 10,000 people including restorers, forgers of documents, smugglers, dealers, collectors, and the tomb robbers themselves. Similarly, a 2000 report by three leading scholars of the illegal antiquities trade found that from 1970 to 1996 "the Italian police recovered more than 300,000 antiquities from clandestine excavations" constituting "only a portion of the total."[17] Looting became so extensive that by the early 1990s the country was losing "the equivalent of a museum a year" through art thefts, "not even counting the objects that disappear most frequently, those dug up and looted from archaeological sites."[18] In the same period when the young Michele was exploring tombs with his father, there was an explosion of interest in Etruscan artifacts by scholars and collectors.[19]

This increased interest seems to have coincided with intensified activity by clandestine excavators in Etruscan cemeteries.[20] When the archaeologist and civil engineer Carlo Lerici (1962) did a survey of Etruscan tombs at a single site in central Italy, he found that 400 of 550 had been broken into. Some of the damage, according to Lerici, was done a very long time ago—possibly in Roman times. People have been digging in Etruscan tombs for centuries to look for artifacts and salable treasure, to seek out holy places, and to explore for fun.[21] Lerici could not say definitively whether the despoiled tombs he encountered had been damaged in the twentieth century or in earlier times. What he confirmed was that clandestine excavation of Etruscan tombs has a long history that predates modern antiquities markets.[22] For Italians who consider artifacts theirs by right, tomb robbing is a long-standing local practice and an "institutionalized part of community life."[23] Because of its widespread practice and tolerance, it is a social leveler—a cultural pursuit that generates non-state, community- and family-level scripts for masculinity, nationalism, and honor.

The state sees things differently: "These criminal events [clandestine excavations] represent one of the greatest blights that afflict Italy and many other countries with a wealth of historic relics."[24] Italian law codifies four major categories of crime against archaeology. The base criminal category is *ricerca abusiva*, or exploitative digging for artifacts, without the necessary permits. This is the law that is often invoked to prosecute a tomb robber. The second core category is failure to file a *denuncia*, to report an archaeological find to the authorities. If police and prosecutors cannot prove a defendant did the digging, they will revert to examining the paperwork. The third category follows: illegal possession of a protected artifact without the presumption that the individual participated in the digging. Finally, attempting to export archaeological material without a permit can be prosecuted as a crime. Each of these four scenarios is potentially criminal, because antiquities and other protected cultural goods are state property based on articles 90 and 91 of the Decreto legislativo 42/2004.[25] These objects are subject to protection by the state regardless of their economic or aesthetic value.[26] Taking possession of artifacts and artworks either from authorized excavations or through accidental discovery is therefore considered a crime. Artifact theft is subject to the same penalty as ordinary property theft.[27]

Catching tomb robbers in the act is difficult. They post lookouts at access points, stash their findings in abandoned farm buildings, and can pass themselves off as legitimate laborers.[28] This is why all four modes of criminal association with antiquities—digging, documenting, possessing, and exporting—are important. Prosecutors face a tough challenge in proving that a defendant personally excavated the objects and did so knowingly, intending to appropriate archaeological material and not just out for a romp on a summer's day. They must demonstrate a plausible correlation between documented possession of artifacts and the initial means of their recovery.[29] That principle was tested in sentencing two men in December 2007 in the District Court of Rome.[30] Precisely because it is an utterly typical case of tomb robbing—fairly mundane in its details—it is worth examining closely.

The defendants were identified in court documents by the initials BM and CSJ, and were both listed as Romanian citizens. They were accused of selling coins from the Punic, Greek, and Roman periods to a jewelry store in the center of Rome for €50. In doing so, they violated the patrimony of the state. That is precisely how it is expressed in Italian: *il patri-*

monio dello Stato, with the state having primary interest in the ownership and protection of cultural patrimony. For BM and CSJ, the offense was "numerous coins" discovered by Carabinieri when they searched the defendants' bags. In keeping with protocol, the Carabinieri presented the coins for assessment by an expert from the archaeological superintendent of Rome. That expert concluded that the coins had historical and archaeological value. This was important because, as we saw with the first national patrimony law in 1909, for an object to have the status of state patrimony, it is not enough that it be ancient. It has to be old and be *of interest* to the state.[31] That criterion having been met, the coin expert had to satisfy one more question: How long had the coins been out of the ground? Was it possible that BM and CSJ found the coins at a flea market or lying on the ground? No, the expert affirmed. Scientific testing revealed that the coins had "an elevated degree of oxidation and evident concretions from underground burial," which indicated that they had recently been obtained from an archaeological excavation.[32] And since they had no excavation permits and were clearly not archaeologists, the men must have been robbing tombs.

It was this last point that the judge hammered on in his verdict. That the defendants were in possession of stolen patrimony was beyond doubt. They could have been prosecuted for this offense alone. But the judge wanted to go further. He wrote, "It cannot be excluded [that they were robbing tombs], precisely because the coins had the characteristics of oxidation and encrustation, which lead one to believe that the excavation had taken place a very short time before, and that the defendants themselves had found the coins, digging them from the ground. In other words, we have no proof that the defendants did not take part in the underlying illicit activity."[33] The state found witnesses to the men's transaction with the jewelry store's owner but no witnesses to the excavation itself. Possessing and selling the coins were sufficient for legal prosecution, but the state decided to pursue the additional charge of illicit digging. It asserted the following: "The defendants came into possession of numerous coins subject to archaeological protection coming from clandestine excavations. As to this fact there can be no doubt, based on the examination of the coins undertaken by the prosecutor's consultant, who drew attention to the traces of earth [*le tracce di terra*] still present and the high degree of oxidation, which suggests a long period underground."

Because of the characteristics of the coins—their age, encrusted dirt, and oxidation levels—it "cannot be excluded," ruled the court, that the defendants themselves "found the coins, digging them from the ground ... and participating in the underlying illicit activity." The judge charged the two men with appropriation of archaeological goods, thereby accepting the necessary correlation between digging and selling artifacts. The men were sentenced to two months in prison and a fine of €300 each, in addition to court costs. As state property, the coins were turned over to the Ministry of Culture. The case shows the effort required to link possessing artifacts with extracting them illegally.

Legal statutes and court cases offer one important optic onto the domestic workings of cultural power and the ways the ideology of national culture is operationalized through formal sanctions and punishment. Alongside the body of law, however, there is a rich and colorful extralegal discourse about tomb robbing as a social problem.[34] This discourse is also important for understanding how cultural power operates and what its underlying assumptions and values are.[35] The Art Squad, for example, describes the challenge of clandestine excavation this way: "Italy has always been flagellated by the wound [*dalla piaga*] of clandestine excavators. For decades this torment has been encouraged by the [art] market, which has no scruples."[36] Embedded in this statement are three important ideas. First, the metaphor of flagellation suggests that Italy is itself a body, a corpus of art vulnerable to constant injury. This is sacred terminology, situating the problem of clandestine excavating in the imagery of patrimonial piety and penance. As we discovered in Quatremère de Quincy's plea for the restoration of Italian artworks taken by France, Italy was long described as a consecrated body. Second, it posits a relation between clandestine excavation and commodification. In the statement above, the Art Squad points the finger at the art market for enticing looters. But there is discontinuity in official and academic discourses about the nature of the relationship. On the one hand, the art market is said to encourage clandestine excavation, presumably by demonstrating the monetary value of artifacts. The reverse is also said to be true: the steady supply of artifacts brought out of the ground by clandestine excavators fuels the market. Both perspectives try to situate clandestine excavation in a tangle of market relationships whose inherent tensions serve as a proxy for the broader set of political relationships within the space of international cultural power.

The third important idea, then, is temporality. The words "always" and "for decades" suggest that archaeological looting has shifted in intensity and focus. Clandestine excavation has always been around, yes, but the Art Squad insists that it underwent a fundamental change in the late twentieth century. They claim a parasitic bond between tomb robbers and the market. In propounding this definition, they make it difficult to imagine tomb robbers outside a system of market transactions. *Tombaroli* and the market are co-constitutive. Linking them are several presumed steps. The authors of a report on the archaeomafia place tomb robbers in an expressly commercial role:

> Among the typical figures who traffic in cultural goods there are tomb robbers [*tombaroli*], who busy themselves with producing the goods [finding artifacts] through clandestine excavation, theft, and counterfeiting; the intermediaries [*ricettatori*], who traffic the goods [*piazzandolo*] in the country of origin for below-market prices or to foreign countries for perhaps medium to high prices; and the clients-intermediaries [*committenti-ricettatori*], who sell the objects to museums, auction houses, and private collections throughout the world. The goods are exported clandestinely—to North America, Australia, and Japan after they have been laundered [*stati ripuliti*] through false documents obtained in their processing "port," such as Switzerland.[37]

The collectors and terminal buyers sit at the top of the pyramid. *Committenti-ricettatori* are intermediaries with direct access to collectors, and the terminology here suggests the capacity to order someone else to make a purchase or acquisition. These second-stage intermediaries can inform the first-stage intermediaries (the *ricettatori*) of what the buyers outside Italy are looking for. It is the job of the *ricettatore,* then, to act as a conduit between *tombaroli* and the *committenti-ricettatori* and move the artifacts discovered by *tombaroli* to the second-stage intermediaries. Tomb robbers, who do the actual digging and stand to profit the least, are the bedrock. Among all these terms, *tombarolo* has a social meaning very specific to Italian culture.

The Social Position of Tomb Robbers

Tombarolo translates as "tomb robber" in English, yet its local meaning is more nuanced. The Italian language offers several terms to describe a person who digs for antiquities without authorization. *Il saccheggiatore,* for example, refers to a looter in the English-language sense of an opportunist who helps himself to goods, while *il clandestino* can be shorthand for a clandestine digger (coming from *scavatore clandestino*), though the word can also refer to undocumented migrants. Clandestine excavators are also called *i ladri* (thieves), *i predatori* (predators), and *i trafficanti* (traffickers) if they are suspected of moving artifacts to market. And yet, within this rich vocabulary of invective *il tombarolo* stands out as particularly illustrative of social relations and the workings of cultural power.

The word is related to a class of Italian words ending with the suffix *-aiolo*, which is associated with crafting or making. A *vignaiolo*, for example, is a winemaker, and an *armaiolo* is a gunsmith. It is noteworthy that many of the Italian terms with the *-aiolo* suffix or its regional, nonstandard variants (*-arolo, -rolo*) also connote mischief or ambiguous intentions.[38] A *mariolo* is a rogue or a rascal, and a *borsaiolo* is a pickpocket—literally, a "bag jostler."

The *tombarolo* is more than a man with a shovel:[39] he is a cultural figure, imbued with a complex of meaning. He is not glamorous in the way of pop culture icons Lara Croft and Indiana Jones (their moral inconsistencies notwithstanding). He is, instead, a bit of loser. This is the figure my informants were responding to, and why they made concerted efforts to instruct me in the proper terminology and draw moral boundaries between them and the archetypal *tombaroli*. The framework of cultural intimacy suggests a reading of this dialogic tension that symbolically validates the *tombarolo* even as it asserts his subordination to state authority and higher-status local concerns. In the case of clandestine excavators, accessing that cultural intimacy was abetted by my tactless questions. I was not intentionally rude; as an outsider, initially I genuinely did not understand the cultural sensitivities around the term *tombarolo*. Because I was foreign and female I was afforded a certain latitude, and my informants were for the most part willing to guide me into an understanding of the *tombarolo* as familiar and affectionately local, yet also mischievous, dark, and embarrassing.

In the archaeological community, looting refers to any removal of an object of historical or archaeological interest without authorization. What the term actually means, however, comes down to context and speaker. Julie Hollowell uses "low-end looter" to refer to the sort of digger Rafal was: an amateur enthusiast who excavates without a permit. Low-end looting is "undocumented excavation in which the products are not headed straight for the international art or antiquities market, but for less lucrative and often less visible markets or for no market at all."[40] The phrase seems to refer both to the minimal market value of the artifacts and the diggers' relative lack of power. Ethnographic work elsewhere reinforces the importance of social context in defining looting. In Jordan, Morag Kersel (2012) found that local community members tolerate unauthorized excavation if it is minimally destructive to the landscape and if the excavators themselves have a reputation as good members of the community with credible expertise in local history and national cultural idioms. In Mali, Cristiana Panella (2014) studied "farmer-diggers"—men who find and sell artifacts—and concluded similarly that they are legitimized through community systems of valuation, commodification, and resource sharing. They actively participate in producing local-level respect for their looting and selling even as state and international discourse impugns them.

Situated in a space of proud local identity inflected by apolitical nationalism, my informants called themselves *collezionisti* and *conoscitori*—collectors and connoisseurs. In insisting that they were collectors rather than tomb robbers, they were participating in a well-established discursive trope.[41] The same trope was mobilized by the defense in a 1973 court case against Professor Pio Fedele, in whose Roman residence authorities discovered more than three hundred Etruscan artifacts of artistic and archaeological interest. Professor Fedele initially defended himself against the state's characterization of him as an illicit trafficker in artifacts, protesting that he was an innocent collector who bought things from the public stands at Porta Portese (a popular flea market in Rome). The case notes specifically mention that Fedele was active in the "antiquaries' circle" and was well known among antiquities traffickers as an "expert, amateur, and buyer" (*intenditore, amatore, ed acquirente*) of Etruscan artifacts.[42] Domenico, like Fedele before him, was distancing himself from the act of illicit digging by pointing to a love of the object that occludes the ambiguities of the excavation process.

My informants' wordplay challenged the way I thought about excavating artifacts without a permit, and it also forced me to make decisions concerning how to write about them. Linguistic exchanges are "relations of symbolic power in which the power relations between speakers or their respective groups are actualized."[43] The labels we give to individuals and the adjectives we apply to their groups inscribe social identities. Words differentiate humans as though such distinctions—Italian or foreign, archaeologist or looter, licit or illicit—were natural. But these distinctions are socially constructed, a fact especially evident in speech registers that originate in institutions whose authority is ordained by state or science or both. Legal discourse, Pierre Bourdieu argued, is "a creative speech which brings into existence that which it utters."[44] When policymakers, elected officials, heads of museums, and Art Squad agents speak about *tombaroli* as though they constitute a verifiable social category, they concomitantly produce the *tombarolo*. This phenomenon is not limited to Italy and tomb robbers. Making migrants illegal, to take just one comparative example, is a sociopolitical process of "fundamental analytic categories that operate pervasively in the formulation of the subject at hand."[45] These arguments further illuminate my choice of terminology. I call my informants "unauthorized excavators," as I explained earlier, in an attempt to describe their activities without imputing a moral flaw or an economic motivation. I arrived at this phrase after testing several others, including "lay diggers" and "off-the-grid diggers." The former I rejected as misleadingly benign, while the latter is simply false because my informants were not off the grid in the same sense that undocumented migrants are; rather, they are active, visible participants in collecting and trading artifacts. I chose not to describe them as collectors, however, because that would exculpate them from the crime of breaking into tombs and appropriating artifacts. "Unauthorized excavator" captures the social and moral distance my informants placed between themselves and *tombaroli,* yet it insists on recognizing their complicity in illicit digging.[46]

The Last Etruscan

> You hear about these men who steal from excavations or sell things to dealers. *They* are the [real] *tombaroli.* They are professional [thieves] and unscrupulous. It wasn't like that with my father. (Michele)

> What they do to the archaeology, to the artifacts, is absolutely horrific. They have no respect for history. Of course they are going to tell you that they collect, they admire, they are careful when they go into the tomb, et cetera. All I can say is, they are good liars. There is no distinction [between *collezionisti* and *tombaroli*]. A *tombarolo* is properly associated with archaeology [but,] practically speaking, a looter is a looter. (Dr. Rita Paris, director of the Museo Nazionale Romano di Palazzo Massimo)

Everyone, it seems, can tell you what *tombaroli* do and why they must be stopped. Few speak publicly about what it means to be one. If Italy had a *tombarolo* hall of fame, Omero Bordo would be its star. In the 1990s Bordo rose to fame as Italy's most talked-about tomb robber. Branding himself the last Etruscan (*l'ultimo etrusco*), he made television appearances, displayed his award-winning replicas of Etruscan antiquities in Rome's Piazza del Popolo and Australia's Melbourne Museum, was the subject of numerous magazine and newspaper features, and in 1997 won a national popularity contest (tied with actor Michele Placido). One magazine article explained that because he was a "true Etruscan" his "vases, bronzes and jewelry are not copies but originals [*manufatti originali*]. Nobody knows how he manages to reproduce the ancient clay mixture, the black paste from which his vases are made. Some finds, identical to his vases, have been found in tombs discovered four years after Omero made his." Bordo's fame brought him sufficient capital to embark on his life's dream: Etruscopolis, a reconstructed "city of the dead" that was celebrated (and lampooned) as a "Disneyland of death" (*Disneyland della morte*).[47] His triumph was redemption for his earlier life as a *tombarolo* in Tarquinia, where he spent twenty years looting Etruscan tombs. In 1978 Bordo was sentenced to five years' imprisonment for making and selling fake antiquities. Despite his subsequent fame he never shook the stigma of having been a tomb robber. Bordo's story—from small-time looting and jail to fame, money, ridicule, and finally obscurity—provides us with a modal *tombarolo* and illustrates the figure that Michele and Dr. Rita Paris, quoted at the start of this section, excoriated during our interviews.

Bordo was born in the vicinity of Tarquinia in 1943, a turning point in the war as American soldiers arrived in Italy and began a sustained assault on German occupation forces. The difficulties rural Italians endured in this period haunt Bordo's recollection of his early years. It was, he says, a period of perilous challenges for rural residents, during which civilians still died regularly from bombs, hunger, and sickness.[48] As a toddler he was sent to his aunt's house near Monterozzi, the famed Etruscan necropolis that was made a UNESCO World Heritage Site in 2004. Reflecting on his first youthful forays into Etruscan tombs, Bordo hits on two themes, somatism and emotions, and these recur throughout his explanations of why he looted tombs. Looting felt completely natural: "As a child I began to breathe the very air and feel the same energy as the ancient rulers and priests, warriors and ordinary people, children of the Tyrrhenians who were still shrouded in mystery." His youthful explorations eventually paid off. At age sixteen Bordo was approached by a man in a bar who asked if he could bring him Etruscan collectibles. Bordo assented and, with a friend, returned the next day with a haul of pottery that earned them 350,000 lire.[49] This was an enormous sum for a rural boy. It was Bordo's first inkling, he said, that the objects he loved held monetary, not just sentimental, value.

In 1978 Bordo was prosecuted for selling fake antiquities, which he made in his atelier and sold to tourists and collectors. He prided himself on the high quality of his reproductions, which he described as being so faithful to the original production techniques that they could fool even the experts. Writing in the third person, he recalls the period leading up to his arrest: "He visits the world's most important museums. Several directors ask to meet him and seek his expert opinion [on the objects] housed by their museums. Very often Omero is surprised to discover many vases produced by his own atelier. He is worried but also flattered on seeing that his work is considered identical to authentic antiques."[50]

Bordo argued that he made replicas—not fakes—and that if his buyers could not tell the difference between his productions and the ancient versions, then it was their own fault. The case worked its way through the courts for months, a period Bordo refers to as "my odyssey," a classical reference that also points to the origins of his name (Omero is the Italian form of Homer).[51] In the prison at Civitavecchia—with support from the prison officials—Bordo began to make Etruscan objects and was given day parole to work in Tarquinia. During this time Chilean artist Sebastian Matta Echaurren invited him to collaborate. Matta was internationally renowned for his surrealist painting, and he professed an interest in learning ancient ceramics techniques from Bordo. Bordo recognized in Matta a shared connection with the ancestors; he was the Incan counterpart to Bordo's last Etruscan: "The outcome [of the collaboration] was a sparkling symbiosis of the vivid imagination of a Chilean Inca with that of an Etruscan of our times." The two men worked together, and Matta opened a ceramics workshop in Civitavecchia, the town where he died in 2002. For Bordo the partnership was evidence that he had transcended the disrepute of tomb robbing and was at last respected for his artistic genius.

Emboldened by his artistic success—Bordo recounts a long list of prizes in his biography—he decided to embark on his life's dream, a full-scale reproduction of an Etruscan necropolis. Etruscopolis was inspired by his sustained contact with what he described as the underground Etruscan world (fig. 15). The exacting reconstruction of Etruscan tombs would be not just a project of scholarly study, but also reparation for the "violations" he had committed on the sacred area of his ancestors.[52] Etruscopolis opened in 1997, with international media interest. The *Los Angeles Times* ran the story under the headline "Grave Robber Creates an Etruscan Theme Park."[53] In Italy, media outlets reported with a mix of humor and fascination the tourist-oriented "city of the dead" in Lazio. Bordo's fame grew, but media stories show that popular reception of Etruscopolis was uneven. Bordo could not escape the public's fundamental distrust of fakes and of collectors stigmatized by the *tombarolo* label. Newspapers stressed Bordo's lack of formal expertise. *La Stampa* was brutal in its assessment: "No, he doesn't seem at all like Indiana Jones, this predator of ancient art: he has the thick, heavy figure of a man who likes a good meal, a crafty look, [and] a slight sleepiness to his eyes" (*La Stampa*, August 17, 1990).

By linking Bordo's physical appearance with supposed intellectual shortcomings, the text drew on a long and repugnant tradition of explaining social deviance as an outcome of "race" or racialized physiognomy. In

FIGURE 15. "The last Etruscan," *tombarolo* Omero Bordo shows the murals he painted in the reconstructed Tomb of the Lioness in his native town of Tarquinia, north of Rome, August 1997. After making a living for three decades by raiding graves in ancient Etruscan settlements, Bordo disavowed tomb robbing and devoted himself to the creation of Etruscopolis, a 15,000-square-meter replica of the world of the ancient Etruscans. Critics derided it as a Disneyland of the dead. Photo credit: AP Photo/Plinio Lepri.

Italian intellectual history, that tradition was formalized in the work of criminologist Cesare Lombroso. It continues today in crude stereotypes about rural Italians' being prone to crime because of deficient morals and failed socialization.[54] Bordo's second flaw, according to the same *La Stampa* article, was ignorance. He was said to have disclosed that he had "no idea" how much to charge visitors after the initial three-month period of free admission subsidized by the regional government. He was quoted as bragging about the independent nature of the venture. "I didn't receive a dime of government money. I built this all by myself." Bordo's boastful independence is an example of *furbizia*—slyness or craftiness. In Italy, a good *furbacchione* is admired for the ability to exploit loopholes and cut corners. Crucially, the *furbacchione* looks down on rule followers as naive. *La Stampa* tried to frame Bordo's failure to collaborate with recognized authorities as ignorance of how Italy's patrimony system works.[55] But Bordo evaded that framing by embodying *furbizia* and thereby harnessing a widespread cultural idiom to legitimize the practices of tomb robbing and make them socially legible.

DELEGITIMIZING BORDO

Professional archaeologists provided their own criticisms of Bordo. Dr. Maria Gabriella Scapaticci, archaeological superintendent for Central Etruria, was interviewed by the Associated Press about the impact of Etruscopolis on scholarly research into the ancient Etruscans and on popular appreciation of them. She did not hold back: "Omero Bordo is a man of low cultural attainment [*scarsa cultura*] and is not an expert. With this business [Etruscopolis] he wants to ingratiate himself with the authorities after many years of many looted [*depredato*] tombs."[56] Scapaticci's comment hits on two recurrent themes. The first correlates expertise with formal education. This theme is especially resilient in archaeology, a discipline that has struggled for more than a century to separate experts from amateurs. We encounter it again in the comments of prominent Etruscologist Lorella Maneschi, who told the daily newspaper *Corriere della Sera* that Bordo's recreated tombs have "no scientific value whatever."[57] Scapaticci's characterization of Bordo as poorly educated in culture is part of the larger project of creating a specific persona for the *tombarolo*. The second theme is embarrassment. For the archaeologists, Bordo's public shenanigans expose a disreputable side of national culture. They can dismiss him as coarse and unscientific, but they know that Bordo represents a mode of cultural production that is widely recognized, if not respected, as constitutive of national patrimony practices.

Bordo's journey from imprisonment and disrepute through media fame and fortune, then back to disrepute and obscurity, sheds light on the workings of cultural power on the ground. His fame should be understood in conjunction with two factors. First, he was a natural showman with an aptitude for self-marketing. He knew how to promote his artworks and his reputation through venues in the art and museum world. Second, as a veteran *tombarolo* he tapped the Italian public's long-standing interest in and instinctive sympathy for a specific type of marginalized figure, the working-class man who resists the state's absolute control of rural resources. Like bandits and political protestors, the *tombarolo*'s membership in the Italian community allows him to push against institutional rules and play with them.[58] Despite the brief wave of popular interest in him, Bordo was always destined for infamy because the construct of the *tombarolo* is firmly linked with pervasive class and regional stereotypes. Bordo's critics effectively exploited these stereotypes and reinforced the shamefulness of the *tombarolo* label. Bordo, in sum, stands for the type of lay digger my informants pointedly distanced themselves from. He is a jokester and a thief, taking himself too seriously as the "last Etruscan" and misusing culture by opening a tourist attraction. While selling antiquities was a major feature of my informants' moral boundary work, so was the idea that there are correct and incorrect ways for unauthorized excavators to demonstrate their knowledge of antiquity. In an interview published after his death in 2018, Bordo was commemorated as a misunderstood connoisseur of Italian antiquity: "I didn't know that my childhood game, which became a profession and a passion [*mestiere e passione*]," he said, "was a crime."[59]

The Good Tomb Robber

Trustworthiness, cultural nous, and appropriate deference to authorities emerged as important issues for my informants, none of whom would identify personally with the story of Omero Bordo. The field of unauthorized excavation is highly structured by rules, ethical boundaries, and codes of masculinity.[60] Deviations from the rules are dealt with internally, and sensitive information is shared only after trusting relationships have been demonstrated and tested. When one dig partner sold an artifact without the group's permission, Michele's father, Piero, expelled him, and news of the man's infraction was quietly circulated among other groups. Henceforth his reputation was besmirched, and he was no longer included in discussions about potential new finds. Michele recalled that the telephone tree would henceforth "skip" the excommunicated digger, shutting him off from the exchange of sensitive information that was vital to their work. Rafal stressed that artifact hunting should be done only with trusted friends so as to avoid "trouble." He recalled that when he dug near Viterbo, "I only went with a friend I knew well because I knew he wouldn't do anything stupid to get us into trouble. When he got serious, I dropped out. He wanted to bring another guy, then another guy; he started to get risky, and I thought, no, that's too much, I'm out. So we didn't go anymore because for me it was getting too crazy."

Whereas Piero removed the deviant from his group, Rafal resigned from his dig group voluntarily once his friend's zeal for tomb robbing became "serious." The two episodes point to different levels of investment in the group, with transparency being treated as a core value among fellow diggers.

Timario highlighted another core value, and I heard it articulated in various ways across my interviews: Respectable unauthorized excavators do not steal from archaeological excavations. Timario was fifty-nine, a semi-retired groundskeeper who had lived in Campobello since infancy and previously assisted with excavation work at a nearby archaeological project. He had a fondness for ancient coins, having found a few by chance in the spoils heaps: "I found a couple, just little things, and if they were in the dirt mound [the archaeologists] sometimes forgot about them so I took one or two. Simple, but very, very beautiful to me. So after this work I had a good eye for coins, and I liked to look for them here and there." Remembering that metal detectors are illegal in Italy, I asked Timario to tell me how he knew where to look for coins. "Well, remember, I spent a few summers with the excavation team, so I know what kinds of things—walls, for example—you look for. But I don't mean the *scavi* [excavations], I mean in the [farm fields adjacent], there, not where [the dig team] works." In a similar vein, Michele swore that his father never "stole" from archaeological sites because he respected the profession of archaeology.

Good tomb robbers can articulate the distinction between theft and gaining artifacts honorably. Striking out on new ground and using one's own knowledge and physical strength to locate tombs define the limits of acceptable unauthorized excavation. Important, too, is having a credible link with the site. In Campobello, claiming that link is additionally important because it distinguishes members of the local community from the foreign excavators who come to the town every summer. Campobello is a small town with a big history: an impressive Etruscan site that attracts one hundred or so archaeologists every summer, bringing commercial business and friendships with locals but also mild strain when it comes to questions about cultural legitimacy and authorized uses of the collective patrimony.

I met Jacopo in the town's main bar. It is a gathering place for the town's elderly residents at all times of day and is especially busy in the evenings when people stroll out for drinks or ice cream after dinner. The bar features an outdoor patio with seating, and the interior is decorated with black-and-white snapshots of local grandees and past events. I had learned from the excavators that several local men were former members of the dig team, replaced by American undergraduate students in the 1980s. Jacopo was in his middle to late fifties when I met him. He was initially not interested in speaking with me, and I realized early in our conversation that I would get nowhere with the protocol questions. We made small talk and slowly warmed up to the topic of excavation and relations between the professional diggers and the locals. Throughout the conversation, he informed me that Campobello residents have experience that significantly predates the arrival at the site of foreign archaeology students and visitors (like me). His growing up near the excavation site, gaining familiarity and sensorial mastery of the area even before it became an official dig site, gave him an advantage, a form of credibility in the production of knowledge and culture. This natal affinity, borne out by his dexterity with dig sites and artifacts, in turn was a core component of Jacopo's local identity. He told me, "We were valuable to the excavations because we know this land better than anyone. My parents and their generation, they could tell you where the burials were by the texture of the soil." Although the local knowledge is still intact, Jacopo told me, "Now they have professionals. Who cares? That's how it goes. We're all friends." Jacopo's insistence on amicability notwithstanding, one senior member of the excavation team told me there are still tensions with local residents who used to dig with the team because they consider themselves passed over for younger, relatively inexperienced excavators.

Jacopo intimated that he still indulged in digging for artifacts, but he did not confirm this, and given the sensitive nature of his community's relationship with the excavation team, I decided not to pursue the matter. Fundamentally, his story hits on a core tension in the production and maintenance of the nation's cultural patrimony. Jacopo has an authentic, lived knowledge of the historic landscape and its material features that the outside professionals do not. His knowledge might count for something, as it once did during paid digging for the excavation team. With expertise increasingly concentrated in the offices and titles of the apparatus of state *beni culturali*, the kind of expertise Jacopo offers is relegated to local history. As a result, he looks for other applications of his archaeological training, including portraying the excavation site as local rather than in national, cultural, or historical terms.

Digging with the Ancestors

Bodily expertise, knowledge of objects, and the structure of the team are inseparable in sustaining unauthorized excavators' work. From Michele, the self-described former child *tombarolo* who participated in unauthorized excavation with his father for more than a decade, I learned that unauthorized dig teams include specialists who perform differentiated tasks. In Michele's experience, the strongest men handled the *spillone*, Michele's father tossed down a rope, and young Michele shimmied down the shaft. If the men agreed, based on Michele's report, that the tomb was worth digging out, the work proceeded rapidly, to evade detection by authorities, but also systematically:

> First my father, because he was a civil engineer, he would figure out how best to dig without having the entire structure collapse. Signore Salerno, he had a good feel for the topsoil, and he'd work with my father's cousin, my Zio Daniele, to clear it. I'd sit up top and look through the dirt piles, hoping to find a coin. So I guess you could say that each of us had a particular task, and we did them independently but also as part of a team.

Dividing the labor along lines of expertise structures the excavation in a couple of ways. First, it guides the pace of the dig. Since organization and efficiency mark off the respectable *conoscitore* (connoisseur) from the dishonorable (because reckless and rushed) *tombarolo,* unauthorized excavators must incorporate organizational routines into their work. Patience is important. Stepping into another man's work area to hasten the digging, Domenico told me, was an insult to the other man. "Each one [of the diggers] knows that speed is important. But if you rush, then you are no better than the messy thieves [*i ladri disordinati*]." Specialized functions and organizational routines thus shape the direction and pulse of the work, and instill patience and anticipation.

Division of labor at the dig site also affects the structure of excavation by making team members dependent on each other. No single team member had the strength and skills to unearth a tomb alone, so it was physically necessary to work with someone else. But it was also cognitively important to do so. Since *conoscitori* take pride in specializing in material types, periods, and localities, they are not supposed to know everything. The reputation of the connoisseur or self-taught expert relies for its effectiveness on strategic ignorance. Timario offered an illustration of this:

> My love is coins. I first learned on the excavation team that coins are very important documents for archaeology. I learned that if you find a coin in situ, it gives you a date for the structure. After that I read a couple of books about ancient coins and became quite good at identifying them. [Fiona: Do you also know about other types of metal artifacts? Tools or jewelry, for example?] No, no. Those things—nothing. I prefer to look for coins. There are so many, many types! I have no time for tools and jewelry.

Timario's insistence that he knows nothing (*niente*) about other categories of metal artifacts shores up his credibility as an expert in numismatics. Because there are so many types of coins, he devotes his time and all his cognitive energy to them. Were he to claim expertise in multiple categories of objects, Timario would threaten his standing as a *cono-*

scitore. And in a small village like Campobello, claims to archaeological expertise are scrutinized. Reputations are vetted by neighbors and fellow archaeology buffs. Strategic ignorance serves the speaker by setting forth modest (and thus socially acceptable) claims and making specialty knowledge more plausible and trustworthy.

Drilling further into embodied archaeological knowledge, in her study of local *huaqueros* (traditional looters) in northern Peru Kimbra Smith identified sensory knowledge as the "tactile familiarity with excavation techniques and artifact types; visual recognition of typical site arrangements and earth stains [and] olfactory knowledge of [the presence of human remains]."[61] *Huaqueros'* knowledge was legitimized through connections with the local community, whether familiarity with local myths about history or with locals' beliefs about sacred objects. Smith suggests a critical point about knowledge forms: they are not evenly distributed. Bourdieu suggested this, too, when he asserted that our social position accounts for the knowledge we embody. But Smith's study points to the inexplicable nature of some forms of knowledge. It was precisely this ambiguity that Omero Bordo cued when he told about meeting King Gustaf VI Adolf. The king was an avid fan of archaeology and was participating with the Swedish archaeological society in an excavation near Tarquinia. Having heard of Bordo's fascinating artifact finds, the king asked him to lead the entourage to an interesting find. Bordo, writing about himself in the third person, described what happened next:

> Omero accompanies him up the slope of a hill. The air is heavy with the pungent aroma of Roman mint. In a peremptory fashion Omero indicates a point to the king, "Dig there, sir . . . yes, right there." The diggers begin working, and after a few strokes of the pickax they come up against a slab of macco, the Etruscan rock par excellence. The rock is the wing of the entrance to a tomb. The king, with an incredulous expression, asks Omero, "Tell me your secret and I'll keep it to myself . . . it's only for me to know." Omero answers, "Sir, there is no secret. I simply feel the presence of my forebears" [*la presenza dei miei antenati*].[62]

With this and other stories in his biography, Omero tests readers' credulity by flirting with the epiphenomenal. In this sense he is comparable to another famous *tombarolo* of the 1980s and 1990s, Luigi Perticarari, whom we met in the previous chapter in the context of the *Scandal at Tarquinia* film. Perticarari called himself Il Mago (the magician), because of his intuition for Etruscan tomb locations and his power to make "beautiful Etruscan treasures" appear simply by touching the soil.[63]

Less important than the accuracy of such claims is their comprehensibility in a long tradition of associating artifacts with magic. For medieval Europeans ancient artifacts had mystical properties: flint tools were "thunderbolts" from heaven, and figurines were the devil's playthings.[64] Revealing themselves suddenly, during routine plowing or trenching, artifacts lay outside the realm of epistemic normalcy. The idea persisted well into the modern period, beyond the point when people understood that artifacts, ruins, and ancient statues were remnants of past civilizations. Instead of devil's toys, artifacts became emissaries of Fortune. The value assigned to the objects—their utility—"depended in part on the chance circumstances of their procurement."[65] Ancient statues derived their status from having been found by chance rather than on purpose. The very unearthing of an artifact was "conditioned in part by circumstances that have their own histories behind them."[66] Artifacts were part of the vast collection of myths, stories, symbols, and sayings that were passed down through generations and shaped the way people made sense of the world.

Tombaroli and *huaqueros* are regarded as credible keepers of sensory knowledge largely because of their intimate ties to a particular place. They understand the landscape and all its nooks and crannies from top to toe, in a way that outsiders with a map could never approximate. Yet the discourse of magical knowledge is not limited to tomb robbers. In earlier fieldwork at an excavation site in Lazio, the chief field director told me that, for Italians, ancient artifacts were their "lifeblood," something felt "in the bones." She could profess her belief in extrasensory perception of artifacts and ruins without jeopardizing her formal credibility because the discourse of magic is widespread and acceptable. Consider that perspective alongside Rafal's story:

> I wrote a novel about them [Etruscans]. It was a couple of years ago. [Fiona: What was it about?] Ah, fantasy. Historical fantasy. Science fiction, sort of. I created some characters and set the story in the last days of Etruria, when the Romans are on the rise. There is a priest [in the book], and he is the hope of his people because locked in his memory are the chants and spells of the ancients. [Fiona: May I read it?] No [laughs]. I would not inflict it on you. No, it was a private project.

Rafal shared this story without prompting. The conversation up to that point was about his grandfather, who had also dug tombs clandestinely. Rafal wanted me to understand that his interest in the ancient past was about more than just digging. He was self-conscious about the quality of his manuscript but not its subject matter. He recognized that the Etruscan religion was a legitimate topic of scholarly study and that the discourse of archaeology as magic was legitimated by Italian culture more broadly.

THE TOMB ROBBER'S "HIGH"

In each of my interviews, I asked subjects about their recollections of the physical sensation of digging. My question, which I posed in Italian, was: "Tell me, what did you like about digging? Can you describe for me what it felt like, physically?" This line of inquiry never failed to elicit an enthusiastic response. My informants seemed pleased to describe in detail their physical strength and endurance, much the way anglers or rafters like to tell about the jumbo salmon they caught on last summer's camping expedition or the fiendishly difficult stretch of class four rapids they tackled on their river trip. For unauthorized diggers, the topic of physical encounters and challenges was also inviting because it allowed them a break from my questions about morals, legality, and identity—topics that were sometimes awkward in the interviews. Informants who otherwise made brief responses suddenly became voluble on the nuts and bolts of scouting dig sites, hauling equipment, digging, unearthing objects, and keeping their operations clandestine.

Strong sensory memories were linked with belonging—belonging to the dig team as well as to a larger group. Recall the "high" Michele experienced while robbing tombs with his father's team. Émile Durkheim (1995) explained this sensation as collective effervescence, the group's experience of a practice or event as otherworldly and unusually exciting (as God or *manna*). It is characterized by embodied, physiological responses. In moments of collective effervescence people feel different than they usually do—more powerful, joyous, and special. Collective effervescence helps maintain group identity and strengthen solidarity because that feeling of specialness, Durkheim argued, is generated through collective rituals, and although it creates the impression of otherworldliness, it is in fact society itself that people are experiencing through rituals.

Bodily practices and somatic experiences provide crucial insight for understanding the relation between antiquities and social identities. Writing on the transmission of Polish national myths, Zubrzycki writes that "discursive tropes, visual images, sounds and music, tactile stimuli, and, most likely, smells as well . . . facilitated the convergence and exchanges between multiple sites of the nation and their modes of sensory perception."[67] This multiplicity of sensory perceptions facilitates synesthesia, the "transposition of sensory images or sensory attributes from one modality to another."[68] Artifacts sit at this juncture of transposition, their meaning crystallized by specific sensory experiences such as the objects' surface feel, weight, size, smell, and color as well as their finders' memories of the physical circumstances in which the artifact was found. Social identities, whether national, local, or in between, are grounded in and legitimized by these experiences. Rafal's remarks reported at the start of this chapter provide an example of this. He feels the objects' weight and shape in his pocket and will display them on a shelf in his home. The antiquities are truly his because they are heavy in his pocket, close to his body. His pieces of pottery, unearthed with his own hands, will forever evoke friendships and excitement. By linking his social identity with the uniqueness of the soil ("how it is in the dirt here") and the specialness of objects lifted from that soil, Rafal applies the discourse of state patrimony to intimate spaces of memory production.

Nonna's Little Pots: The Social Ethics of Illicit Collecting

What happens to the artifacts tomb robbers bring out of the ground? Because my informants made a point of exculpating themselves from antiquities trafficking and sales, I could only assume they were keeping their finds. With the division of labor so neatly articulated, it was reasonable to imagine that the artifacts, too, were divided fairly. Jacopo hinted at this when he stated that dishonest lay diggers were disrespected and sometimes expelled from a dig group. Each interview subject answered my question differently, yet they all pointed to home as a significant space for handling looted artifacts. Michele, the former child tomb robber we met at the start of the chapter, recounted what happened when he found something particularly valuable. The adults who sent him down the shafts were particularly interested in jewelry and pottery. His father, Piero, had a collecting interest in *bucchero* wares, a distinctive pottery type from Etruria, and Michele liked to be able to bring the good news that he had found some: "That is when the adventure really began [Michele laughed]. My father would carefully wrap it, and when we returned home we'd look at it together. And my mother would say, 'Who is this one for?' because the house was starting to fill up with his treasures."

His mother had a legitimate concern. Her husband's collection of Etruscan artifacts grew so large that it filled the shelves in the living room, a cabinet in the bedroom, and boxes in the outdoor storage shed, which had been cleared of bicycles and garden tools to make room for the urns, pots, and statuettes. I asked Michele what Piero did with the objects once they were home. His answer revealed an organized in-home curatorial system: "First of all, we would bring the things to the kitchen. There was a table there and we would spread out the things on it. We looked over everything and sorted them into piles. My father stayed up late. Sometimes when I woke up he was still there, hunched over some pottery fragments, trying to piece them together." The way Michele tells it, piecing together fragments of pilfered ceramics is a routine aspect of family life, as normal as playing a board game or watching TV. Piero did his sorting in the kitchen, the symbolic heart of the domestic space. He worked in full view of the family, signaling his confidence that he was doing nothing wrong. Michele's uncertainty about the legality of his father's actions is understandable in light of this openness.

Elisa, a Rome-based friend with an apartment north of the city, was sheepish about showing me the Etruscan antiquities displayed in her living room. Her father bought the apartment thirty years ago, when the neighborhood was still cheap to live in. Elisa, her husband, and their young child moved in when Elisa's father retired and moved back to his native city in southern Italy. Elisa's father loved art and, she told me, had a habit of purchasing things that he probably knew were illegal:

> I mean, look at this stuff! Do you know what that is? [Points to a shelf above the bookcase.] That's an Etruscan vase. It's complete [intact], probably taken straight from a tomb. There is no way he should have it. [She laughs.] I probably shouldn't tell you this, given what you study. But look, there's more. More pots, this thing here looks like the lid of an urn, and then he has some little figurines, but I don't know if they are Etruscan or came from some other place. He just loved to collect things. A lot of it, he bought before I was born, so maybe it was legal, or more likely people just didn't care as much. I wish he would come and get these things. I need the storage for our stuff, and also then I wouldn't feel *guilty* about having them here. What will happen when he dies? God only knows what I'm supposed to do [with it all].

As she spoke, Elisa gestured toward the objects. All the artifacts were on a high shelf, about two feet from the ceiling. They were arranged neatly and occupied their own display space. The rest of the room was outfitted with the furnishings and personal possessions found in any family household in Italy: TV, couch and loveseat, glass-top coffee table with magazines, unopened mail, and the TV remote; a dining room set, the table used for folding laundry and organizing the contents of the child's school backpack; and a bookcase with glass doors. This was, in other words, a thoroughly modern space. Nevertheless, the antiquities did not seem out of place. My conversation with Elisa turned into an impromptu guided tour, and it became clear that the Etruscan pieces were connected to other things in the room. The bookcase contained a row of her father's books on ancient art. These were the books, she told me, that he studied when he bought a new piece or saw an interesting piece at a market or in a museum and wanted to know more about it. Two small *bucchero* pots were the same charcoal gray as the frame of the coffee table, a detail Elisa pointed out as evidence that the room was perhaps not as hopelessly uncoordinated as she feared. The urn lid showed a reclining figure, a visual reminder of the intended function of the dining table below.

Elisa was careful to balance humility with pride. She expressed remorse for her father's decision to purchase antiquities with questionable provenance, yet this remorse was socially obligatory. She knew that *I* knew there was a high probability the vases and urn lid had been looted from a tomb. She acknowledged this difficulty right away ("There is no way he should have it"), but she also cut him some slack ("maybe it was legal, or more likely people just didn't care as much"). After all, her living room was not so unusual for having antiquities:

> It's actually fairly common, especially where my dad is from where you visit homes, just ordinary homes, not fancy or anything—believe me, there is nothing fancy in his village—and you see antiquities on a shelf or maybe the ashtray on the coffee table is actually an oil lamp. [I'm startled.] I know! It's true. But there is all this stuff, all these antiquities swimming around, and I'm not saying it's right, but I am saying it's sort of no big deal.

When would it become a big deal? I ask. When would a small domestic antiquities display become questionable enough to get the police involved?

> Honestly, in my dad's village everybody knows each other's business. You can't hide secrets. Nobody cares about Nonna's little pots enough to call the Carabinieri. The Carabinieri are a joke, anyway. . . . I guess if someone actually showed up with an earthmover and bulldozed a tomb and sold enough stuff to get rich, the police might get a call.

Elisa here contrasts two scenarios, "Nonna's little pots" with a classic image of looting for profit. The succession of tropes (earthmover, bulldozed tomb, getting rich) demonstrates Elisa's fluency in the popular discourse of tomb robbing. With the phrase "Nonna's little pots," she nicely orients us to an idiom with deep shades of local identity. *Nonna* is the Italian word for Grandma. In Italy as in many places, the grandmother is revered as a figure of domestic continuity and transfer of tradition. As stressed in Elisa's phrase, inherited antiquities are harmless tchotchkes that fit within the framework of socially acceptable antiquities ownership. Throughout our interactions, she showed awareness of state regulations but demonstrated no fear of the consequences of violating them.

The phrase "Nonna's little pots" originates with Elisa, yet the idea behind it came up several times in other interviews. Jacopo, for example, challenged me to say why he and his neighbors should not be allowed to keep the artifacts they find by chance or already have in the family. In doing so, he invoked a grandmotherly figure:

> Take "Signora Rossi," the old widow who lives over there [points to a small house across the piazza]. She has amphorae in her home. Two or three of them. She uses them [for] storage. Kitchen storage. Who knows. And so what? You are going to tell me that Rome needs them? Or maybe the archaeologists need them to do their work? Come on.

Jacopo was hinting at the absurdity of even suggesting that Signora Rossi should have to prove she has legal title to the amphorae or else surrender them to the state. His elderly neighbor is not a looter. She is not a participant in the antiquities trade, and she does not stoop to the level of Omero Bordo. Instead she is a fixture in the neighborhood, and her pots are companions, silent helpers to an old woman in her kitchen. For Jacopo, she represents a relationship with artifacts that falls outside the state framework of *beni culturali*. He took this conversation as an opportunity to lecture me that Signora Rossi's way of using amphorae was closer to their original function: "You know, it is *good* for the ceramics to have oil inside, or grains. That is what they were meant for. It keeps them from drying out." The authentic uses she put them to further confirmed Signora Rossi's claim on the pots, with local, conventional meaning trumping the abstract categories and rules of the state.

Michele, Elisa, and Jacopo each pointed to the role of women in shaping a domestic narrative about lay digging and collecting. By cleaning, sorting, and then using artifacts taken from archaeological contexts, Michele's mother, Jacopo's neighbor, and Elisa's imaginary Nonna integrated artifacts into the home. Using pots for kitchen storage is one way of naturalizing them, something Italian women are especially empowered to do given their traditional authority in the household. Domesticating and feminizing the retention of looted artifacts makes the practices innocent by contrast with the harsh interventions of the state. In this context, moreover, the objects are no longer comprehensible as commodities or items of state property or national symbolism. Jacopo's challenge to me had its intended effect, and not only because he rhetorically enlisted a kindly old lady whose pots I was hardly prepared to question. Jacopo placed the amphorae in a context of local meaning, within which questions of legality seem not so much tactless as pointless. "Rome," he suggested, gains nothing by raiding Signora Rossi's kitchen and confiscating her amphorae. In emphasizing the interests of the nation's capital, with its marquee museums and formal offices of cultural power, Jacopo also left open the possibility that Italian cultural power draws strength from local practices and traditions of making meaning from archaeological objects. State-driven processes are incomplete without those local idioms.

The unauthorized excavating and collecting of artifacts complicates the formal workings of cultural power in Italy through creative play with the laws. At the same time, unauthorized excavators produce patrimony by generating a critical mass of mundane objects that are circulated locally, often in homes and through kinship networks where they sustain intimate links between artifacts and ordinary people. For Jacopo, Signora Rossi's amphorae exemplified the substantiation of the patria, linking her and her community with their locale. The state has to let them go because total enforcement is logistically impossible and symbolically ruinous. In this setting, the *tombarolo* reflects inconsistencies in the official, idealized presentation of citizens' enjoyment of cultural heritage. The following chapter moves beyond the practical organization of tomb robbing, and the folkloric and local practices that shape it, to a broader understanding of tomb robbers' value for the state and what this means for the growth of patrimony capital in the early twenty-first century.

✷ CHAPTER 5 ✷

Made in Italy

Consider the following four events, which together make up the focus of this chapter:

First, in February 2006 the Metropolitan Museum of Art agreed to return to the Italian Republic twenty-one antiquities, including the fifth-century BCE painted ceramic vessel known as the krater of Euphronios. The Met paid $1.2 million for the vessel in 1972, and the circumstances of its acquisition were immediately scrutinized by Italian officials. The restitution agreement was a stunning reversal of fortune for the museum, which had rejected the repatriation claim for years.

Second, Prime Minister Silvio Berlusconi flew to Libya in August 2008 to return a first-century BCE marble statue of the goddess Venus that had been taken to Italy in 1915 by colonial officials. The Libyan repatriation request was nearly derailed by an Italian cultural heritage group, which claimed that the statue was the rightful patrimony of the Italian people. At the handover in Benghazi, Berlusconi joked that he was returning Qaddafi's sweetheart. The repatriation coincided with a multi-million-euro trade deal between the two countries.

Third, in January 2015 the Ministry of Culture announced the conclusion of a multiyear, multiagency investigation of a looting and smuggling ring that operated in Italy and Switzerland. More than five thousand antiquities were captured, estimated at a collective value of €50 million, making "Operazione Teseo" the largest such raid in the nation's history. At the press conference, the Swiss ambassador to Italy symbolically restored the objects to the Italian patrimony and pledged his government's earnest commitment to clean up the Swiss art market.

Finally, in July 2016 luxury fashion company Tod's hosted an evening concert at the Colosseum in Rome to mark the first phase of refurbishment work, paid for by the company. The audience included Italian prime minister Matteo Renzi and Tod's CEO Diego Della Valle. When the state announced its partnership with Tod's in 2011, to the tune of €30 million, the backlash was swift. "What pisses me off," said one critic, "is that this is the same state that invests billions of euros in nuclear power plants [but] won't lift a finger for patrimony."

How does the world's greatest cultural power benefit by winning or losing repatriation claims? What does it mean to say that antiquities that were never actually on the market have a market value of millions of euros? Why is it acceptable for Tod's to link its brand to the Colosseum but unacceptable for tomb robber Omero Bordo to build an "Etruscan Disneyland"? These questions ask us to think about the interplay of political, economic, and cultural interests as patrimony capital is accumulated. Cultural patrimony is a nation's priceless endowment, yet its monetization—its direct and indirect pricing—can be strategically manipulated to stretch the state's reach into domains beyond archaeology and culture. This binds the state to institutions and foreign entities via long-term partnerships that can expand to further projects.

After the 2008 economic downturn, Berlusconi greatly reduced overall government spending and oversaw an unprecedented government divestment of the heritage and culture sectors. Facing down political opposition to the cuts, his minister for heritage, Sandro Bondi, fired back, "People can't eat culture." To replace state money, Berlusconi restructured the Constitution to allow for expanded market involvement. The sphere of cultural patrimony was divided into two separate domains: protection and valorization. Patrimony protection was no longer a national project; it was, instead, a market project. "Corporate Medici," or philanthropic CEOs, were enticed with tax breaks and publicity incentives to foot the bill for conservation work. Cultural patrimony "now had to demonstrate a socioeconomic value in order to justify public spending."[1]

Today, public-private partnerships dominate Italian cultural politics. The move from state spending to private capital was made possible by a broader shift from state/public power to state/private *governance*—an expanded configuration of the state that includes market forces and key elements in civil society. This shift is one of the defining characteristics of the neoliberal "heritage game."[2] Artifacts' material, aesthetic, and historic qualities make them uniquely amenable to manifold valorization. In this sense, archaeological patrimony fits the classic definition of cultural capital as "an asset which embodies, stores, or gives rise to cultural value in addition to whatever economic value it may possess."[3] Guided by these four events, this chapter examines the work of patrimony accumulation through repatriation, reintegration, and branding. Artifacts and monuments are locked into a constant system of value extraction and continued investment to perpetuate the elite status of Italian heritage.

Accumulation by Repatriation

Repatriation is the return of a person or object to its country of origin.[4] In Italy, artifact repatriation claims are pursued by the Ministry of Culture based on evidence provided by the Art Squad.[5] One of the most visible practices of the Italian model of cultural patrimony, it is also one of the most controversial. It has been decried as "trophy hunting," with "unreasonable, and sometimes blatantly extortionary, demands" made on the museums and collectors who stand accused of wrongful possession. The prominent essayist who wrote this particular critique suggested that Italy already had "more than enough antiquities of its own to worry about"—cueing a familiar trope about Italy's lacking sufficient resources to provide proper conservation treatment and curatorial care for its cultural goods.

Similarly, James Cuno, who has directed some of the most prominent art museums in the United States, has rejected Italy's suggestion that "the cultural patrimony represented by [archaeological materials] is a source of identity and esteem for the modern Italian nation." Repatriation is retentionism, he argues, and as a means of enriching patrimony it backfires because it "devalues" cultural property by limiting its circulation to a single nation of origin.[6] In Cuno's view, the only plausible explanation for repatriation is politics: "Governments can use antiquities—artifacts of cultures [that are] no longer extant and [are] in every way different from the culture of the modern nation—to serve the government's purpose. They attach identity with an extinct culture that only happened to have shared more or less the same stretch of the earth's geography. The reason behind such claims is power."[7] Retentionism, bullying tactics, and politics: what all three criticisms acknowledge is that the power of the Italian state is rooted not only in its capacity to control the flow of cultural resources but also in its ability to increase the state's patrimonial largesse through artifactual relations.

THE EUPHRONIOS KRATER

The krater signed by the Greek painter Euphronios (fig. 3) was described by Thomas Hoving, former director of the Metropolitan Museum of Art, as "one of the two or three finest works of art ever gained by the Metropolitan."[8] In November 1972, at the behest of its director and chief curator of Greek and Roman art, the museum paid more than $1 million for it, making it the most expensive single work ever purchased by the Met. Dietrich von Bothmer, the museum's curator of Greek and Roman art, recalled that he was left "speechless, bowled over" when he was first shown the inscribed ceramic pot. But the purchase immediately came under suspicion by Italian authorities, who questioned the circumstances under which the krater had traveled from Italy to New York. As press interest in what came to be known as the "hot pot" intensified, Bothmer defended the integrity of the purchase. Speaking to a *New York Times* reporter, he asserted that the circumstances of the krater's disinterment should be subordinated to its aesthetic and historical qualities. "Its intermediate history is not important to archaeology. Why can't people look at it simply as archaeologists do, as an art object?" he asked. Whether the vase had been in a private English collection for fifty years (as its seller insisted) or was actually the product of a recent clandestine excavation in Italy, "It doesn't make any difference ... whether it was the 3,198th vase or the 3,199th found there."

Arguments put forward by the Metropolitan in 1972 emphasized the institution's moral authority to acquire unique cultural objects without regard for their provenance (the record of ownership and exchange that constitutes a work's social history). In the prevalent art historical and museological thinking of the time, provenance was of interest only insofar as it revealed something about prestigious past owners, patrons, and makers. Still in its infancy was the idea that provenance should be structured as a history of power relations and of possible cultural exploitation. Lacking concrete evidence of the krater's illicit removal from Italy, the Italian authorities shelved the case, and the pot became the crown jewel of the Met's Greek and Roman collection.

The case was reopened in the 1990s when new evidence showed that the krater had indeed been smuggled out of Italy and into Geneva Free Port, a storage facility near the international airport in Geneva, Switzerland. The Free Port was an ideal place to store contraband because it was not subject to inspections by Swiss customs authorities. Italian authorities claimed the krater had entered the Met's collection in 1972 through a network of illegal looters and unauthorized art dealers extending into the dusty outback of central Italy.[9] In the face of this new evidence, the Met's director, Philippe de Montebello, was unmoved.[10] He maintained that the museum was in the best position to guarantee superlative conservation and curatorial treatment for the krater. He insisted that the krater's exemplary aesthetic and historical status merited inclusion in a world-class institution. Montebello's implication was not lost on the Italians. He was suggesting that the piece was better off in the Met than in an Italian museum. Even after the accord was signed, he complained that "the whole process of how Italy prosecuted its case in the United States was shabby" because the evidence was circumstantial.[11] But what really drew his ire was the Italian authorities' savvy use of news outlets to leverage public support and sympathetic media attention to the krater's plight. As Montebello saw it, the Italians violated norms of international cultural diplomacy by communicating primarily through mass media rather than through direct, private discussions with his office. That strategy, he suggested, blindsided museum leadership and biased the outcome. "I am puzzled by the zeal with which the United States rushes to embrace foreign laws that can ultimately deprive its own citizens of important objects useful to [their] education and delectation," he said in an interview with the *New York Times*.[12] For him the case remained "an irritant . . . a vexing issue [to be put] behind you."[13]

The February 2006 agreement stipulated that the museum would return twenty-one objects to Italy, including the Euphronios krater and a Hellenistic silver hoard thought to have been taken illicitly from Morgantina, in Sicily.[14] In exchange, Italy would lend the museum several significant artworks. For a two-year period, the twenty-one repatriated objects could remain in the museum for display—a conciliatory gesture that allowed both sides time to prepare for the transfer of possession and replacement of display materials. Property is not all that was being transferred; prestige and moral authority were also being scrutinized and balanced. Italy agreed that the museum had acted in good faith, thus backing away from outright accusations of theft, but the two parties also agreed that the museum was responsible for past improprieties. Structuring the mutualities this way allowed the current museum leadership to distance itself from decisions made thirty years ago, and Italy to maintain that the museum had acted improperly. The agreement, in short, presented the new calculus of power in the global cultural space. In January 2008 the Euphronios krater was officially repatriated to Italy. In a conference room crowded with journalists, academics, politicians, and representatives of the Ministry of Culture, an archaeologist from the Soprintendenza Archeologica and an agent from the Art Squad removed a white sheet to reveal their triumph (fig. 16). Rocco Buttiglione, the former minister of culture who had pushed for the krater's return, was euphoric: "The Italian state has won."[15]

What did it win? The krater, the archaeological artifacts, and the silver hoard were Italy's. The krater would remain in the museum for a further two years, but on condition that a sign be displayed next to it reading "Lent by the Republic of Italy" (*Agreement*, 4.1[a]). Similar signage

FIGURE 16. Unveiling the Euphronios krater at the state's attorney's office in Rome after its repatriation from the Metropolitan Museum of Art in New York. Archaeologists and Art Squad agents flank the sixth-century BCE bowl as part of the repatriation ceremony, which was held at the prosecutor's office to underscore the role of legal expertise and law enforcement in pursuing the claim. January 18, 2008. Photo credit: AP Photo/Plinio Lepri.

was required for the silver hoard. The costs of future loans from Italy to the Met would be covered by the museum, including expenses associated with the Ministry of Culture staffer escorting the lent objects from Italy to New York. Material gains, however, pale compared with the symbolic ones. The agreement omitted monetary values of each artifact; the closest the text came is in declaration A, which described the Italian archaeological heritage as "the source of the national collective memory and a resource for historical and scientific research." But talk of money was prominent in media coverage. Many outlets mentioned the price paid by the Met for the krater, and some included additional details such as that it was, at the time, the single most valuable item in the museum's collection. With the price a matter of historical record, Italian authorities could adopt a posture of disinterestedness and leave the media to speculate about the worth of Italy's victory. Together, these activities and discursive elements created conditions in which the krater could be *thought* about as having enormous market value. What the Italian state won, finally, was the symbolic transfer of what the Met paid, plus interest.

The krater was returned to Rome in a highly publicized procession and then publicly displayed in the Villa Giulia museum in Rome, where countless visitors came to see it. The Villa Giulia display told the story of the krater's illegal removal from Italy and its dramatic, and just, return. Through the years, the vessel became the centerpiece of museum shows about looting, the art market, and Italian patrimony. The krater had never previously been publicly displayed in Italy, so the state created a patrimonial narrative that valorized it as sought-after treasure. It also valorized it as unambiguously *Italian*. Museum materials explained that archaeologists believe the vessel was unearthed from a tomb in Cerveteri (central Italy).[16] They did not explain how it got to Italy or how long it had been there. Had it been used and cherished in Athens for a century before it came to Italy? Was the eventual owner a Greek speaker or a Latin speaker, and did he or she identify as Roman, Etruscan, Oscan, Greek, or something else entirely? These questions went unasked and unanswered. Greek authorship of the vessel was absorbed into its Italianness. Through a dramaturgical and symbolic repertoire that glossed over multicultural complexities, the krater was added to a purely Italian state patrimony.

VENUS OF CYRENE

When Silvio Berlusconi flew to the coastal city of Benghazi, Libya, in August 2008 to meet with Libyan dictator Muammar Qaddafi, the two already had a long history. It was partly personal. Both men enjoyed the company of young women, and Berlusconi was known to be an eager host to Qaddafi's whims. But it was also political. Libya gained its independence in 1947 and, as part of a long process of ameliorating postcolonial relations between the two countries, agreed to a reparations package with Italy in 2008. On August 30 of that year, Berlusconi and a contingent of Italian lawmakers met with Qaddafi and his courtiers to celebrate the Treaty on Friendship, Partnership, and Cooperation between Italy and Libya. The treaty's focal points were an economic development package for Libya, eventually totaling US$5 billion, and the sensitive matter of apologizing for past colonial occupation. Qaddafi hosted the treaty signing in a tent, a key symbol for his image as a modern tribal leader. Media coverage focused on the economic measures being negotiated, but the real star of the show had nothing to do with trade or tariffs.

The Venus of Cyrene, the headless marble statue dating to the second century CE, had been the subject of Libyan diplomatic efforts since 1989. We encountered this statue in chapter 3 (fig. 5): discovered in 1913 by Italian troops in the ruins of the ancient Greco-Roman city, it was moved to Italy two years later and exhibited at the National Museum of Rome. In July 1998 the two countries signed a joint declaration according to which Italy agreed to return "all manuscripts, artefacts, documents, monuments, and archaeological objects brought to Italy during and after the Italian colonization of Libya," pursuant to the 1970 UNESCO Convention. Eighteen months later, during the first meeting of the Committee for the Italy-Libya Partnership, the Venus of Cyrene was one of the objects identified for repatriation. On August 1, 2002, the Italian Ministry of Culture issued a decree commanding the

> passage from the demesne of the patrimony of the state [*il passaggio dal demanio al patrimonio dello Stato*] of the headless marble statue of Aphrodite, also called Venus of Cyrene, in the custody of the National Museum of Rome, in light of the transfer of the sculpture to the museum institutes of the Republic of Libya, considered a scientific and cultural opportunity to place the find in its original context of belonging [*presso il contesto culturale di appartenenza*].[17]

The final word of the decree, *appartenenza,* can also be translated as "membership," and it acknowledges that the statue is part of a group. The terminology of the first clause, "passage from the demesne of the patrimony of the state," requires further parsing. *Demanio* in modern usage refers to state property, and the word's origins lie in feudal land claims. The demesne was the land made available to the lord, adjacent to or extending from land he directly occupied. The land and its resources were theoretically at his disposal. The inclusion of *demanio* in the 2002 decree was in keeping with standard legal parlance. But by applying the concept of landownership to patrimony, the decree created a scheme of cultural sovereignty, in a way that identified the graded structure of place-based claims.

Before the transfer could take place, there was a surprise legal move. In November 2002 the Associazione Nazionale Italia Nostra, a nonprofit organization, filed suit to annul the decree. Italia Nostra is Italy's oldest association devoted to the protection of Italy's cultural, historical, and environmental patrimony. The group objected to the state's "excessive and abusive use of power." In the suit the plaintiff argued that removing the statue from the state demesne was a contradiction in terms.[18] Although the decree named Libya as the statue's original context of belonging, Italia Nostra insisted that "a Roman copy of a Greek original from the Hellenistic era is more in keeping with our artistic context than an Islamic one [*più pertinente al nostro contesto artistico che a quello islamico*]."[19] The

Venus of Cyrene was Roman, not Libyan, and should therefore remain in Italy as part of state patrimony. The Ministry of Culture, which had endured criticism from foreign institutions for being too zealously nationalistic in its prosecution of repatriation cases, was now being accused by a domestic group of not being nationalistic enough.

Italia Nostra asserted that the statue should be considered Italian due to its twentieth-century provenance and stylistic features. Just *look* at it, they suggested. The style of the statue made it perpetually Roman, marking it as material from Roman cultural practice, and modern Italy was the natural heir to classical Rome. Further, the group objected to the legal instrument the Ministry of Culture employed to discharge the statue's release. Federal law, rather than ministerial decree, was the only valid mechanism; according to the Italian civil code, cultural patrimony goods were subject to

> a regime of absolute inalienability [*inalienabilità assoluta*], since the character of demesne invests universality in movable cultural goods only insofar as they constitute a museum collection, considered as a whole, and not as individual cultural assets [and they remain] susceptible to losing such character if the absence of the bond itself is ascertained [*di perdere tale carattere ove venga accertato il venir meno del vincolo stesso*].[20]

The bond (*vincolo*) between statue and museum collection was creatively reimagined as a bond with the entire theoretical collection of Italian patrimony. Note, too, the emphasis on inalienability, a concept we encountered in chapter 2 in the context of the 1909 legislative debate.

Italia Nostra lost the case. In its ruling, the court determined that the Italian government did not have sovereignty over Libya in 1923 and was wrong to take the statue. When the Venus was pulled from the ground, it was Libyan ground, not Italian ground. It also remarked that the statue was stylistically and materially related to the Libyan cultural context and pointed to the architecture and decoration of the cities of Sabrata and Lepcis Magna and to portraits of the emperor Septimius Severus. Although the group lost this particular case, it had made an important political gain. By having its claim validated and brought before the Tribunale Amministrativo Regionale, Italia Nostra gained recognition as a legitimate non-state authority on patrimony decisions. The tribune agreed that heritage does not belong "to the exclusive competence of the State. On the contrary, the imperative of safeguarding national heritage does not preclude the collaborative contribution of non-State entities."[21]

FIGURE 17. Muammar Qaddafi and Silvio Berlusconi shake hands after Italy officially hands over the Venus of Cyrene marble statue to the government of Libya. The exchange was part of a multibillion-dollar trade accord as compensation for Italy's colonial-era exploits in the country. Benghazi, August 2008. Berlusconi was quoted as saying, "Muammar, I brought your girlfriend back." Credit: Reuters/Livio Anticoli–Italian Prime Minister's Press Office handout.

The door was now open to nongovernmental organizations, community associations, and the private sector on patrimonial matters of the state.

The handover took place in the tent in Benghazi as a prelude to Berlusconi and Qaddafi's bilateral treaty ceremony. In a widely circulated press photo, Qaddafi, Berlusconi, and the statue stand in the foreground with a crowd of dignitaries, reporters, and security personnel behind them (fig. 17). Qaddafi's snow-white robes visually echo the warmer white marble drapery artfully arranged beside the nude Venus. Clasping hands with Berlusconi and facing front, Qaddafi occupies the center of the scene and signals that this is his venue, his Venus, and his diplomatic victory. Berlusconi's expression is inscrutable. He may be listening to Qaddafi, squinting against the sun, or looking wistfully at Venus, headless, armless, and naked—the vulnerability of the statue consonant with Italy's posture of humility. The statue was not included in the friendship treaty. Its presence in the desert tent that day has been explained as a deal sweetener—an "expedient" to get the treaty signed, a sign of Italy's goodwill and an affirmation of cooperation.[22] But there was something else going on. The body of the statue—lithe, broken, sexualized by comment and subtext—is unmistakably classicizing. The statue came back to Libya, but only after it had been firmly embedded in a specifically Italian cultural tradition—a tradition characterized by public nudity, pagan gods and goddesses, fertility, and profligacy. "My dear friend Muammar," Berlusconi said, "I brought your girlfriend back."[23]

Berlusconi's quip diminished the statue's significance and, by extension, the seriousness of Italy's colonial transgressions. In the context of two vigorously—even ostentatiously—heterosexual male leaders, a sexualized, effeminate statue is a conquest and a lust object that has no standing apart from the men who (temporarily) possess her. The quip did something else: it conveniently restaged the statue as national *and* universal. Coming as it did after a protracted legal fight about its proper cultural context, the Venus statue was indelibly marked as descending from the Roman classical tradition. Italia Nostra had argued that the statue was "more in keeping with our [Italy's] artistic context than an Islamic one." That suggested that Libya lost its share of the classical inheritance when it embraced Islam. Matricial thinking—that objects found in this soil belong to the social community that inhabits it—was *not* extended to Libya. Italy has constructed itself as the rightful heir to the Roman classical tradition, in spite of the fact that were we to overlay a map of the Roman empire onto a map of the modern world, fourteen modern nation-states in Europe and North Africa would be included.

Ten days after the Benghazi meeting, Berlusconi was in London for a meeting with British Prime Minister Gordon Brown. Asked about Italy's cultural assets at a press conference, Berlusconi replied that "72 percent of Europe's cultural patrimony is found in Italy, and a good 50 percent of the world's [cultural patrimony] belongs to our country."[24] The statement highlighted the subtext of the entire performance of the Benghazi handover: *We can shift an ancient masterpiece from our patrimony to yours because we have plenty more like it.* Berlusconi's statistical claim shines a bright light on one aspect of the logic of sovereignty in Italian cultural power. What counts as the world's "patrimony"—as *valuable* patrimony, meaning the artifacts and artworks that we regard with reflected glory—happens to align perfectly with what artisans on the Italian peninsula have been making for millennia. The consecration of a certain body of works as "Italian," and the reciprocal consecration of Italian works as a corpus of characteristically significant pieces, sets up the equation so that the outcome is always in Italy's favor.[25] Berlusconi can benevolently hand back the stone Venus because of the mass of patrimonial objects still in hand. In giving the statue back, the Italian premier was reasserting Italy's authorship of the statue and casting his sights on a broader role for Italy in trans-Mediterranean relations.

Through heritage politics and artifact repatriation, Italy can distance itself from the stain of Fascism and imperialism and act in the guise of moral leader.[26] In managing its cultural ties with its former African colonies, Italy has dropped the rhetoric of the *colonia prediletta*, or the favored colony yoked to Italy by Roman archaeological materials. Instead, it emphasizes shared government commitments to heritage valorization. In chapter 3 we encountered the Axum obelisk, which Italy agreed to return to Ethiopia as part of a broader postcolonial repatriation process. This obligation was at last fulfilled in 2008. The repatriation process broke down over divergent understandings of which government—Italy's or Ethiopia's—should pay for its transport from Rome to Axum. (In 1937 Italy had used a private shipping company to move the obelisk from the port at Massawa, Eritrea, to Naples, from which it was shipped to Rome by truck.[27]) Media coverage of the handover praised Italy's archaeological and engineering expertise for making it possible:

> When it was removed by the Italians, the obelisk was in fragments, having been toppled during a sixteenth-century Muslim rebellion. The weight of the fragments pushed the limits of military vehicles and makeshift roads and bridges built by the Italians. Once in Rome, it was restored with metal rods embedded in concrete. The restoration made it difficult to disassemble, but at the end of 2003 the obelisk was dismantled from where it stood near the Circus Maximus in central Rome.[28]

The restitution, one Italian official emphasized, was "an obligation" (*un atto dovuto*), and not the first of its kind.[29] The obligation was legal, but the language that was used presented Italy as a moral leader.

As with the Venus of Cyrene repatriation, the Axum obelisk handover was a staging ground for geopolitical diplomacy. After the homecoming celebration Alfredo Mantica, secretary of state, had a private meeting with the Ethiopian prime minister, Meles Zenawi. "Very cordial and friendly," Mantica said afterward, "although [Zenawi] criticized the international community for leaving Somalia alone for Ethiopia to deal with. But on that issue he also thanked Italy for the efforts we have made to reach a peace agreement between the various warring parties."[30] Repatriating artifacts to the former colonies involves a power imbalance. Italy's paternalism and technical supremacy are implicitly compared with the recipient country's capacities, and any vestiges of cultural affinity between the two countries are relegated to antiquity. Discrepant framings—of history, culture, sovereignty, and materiality—take us into the contemporary political imaginary of the open-air museum, in which Italy's cultural capital once more extends across the Mediterranean.

OPERAZIONE TESEO AND THE ART SQUAD

At repatriation press conferences when objects are transferred back to the Italian Republic, the artifacts and efforts of uniformed law enforcement are jointly celebrated. They recycle performative devices: objects laid in rows and grouped by type; an absence of individual object labels; prominent display of the Art Squad logo and flag; and the presence of Art Squad agents turned out in full-dress uniforms and sternly protecting the artifacts. This is the visual lexicon of repatriation, and it offers the public an experience of the collective past that is expansive, enumerated, and accounted for.[31] When recovered antiquities are heaped in rows and stacks, they testify to the magnitude of crimes against patrimony and to the state's effectiveness in combating them (figs. 2, 4).

Among the most visible Art Squad tactics is the "blitz," or police raid. Blitzes can require delicate politicking. When a blitz disrupts a smuggling operation that originates in Italy and moves across national borders, international diplomacy is carefully managed to showcase Italian authorities' professionalism and the art market's predations. Let us look more closely at Operazione Teseo (Operation Theseus). Unveiled in January 2015, it was billed as the largest recovery of stolen artifacts in the nation's history.[32] A total of 5,361 artifacts taken clandestinely from sites in Puglia, Sicily, Sardinia, and Calabria, with an estimated value of €50 million, were brought back to Italy from Switzerland. The assemblage was too big for a single display, so selections of artifacts were set up in shifts in the museum of the Baths of Diocletian. Present at the press conference were special prosecutor for the Republic of Rome Giancarlo Capaldo; the minister of culture, Dario Franceschini; the commander of the Art Squad, General B. Mariano Mossa; the head of the Special Superintendency for the Archaeological Heritage of Rome, Maria Rosaria Barbera; and the ambassador of the Swiss Confederation in Italy, Giancarlo Kessler. A press release issued by the Art Squad explained the significance of the event:

> The Carabinieri Art Squad, after a long and complex investigation—coordinated with the public prosecutor of the Republic of Rome—restored [*restituito*] to the national cultural patrimony more than five

> thousand exceptional archaeological artifacts from the era between the eighth century BCE and the third century CE, repatriated from Basel (Switzerland), but having originated in clandestine excavations [*provenienti da scavi clandestini*] carried out in Puglia, Sicily, Sardinia, and Calabria.[33]

Kessler, the Swiss ambassador to Italy, was present to hand back the artifacts symbolically and to signal his government's willingness to cooperate with the Italian government to complete the investigation and take steps to clean up Switzerland's antiquities market. We might recall the strenuous efforts of lawmakers in the early 1900s to address the art market and the export of prized patrimony goods. In a sense, the market has always been part of the equation. Italy would not be the cultural power that it is without the antiquities market, its worthy foe.

The estimated value of €50 million is a symbolic number. The captured antiquities cannot, by Italian law, be sold. We will never know whether they would actually fetch that amount, and that is the point. The objects are priced, but in ways that distance the state from the actual work of pricing—work that would undercut the state's official antinomy toward the antiquities market. Put differently, there is considerable benefit to attaching monetary values to archaeological artifacts, but because they are part of the national patrimony, they are separated from the realm of money. Symbolic prices promote the state's profile as a cultural power and suggest the scale of injury to the national community. They resonate with a broad public because they are easy to understand. Symbolic prices can then simplify the complexities of cultural identity in a pluralistic society. The state is seen to be doing good because it is winning back valuable things for the public from thieves.

It is an easy story to love. It is also a story that relies heavily on tomb robbers to dig up new treasure. That is something the state cannot do easily, in part because professional archaeologists do not dig for treasure: they excavate layers for knowledge. Artifacts previously unknown to the patria—because still buried—did not develop their patrimonial valence through chains of community relations. Their value was locked in the soil as *potential* patrimony, as yet unseen and all the more powerful for its unknown qualities. But because the illicitly excavated artifacts cannot be returned to the soil and may or may not possess aesthetic or material brilliance, the process of reintegration emphasizes the injury done to the patria. One of the ways this is accomplished rhetorically is by likening artifact theft to religious martyrdom.[34] Here the national body presents itself as suffering from the violence of tomb robbers, who care nothing for

FIGURE 18. *Missione TPC* video game. The youth-oriented online game takes players on an adventure to learn the rules and mission of the Art Squad. The game is staged through a sequence of rooms in the Art Squad headquarters, which boasts symbols of the state.

the well-being of Italian patrimony. Tomb robbers, in this sense, provide a foil to the fantasy of patrimonial order.

No Italian citizen is too young to join in the fantasy of restoring and recreating the country through patrimony. A youth-oriented video game, available free on the Art Squad website, encourages Italian children to learn the proper rules of engagement with the nation's material culture. The Art Squad website introduces *Missione TPC* (fig. 18) as an educational game, primarily targeting children six to twelve years old, in which Sandrino, accompanied by Marshal Lightning, will have to discover the meaning of the acronym TPC by exploring the specialized command of the Carabinieri of that name and learning the main issues relating to the protection of cultural heritage.[35] The game allows the player to take a tour of the head office in Rome with an animated Art Squad agent. Where the wildly popular American game *Tomb Raider* has players traversing action-packed caverns in search of valuable artifacts, *Missione TPC* has them navigating bureaucracy. Here the player adopts the persona of a boy (male sex is standard) with brown hair and brown eyes. The broad-shouldered blond, blue-eyed agent towers over the boy. Players can choose which rooms of the Art Squad office to visit. In the conference room they can click on a map of Italy, which shows them where the other Art Squad offices are, and can learn about noteworthy *beni culturali* from a selection of Italy's regions. Presidential decrees thanking the Art Squad members for their work decorate the virtual pressroom. A general's office boasts a fine Renaissance painting; clicking on the painting reveals the story of the painting's creation, its shocking theft from Italy, and the Art Squad's efforts to bring it back.

In *Missione TPC* the state, and above all its Art Squad, is presented as the force for good *because it follows the rules*. Foreign museums and homegrown looters are presented as enemies of culture and therefore of the state. But the way to fight those enemies is surprisingly banal. The video game does not allow players to patrol archaeological sites or raid smuggling rings. There are no high-speed car chases. Instead, they score points by demonstrating their knowledge of the bureaucratic arrangements and organizational routines of the Art Squad. Players are rewarded, in other words, for learning and following the impersonal rules that characterize modern states. This is Indiana Jones with triplicate government forms, and it stands in stark contrast with the muscular version of Mussolini as *Homo autotelus*, who had the mythical capacity to generate new realities apparently ex novo—"miraculously, out of [his] own substance."[36] For a state that constructs itself as a cultural power, both figures are important. With the rules-oriented Art Squad official, patrimony management is depoliticized and becomes the dispassionate specialty of professionals. With the romanticized and larger-than-life birther of cultural life, patrimony itself exceeds the strictures of bureaucracy.

Made in Italy: Reintegrating Artifacts into the National Community

The conclusion of a repatriation case is marked by an exchange of objects, words, and gestures between the possessor and claimant. At this point, interparty mutualities recede into the background as a new mode of cultural production begins in earnest: reintegration—the object's absorption into its community of origin. In the Italian case, the community of origin is presented as both a political-legal unit bound by territorial limits and a family space held together by shared culture and history. The community of origin therefore insists on sovereignty in a double sense: legal jurisdiction over the national soil and cultural jurisdiction over the objects that emerged *from* that soil and, in this case, have traveled beyond national borders. At this point the legal argument has been settled and Italy's cultural sovereignty is reaffirmed. The gestures, words, and

FIGURE 19. Officers with the Lombardy region Art Squad hold three works by eighteenth-century painter Gaspare Vanvitelli. The works were stolen in January 2007 and surfaced on the international art market two years later. They were eventually recovered by the Art Squad from a bank vault in Switzerland. Monza, Italy, 2010.

rituals that make up this repertoire can be seen in the many press conferences and museum exhibitions that the Italian government organizes in the aftermath of repatriation settlements (fig. 19).

To have its full symbolic effect, reintegration must be made to feel expected, natural, and collectively sustained. Objects must be named, categorized, and evaluated, story lines must be created, and points of origin must be assigned and delegated. If physical return to the precise point of origin is not possible—say, the Cerveteri tomb where the Euphronios krater was found—museums are the logical repository. Museums are centers of cultural authority, and they use a range of curatorial practices to imbue objects with meaning. They also encourage ideological compliance.[37]

Frequent, well-publicized museum exhibitions with such titles as *Art Held Hostage* and *Recovering Our Culture* play up the worth of state patrimony. In November 2012 the Villa Giulia Museum hosted an exhibition titled *I predatori dell'arte . . . il patrimonio ritrovato* (Predators of art . . . the rediscovered heritage). The display featured artifacts recovered by Italian authorities from the illicit trading network of Giacomo Medici and Robert Hecht, two prominent art dealers who were indicted by the Italian government for the illegal export and sale of Italian cultural objects.

Medici went to prison for ten years and paid a fine of €10 million, one of the largest penalties for antiquities crimes in Italian history. Many items were found in the Geneva Free Port, awaiting export to private collectors and auction houses in Britain and the United States. A museum press release announced the exhibition as an opportunity for members of the public to become familiar with the extraordinary work undertaken by the Swiss magistrate, the Art Squad, the Guardia di Finanza, and state archaeologists. Two themes dominated the exhibition: the immorality of the predators—who include the *tombaroli*, antiquities dealers and private collectors, and unscrupulous foreign museums—and the heroism of the state authorities who stood up to the predators and restored the artifacts to their rightful home.

Italian-speaking visitors were recruited to support the Art Squad's mission at the entrance to the exhibition, where they were told that the museum's directors knew the visitors could be counted on as "important allies for the care and enrichment of the archaeological patrimony of the Etruscan world." The opening panel in the exhibition reminded Italian speakers of their government's duty toward patrimony, reprinting in bright yellow script a passage from article 9 of the Italian Constitution. This text did not appear on the English-language panels. The English text wished visitors a pleasant tour of the exhibition and requested that they show respect for Italy's archaeological and cultural heritage. The discursive divergence continued throughout the exhibition. Italian-language readers were encouraged to identify with the objects and institutions through the first-person plural pronoun and frequent invocations of national pride. English readers were given a more detached and scholarly description of the objects and their recent mistreatment. The disjuncture between what was said in the two languages reveals the effort to construct a zone of self-recognition and intimacy for Italian readers, most of whom, the didactic boards assumed, were Italian citizens.

Non-Italian visitors were acknowledged, but they were restricted to a non-intimate zone in which English was the sole non-Italian alternative. Discourse flattened national differences among the external observers and essentialized and celebrated national sameness among the insiders. Intimacy does not "flow" effortlessly out of a familial space, but is "perceived against a backdrop that accentuates the experience of difference (in and beyond domestic spaces) and orients that experience toward the task of ranking, comparing, accommodating, impressing, persuading, or excluding an 'audience' of real and imaginary onlookers."[38] The presence of the English and Italian text on the same didactic boards reminded Italians that their country and its cultural treasures were on display. The exhortation to Italians to be "important allies" of the state must be understood against this backdrop. When the country is accused in the foreign press of neglecting its patrimony, that accusation is an indictment of every Italian.

The recovered objects, mostly Etruscan and Greek in origin, were presented as members of the Italian family. Their recovery from foreign museums was a homecoming: they had been on a long and "involuntary" *giro del mondo* (world tour) that ended, "fortunately, where it was begun." A bronze figurine of Heracles had "returned to his home in Italy, where he originated" (*è tornato a casa in Italia, da dove proviene*). The Italian text commandeers the technical term *provenienza,* or provenance, which archaeologists use to describe the location of an object's discovery or origin. The word choice is deliberate; the more common phrasing would be *da dove viene* ("where it comes from"). By using *proviene,* the museum curators enlisted the figurine in the state project of patrimony. The display emphasized the artifacts' victimization by the black market and by powerful foreign museums with an appetite for Italian art. In four separate panels, foreign institutions' transgressions were laid bare: "Many museums were involved, from the largest and best-known museums of Europe and America to small university museums." As examples, the information panel named only American offenders: Boston's Museum of Fine Arts, the Princeton University Art Museum, the Cleveland Museum of Art, the Metropolitan Museum of Art, and the J. Paul Getty Museum in Los Angeles. In a sentiment that would be repeated three times in the one-room exhibition, readers were told that the corrupt American institutions had the tactical advantage in the illicit antiquities trade because "the American museums . . . enjoy significant economic resources." For decades, the implication goes, these resources had allowed US museums to purchase Italian antiquities illicitly with impunity.

In the face of the American museums' outsized financial capital, Italian institutions were shown taking the moral high ground. A series of interactive miniature computer screens was installed throughout the exhibition, playing film clips and still photos from the recovery operation. In a sequence of photos, Art Squad agents in dress uniform inspected vandalized sites. Sometimes they appeared with plainclothes Finanzieri (agents of the Guardia di Finanza) or archaeologists in white lab coats. Other photos presented Art Squad agents at press conferences with recovered items on the tables in front of them. The accompanying text made clear what they were up against. Although looting and heritage crimes occur throughout the world, "It is our country that is most exposed to the raid [*razzia*] on cultural patrimony." The determination and moral investment of Italian authorities were credited with the safe return of the purloined antiquities and the defeat of foreign economic power and looters' depravity.

In the *Predatori dell'arte* exhibition, the recovery of archaeological materials was presented as involving powerful foreign (above all, American) institutions in conflict with Italians and the state's Art Squad. The emphasis on conflict, foreigners' greed, and the artworks' suffering allowed the Italian state to emerge as the righteous savior. In this reading, the state agents involved in the repatriation operations play the part of a culturally correct David in the face of the American museums' culturally impure, bullying Goliath. There is an unsubtle subtext here: non-Italian museums are so desperate to compensate for their own poor material cultures that they are willing to stoop as low as contravening international law and knowingly depriving the Italian people of their rightful heritage.

The exhibition also stressed the familial nature of the national culture.[39] The Heracles figure was not simply returned to Italian soil or to a Roman museum; it was returned to its rightful "home," from which it originated. A collection of terra cotta pots was said to have had its "homecoming" at last. And two female bronze figurines were sisters "lost" to their *nazione* in Italy and relieved to be "home." The objects, then, were animated with human characteristics by being given family roles and a footing in the Italian national community. A single line explained how Greek objects became Italian: "Ancient Romans were in constant contact with Greek artisans, and countless works of art were brought to the Italian soil where they were integrated into local communities—some of which developed their own manufactures for Greek-style objects." That sentence vastly simplified what is in fact a complicated and unsettled process. Archaeologists often struggle to fix an object's provenance with certainty, and there is great disagreement concerning whether place of manufacture or place of use should be weighted more heavily in determining provenance. In the *Predatori dell'arte* exhibition, the Italianness of ancient Greek objects was beyond dispute.

Italy is in good company in describing antiquities as members of the national family. In the dispute between Greece and Great Britain over ownership of the Parthenon Marbles (or Elgin Marbles), familial rhetoric is frequently invoked by Greek officials and proponents of repatriating the marbles. The dispute centers on a set of carved marble figures from the *cella* frieze and pediments of the Temple to Athena Parthenos on the Acropolis in Athens. The figures have been in London for two centuries, but there have been loud calls for their return to Athens since at least the time of Greece's independence in 1832.[40] In 2009 the Greek government completed work on a new Acropolis Museum in Athens to showcase archaeological finds from Acropolis excavations. Greek officials initially hoped that the museum would become the new home for the marbles in the British Museum, but the British government refused to part with them. At the opening of the Acropolis Museum, Greece's culture minister, Antonis Samaras, likened the museum's Parthenon Gallery to a family portrait with "loved ones missing." A caryatid (female statue) that was removed from the Acropolis and shipped to Britain in the early 1800s has long been said to be a "lost sister" to the remaining sculptural pieces. In the idiom of cultural repatriation, antiquities are imagined as the original family members and have a mythical status as autochthonous objects originating in the soil. There is no more authentic way of being Made in Italy.

Paying for Patrimony: The Transactional Life of Artifacts

In 2020 the Ministry of Culture projected a total expenditure of €2.45 billion, a decrease from €2.74 billion in 2019.[41] The money included contemporary art, theater, dance, tourism, archaeology, museums, and patrimony conservation, with €63 million dedicated to archaeology staff, materials conservation, and the "protection and valorization" of archaeological sites.[42] An additional €7.5 million was earmarked for the Carabinieri's activities to protect cultural patrimony.[43] This €2.45 billion is a small fragment of the entire annual state expenditure. Italy spent less on recreation and cultural activities in 2018, as a percentage of GDP, than every other EU member state except Ireland and Bulgaria.[44] Cultural patrimony contributes a small portion of the country's GDP, about 0.2 percent in recent years. But when considered as part of a broader cultural sector of creative activity, the contribution grows to 6 percent, or about €95 billion. There is, in addition, a multiplier effect: an estimated €170 billion is generated nationally, every year, by activities associated with the system of cultural and creative production, making the total value-add €265 billion, or about 17 percent of the economy. Within the cultural sector, cultural heritage punches above its weight and increases its value through activities directly stemming from it.[45] For these gains, Italy's position as a cultural powerhouse has to be renewed. We will see in the subsequent examples that money follows everywhere there is antiquity, from small-town hotel packages that skim money off foreign cultural tourists to lucrative sponsorship deals with colossal private corporations. What they have in common is a marriage of state patrimony to private capital to generate mutually beneficial perceptions of superior quality and authentic tradition.

GRAFT AND GREED AT CAMPOBELLO

After I got to know Mike at Campobello, I asked whether tomb robbers were a problem. Nah, he said. Campobello artifacts had scientific value but no market value to speak of. *Tombaroli* knew that and had moved on to greener pastures. "So the archaeological site isn't enough of a jackpot to bother with, eh?" I asked in a tone of commiseration. "It all depends on how you see things," he replied. And he told me the following story.

When Mike took over as dig director, he had to negotiate contracts endlessly: with the archaeological superintendency and its permit office, with his home university, and with local businesses. His students and staff needed accommodations, meals, postage stamps, shampoo and toothpaste, tools, and rides to the train station. The *pasticceria* (pastry shop) owners, the butchers, greengrocers, barkeeper, and taxi driver regarded the archaeological site as a paycheck. Mike explained that the mayor of the town where Campobello is situated wanted the field school to relocate to a town ten kilometers away. A friend of his owned a hotel there, and the mayor would get a commission if he could guarantee summer occupancy. The mayor evicted the field school from the building it had been renting from the *comune,* on the pretext that it was unfit for occupation, in need of costly repairs. Mike had not complained about the building or requested repairs, and the mayor's provocative political move presented a practical problem. Ten kilometers was too far to walk to and from the dig site, so he would need to pay for two buses every day.

More distressing, he would be at the mercy of the patronage system in the other town, which had a tense rivalry with Campobello residents, and would risk squandering his social capital among the Campobellese. Mike stalled, and the Campobello business owners, who stood to lose their lucrative contracts with Mike, went to the mayor's office. They argued that moving the dig team to another town would diminish the local residents' relationship with their history. Having the excavators live *in* Campobello encouraged impromptu conversations and increased opportunities for exchanging knowledge with locals—the very people Mike had described to me as "irritated" about being displaced by the American students. While this was happening, Mike was in negotiations with the "Mozzi" family, who owned the town's only hotel. Mike was able to strike an agreement with the Mozzis by which he guaranteed a certain accommodation load every summer *and* promised to buy a portion of the school's fruit and vegetable order from the Mozzis' nephew.

The mayor's scheme backfired. He had miscalculated the townspeople's capacity to put aside their grievances and cooperate. He held no sway over the Mozzis. Pragmatically, he could not close down their hotel because there were no alternatives for tourists in Campobello. Symbolically, he could hardly reject the Campobellese invocation of cultural identity. It was a performance, and he knew it, but some matters, Mike told me, are sacred even for a corrupt mayor. Because I was staying at the Mozzis' hotel, I got to know the owner's grandson, "Francesco," a college student who helped at the hotel during the summer. One day I asked him if his grandfather ever regretted the agreement with Mike. It was, after all, a lot of work to look after so many guests. No, Francesco said. Not at all. When his grandfather got wind of the mayor's scheme, he said to his neighbors, *Facciamo casino*—let's raise hell. Francesco laughed at his own joke. *Casino* in this sense is racy language, playfully hinting at the elder Mozzi's mischievousness and suggesting that his bargain with Mike was as much an act of civil disobedience as of shrewd fiscal management. The mayor and his friend the hotelier saw the archaeological site as a *casinò*, a place to gamble and perhaps make a fortune (recall the scratch-and-win metaphor for artifact hunting from chapter 1). For Mozzi, the rejoinder was *facciamo casino*, and he and his allies commandeered patrimony discourse to beat the mayor.

"TODAY'S PATRONS FOR TOMORROW'S ITALY"

The Mozzi story distills the basic ingredients of brand heritage in its Italian iteration. The mayor and hotelier both stood to gain by a partnership that would generate short-term tourism earnings and longer-term revenues from associating the hotel and municipality "brands" with the Campobello site. At the national level, this type of partnership involves the state and private firms. It drives, and is driven by, the *cultural heritage effect*, or "the influence of the cultural heritage image on consumers' perceptions of and attitudes toward heritage-related national products and services."[46] Economists and marketing scholars have studied the monetary value of the heritage effect for firms. My interest is in the impact of this effect on state power.

On July 31, 2014, a new law established tax incentives for both individuals and firms that donate money to the protection and promotion of specifically designated sites and objects of cultural interest.[47] The title of the law stressed the gravity of the situation: "Decree 31 May 2014, no. 83: Urgent Provisions for the Protection of the Cultural Patrimony, the Development of Culture, and the Revival of Tourism." Explaining the necessity of the legislative provisions, the opening paragraphs emphasize

FIGURE 20. Logo for the Art bonus fund-raising campaign. Credit: Art bonus.

"the extraordinary need and urgency to find resources, including through tax subsidies, to guarantee the protection of the cultural heritage of the nation and the development of culture, [and] offer immediate remedy to the state of emergency and degradation in which numerous Italian cultural sites find themselves, with particular regard to the archaeological area of Pompeii, [and] to all areas affected by natural disasters such as the Abruzzo Region and the city of L'Aquila." The tax credit encouraged cash donations to support culture during the fiscal years 2014 through 2016. To be eligible, donations had to go toward maintenance, protection, and restoration of public cultural property and had to be directed to nonprofit cultural institutions. Up to 65 percent of the donation could be claimed back as a tax credit. Several major cultural projects were highlighted as urgent beneficiaries, and many more were listed in the government's wish list.

Art bonus (as it is referred to in Italian) had a nationwide media launch with a bespoke logo and professional advertising materials that promoted a "Call to the Arts" (fig. 20). In the promotional materials, music, drama, literature, and antiquity were minimalist figures, and *Art bonus* was written in characters taken from the signatures of some of Italy's most famous artists. The campaign slogan, "Today's patrons for tomorrow's Italy" (*Mecenati di oggi per l'italia di domani*), urged private citizens of any income level to become patrons of the arts. *Mecenate* is a specific allusion to Gaius Maecenas, friend and political adviser to Julius Caesar and a generous supporter of artistic life in Rome. The word reinforces Italians' shared cultural history and reproduces a theme of obligation to patrimony. The

Art bonus website offers a user-friendly interface in which individuals browse for sites and object types that they might like to donate to. There are large and well-known museums on the list, including the Uffizi Galleries in Florence, and smaller endeavors, including the restoration of Roman-era terra cotta sculptures in the conservation department of the Museum of Reggio Calabria. The initiative raised €20 million in its first four months, and €100 million in 2015.

Responses were mixed. Some applauded it as creative crowdsourcing, creating a mutually beneficial arrangement for culture fans and cultural institutions. Others decried the government's shirking of public duty, insisting that the lack of funds was the outcome of decades of slashing budgets in the cultural sector. State officials defended the corporate partnerships and Art bonus campaign as both materially necessary and morally sound, given the collective obligation toward Italy's universally appreciated art. Ignazio Marino, a former mayor of Rome, said, "I don't think this is a responsibility that belongs to Rome or Romans only—it belongs to mankind. Large parts of Western civilization started here."[48] Marino's argument reveals something important about the vulnerability of the cultural power in the current moment. The state retains final say over the value and meaning of its artifacts. While claiming full ownership, it also wants to split the bill. *We own them, but if you say you enjoy them and want to protect them from age and theft, you must pay for them.* The real looters, critics alleged, are private-sector financial interests.

DELLA VALLE'S COLOSSEUM

Mixed up in all of this was the government's 2011 partnership with Tod's, the luxury shoe and accessories firm. The Colosseum in Rome is an emblematic structure: built in the late first century CE under the Flavian emperors, it was the largest amphitheater in the Roman world and once hosted dazzling gladiatorial games and other spectacles. Today it is the most-visited heritage site in Italy, with some 5 million visitors a year. But age and the crush of tourism took their toll, and by the end of the twentieth century the Colosseum had major structural issues. Tod's agreed to contribute €30 million to cleaning and refurbishing the building. In return, the company would enjoy high-profile association with the structure. "This is one of the most significant restorations of our era," explained a Ministry of Culture employee in a media interview. "It was made possible because of the synergy between the state and the private citizen—two different but complementary worlds."[49] Tod's CEO,

FIGURE 21. Diego Della Valle, Tod's CEO and Colosseum benefactor. Tod's patronage agreement with the Italian government was widely criticized as a corporate takeover of public cultural heritage. Credit: ANSA/Guido Montani.

Diego Della Valle, rejected suggestions that it was a marketing ploy. "I'm a very proud Italian, and my group too. It's because of love for one of the most important Italian monuments—representing Italy all around the world. When we are able to contribute, why not?" *As long as the work gets done*, went the subtext, *it's fine that the money is coming from a corporation*. Skeptics suggested that there was more to it and derided the endeavor as "Della Valle's Colosseum" (fig. 21).

Massimo Consorti, a culture critic and media presence, was scathing. "Italy's resources are subjected to looting and speculation of all types and nature," he wrote, "such that the state suffers daily from the attacks of those who consider the country a cash cow overflowing with milk quotas, assuming that, at the end, someone else will pay the fines of the EU." It's not so much that Della Valle had an exclusive agreement with the Ministry of Culture. That was irritating rather than upsetting. The problem, Consorti argued, went deeper:

> What pisses me off [*chi ci fa incazzare*] is that this is the same state that invests billions of euros in nuclear power plants, in the bridge over the Strait and in the Transpadana, and does not lift a finger for a patrimony that does not cost it a cent and he finds himself thanks to those who spent

blood, sweat, and tears building that patrimony through centuries of history. . . . Of course the state sells off culture. It sells at the end of the season, like a frantic clearance at the Standa [department store].[50]

The title of the blog entry, "Alemanno is not Totò, the Colosseum is not the Trevi Fountain, but Della Valle is Tod's," refers to a famous scene from the 1961 film *Totò truffa 62,* where the Neapolitan comedian Totò scams a tourist by making him believe that he owns the Trevi Fountain and will sell it at a bargain price. In his essay, Consorti stresses that Totò did not know that the scene—absurdly funny in 1961—would come true fifty years later, with Gianni Alemanno, the mayor of Rome, "selling" the Colosseum to Della Valle. By recalling the film, which criticizes Italian politicians who feel entitled to sell something public to private companies, Consorti contrasts the comedic element of Totò with the tragedy of contemporary Italy, where private heritage is a sign of decadence and a loss of agency for a state that does not effectively care for its historical resources. In an online essay published two years later, art historian Tomaso Montanari criticized the state's reliance on Della Valle as desperate wishful thinking—a miraculous act of healing (*la taumaturgica apertura*) that would eventually be the natural strategy for funding health care and schools. The problem is not Della Valle's motives, Montanari asserts; he is doing what any corporate mogul does to promote his company, and he may very well admire and esteem Italian culture. The problem is the state, which no longer exists. Della Valle cannot be a father of the country because the country has committed suicide (*perché la Patria si è suicidata*).[51]

Whose interests are actually given priority in public-private cultural ventures? If political humor is anything to go by, it is the politicians and patricians who benefit. A 2017 comic strip by graphic artist Donald Soffritti offers a searing critique. In the first panel, Massimo D'Alema, the prime minister, and Mayor Alemanno connive to make money from the tourists who are there to take photographs of the Colosseum. The first panel shows D'Alema, in casual dress and with hair slicked down, coaching Alemanno on the correct pronunciation of the city's name. It's *ROHma,* he suggests, not *Rahma,* a regional pronunciation reflecting Alemanno's roots in Bari, a city in Puglia on the east coast of Italy. Alemanno gives it a shot ("Ròma! . . . Ròma . . ."), but then he gives up. "Bloody hell! It takes a superhuman effort [*è uno sforzo sovrumano*] and I'm tired of it. When do the tourists come?" For Alemanno it's a huge effort just to get "Rome" right. He's too lazy to buckle down and learn the local culture; in the comic, his real interest is the tourist hustle. D'Alema

FIGURE 22. Excerpt from a cartoon lampooning the "sale" of the Colosseum by corrupt Italian officials to the unsuspecting shoe magnate Diego Della Valle, CEO of Tod's. *Misfatto* N. 58-Gli Facciamo Le Scarpe (Corradi-Soffritti). Credit: Emanuele, Donald Soffritti and Roberto Corradi (by kind permission of the artists).

exits the frame and nudges Alemanno toward a group of tourists. Off to the side is a well-dressed man in glasses. It is Diego Della Valle, chairman of Tod's. He looks puzzled. Alemanno seizes the moment. He walks up to a group of Asian tourists and announces that each photo of the Colosseum will cost €20. The bespectacled man overhears and approaches him: "Twenty euros? But why? Is this building yours?" Yes, affirms Alemanno: "The Colosseum is certainly mine because I am the mayor of Rome. It's all mine!" The conversation turns to a proposal from Della Valle. He has been looking to settle down in Rome, he says. Will Alemanno sell him the building? Just then D'Alema returns, pretending to be a foreign tourist himself, also interested in buying the Colosseum. He offers €1 million. Della Valle cuts him off: "I was here first." He is determined to get the building, and he offers €25 million. "Holy shit!"

Alemanno is jumping up and down. He can't believe his luck. "See? What did I tell you?" D'Alema whispers. In a final panel, Alemanno asks Della Valle to sign the contract, without telling him that by signing he agrees to take care of restoring the Colosseum. Della Valle agrees and asks Alemanno if he can restore the building in whatever way he wants. "Certainly!" says Alemanno. "It's up to you, as long as you restore it. See you later!" Della Valle is pleased. The comic strip ends with the Colosseum transformed into a massive shoe bearing the Tod's logo (fig. 22). Alemanno and D'Alema walk away grinning. *"Gli abbiamo proprio fatto le scarpe!"* says the mayor. "We double-crossed them." The wordplay on "took their shoes away from them" captures the accessories magnate's naïveté and the politicians' connivance. Alemanno, with a fat roll of bills, still can't say "Roma" correctly.

What is being laughed at here is the absurdity of national culture—that something supposedly sacred to the national community, which *should be* the solemn obligation of elected officials, is being bought and sold with little concern for actual public culture.

Since the creation of the Tod's-Colosseum partnership, similar agreements have been announced with Fendi (refurbishment of the Trevi Fountain), Bulgari (Spanish Steps), watchmaker Panerai (the Paolo Uccello Clock in the Duomo at Florence), and cashmere brand Brunello Cucinelli (the historic center of Solomeo, the Umbrian town where the company is based). Through the partnerships, refurbishment work *does* get done, but mostly in favor of iconic structures and at the expense of mundane sites or invisible foundation repairs. The result is a form of "monument inequality."[52] Beauty and aesthetics being the two qualities that foreign consumers most readily associate with Italy, firms link their logos, websites, and advertising campaigns with the form and style of the monuments they adopt.

Tod's, for example, developed a "Tod's for Colosseum" media campaign, and the company features a small version of its logo in digital and print materials related to the building's conservation. These are firms that promote their products to global consumers as "Made in Italy" even though only two stages of production, textile sourcing and final packaging, have to be based in Italy in order to make that claim. The situation has generated confusion and frustration among consumers, to say nothing of the labor market exploitation via cheap overseas workers and domestic piecework without benefits. By linking themselves with ancient monuments and heritage sites, however, firms can divert attention from manufacturing inequalities to "Made in Italy" as a rhetorical claim to pre-national cultural tradition grounded in the country's land and past peoples. In this regard, the Fendi CEO Pietro Beccari suggested that corporate Medici occupy a role once intended for the state:

> In Italy, there's a piece of art that anywhere else in the world would belong to a museum; but instead, in Italy, it's probably sitting in a corner of the church, just like that. When the state is not in the greatest shape, we need to help, to do what's usually been done by the government.[53]

That the state's constitutional obligation is now being fulfilled by private capital has sparked fierce opposition in local political activity. The Comitato Pompeimia (Committee My Pompeii), a community action group founded to safeguard the ancient city of Pompeii, uses civil disobedience tactics to block development initiatives. Their protests and social media campaign have made national headlines. The local residents seek site conservation but insist it should be done with money from the public coffers. The recurring theme, in the Colosseum comic as in the Comitato Pompeimia, is loss of agency. But even with recent pledges to increase state spending on cultural patrimony, the costs will exceed what the state says it can afford. Nearly a decade after the Tod's partnership was initiated, the model it represents has been normalized. The accumulation of capital through culture is too useful—too enriching—to be disbanded. The director of the Vatican Museums was forthright:

> Behind every pair of shoes and every machine tool, behind every skirt and all belts sold in Sydney or Vancouver, in Tokyo or Los Angeles, there are the images of the Chianti hills, the sea of Taormina, the Botticelli paintings in the Uffizi and Michelangelo's frescoes. If we could calculate the influence of [this] miracle of art, life and nature on consumers around the world, we would realize that it is a contribution of far greater importance than is brought to the economy of our country.[54]

The quarry of national patrimony is now replenished by Made-in-Italy belts and shoes.

At the beginning of this chapter, I asked why the Tod's Colosseum partnership was backed by the state but Bordo's Etruscopolis was not. Bordo, recall, was dismissed by experts for his lack of culture and his profit-seeking motives. But Tod's is a profit-seeking venture too, and its expertise, luxury fashion accessories, has nothing to do with archaeology. What the Colosseum partnership had in its favor was an interconnected system of capital networks that created an infrastructure for large-scale state projects. Bordo, working outside the state and in a limited private capacity, could not offer anything like the building and branding power of Tod's. Had he been a corporate raider rather than a tomb raider, his project may have taken a very different trajectory. An expansive capital infrastructure was the fundamental goal of the Art bonus, and in ensuing years it has become the vehicle for a new iteration of cultural power—as heritage branding.

I have argued throughout the book that nationalism, as a critique of ideology or a categorization of cultural practice, is not sufficient to capture the origins and logic of Italian cultural power. Italian cultural power is not exclusively, or even primarily, focused on identity or ties of solidarity. It is also not the privileged domain of the state or of archaeologists and museum curators. Antiquities are strategic resources constituted and leveraged by tourists, hotel owners, art collectors, and gallery owners, by government officials and business developers, and by ordinary Italians, some of whom dig up artifacts, then keep and sell them illegally. This tangle of relations is messy, and it moves us from the tidy divisions between nation and state, Italy and Other, and public and private—divisions that are a staple of sociological accounts of nationalism. But the tangle is a more representative depiction of how cultural patrimony functions as a distributed form of sovereignty. The open-air museum is complicated and thoroughly modern. Weaving through ritualized practices and official discourse, emblematic statues and idioms of meaning making, there are hotel hustles, shoe magnates, small-time artifact thieves, and transnational diplomatic showbiz. These things should not be thought of as the seamy underside or unfortunate by-product of "real" heritage. They are integral to it. Extracting artifacts from the soil and moving them among relational matrices of time, space, and culture stretches cultural sovereignty to ever further sociopolitical horizons.

✷ CHAPTER 6 ✷

Farewell to the Tomb Robber

Omero Bordo died in November 2018 at age seventy-five. Family, friends, and local dignitaries attended the funeral in the duomo of Tarquinia. The former mayor of Civitavecchia spoke, remembering Bordo as a true Tarquinian artist who carried on the best traditions of Italian art workshops by offering an Etruscan cultural experience. He pledged to republish Bordo's autobiography and share it with Italian youth as an example of "challenging one's destiny." In his eulogy, art critic and TV personality Vittorio Sgarbi mused, "If we'd never had him, we would know so much less about the Etruscans. And it is for this reason that we must acknowledge him as the last of the Etruscans."[1] A local news outlet recalled that he had lived his life "convinced that the descent of his ancient countrymen [*la discendenza dei suoi antichi conterranei*]" was his exclusive right.[2] Far from the harsh criticism and haughty dismissal of the professional archaeologists in Rome, the local media praised his messianic vision of the past:

> Bordo abandoned the "errors of youth" to become a true archaeological entrepreneur, reproducing objects that the Etruscans made thousands of years ago.... He introduced many young people to Etruscan pottery techniques [and] fulfilled a lifelong dream of Etruscopolis, of recreating the tombs. "I realized that no one really knew how to explain their history," Omero explained.... With the writing of the book "Omero: my life with the Etruscans," finally the restless tomb robber gave way to the artist with a courageous path, common to all art, making reproductions and replicas with passionate conviction that they had the power to pass on the story of an otherwise overlooked people.[3]

Death has a way of affixing meaning, and Bordo's obituary gracefully accentuates the artistry of the reformed tomb robber's life. A remarkable feature of the celebration of his life, however, is that it affirms him as a local hero and servant of cultural heritage in contradiction of the law. He cherished Etruscan culture when, by implication, no one else did. He bothered to teach young people the ceramic skills of their ancient countrymen because if he didn't, no one else would. He recreated Etruscan tombs to explain them to non-specialists. And if Etruscopolis is still derided on travel websites as a "folkloristic Disneyland-type reconstruction," it also strikes a chord with visitors. It makes the tombs, and the long-ago people who inhabited them, approachable and real.

Bordo, who as a young man slyly performed for the camera in *Scandal at Tarquinia*, was the archetypal trickster. Figuratively speaking, he is the mischevious sidekick to Berlusconi and Qaddafi: "I brought your girlfriend back," the knowing wink of one virile collector to another. Bordo could never be an insider the way Berlusconi can. The stigma of working-class rurality, a marked accent, and a criminal record obliterated that possibility and relegated him to the internal Other. Look again at Berlusconi and the Venus sculpture, however, and note where the power resides. Without Bordo the tomb robber, Berlusconi's custodial conceit is worthless. Without a Bordo to interpret—to tell stories that regular people can understand and latch on to—Venus is just another marble torso, distaff of a fallen empire whose treasures are hermetically sealed in museum vitrines.

Bordo's body lies in repose near the tombs he raided for four decades.

❋

In the opening chapter, I asked whether the tomb robber has something to teach us about state power. The answer is yes. In a country whose entire apparatus of cultural patrimony has been built in contraposition to the art market, tomb robbers provide an illicit market figure and hence an internal enemy whose predations justify the application of state force. Tomb robbing is an eternal social activity in Italy, and it has been morally and politically restaged at various historical moments to suit current state conditions. In the early years of the unified nation-state, peasant diggers were paid for bringing artifacts to the national museums. In the early twentieth century, these diggers were tarred as feckless abettors to the art market. By the 1960s they were called *tombaroli*, and with that label they acquired different notoriety. Now they were characterized as black-market suppliers whose personal greed violated collective norms of citizenship and patrimony. Embarrassingly, they also revealed the state's failure to discharge its obligation to protect patrimony. Today, the figure of the *tombarolo* has evolved yet again. Portrayed as the first (and lowest) level of production in the illicit antiquities trade, the *tombarolo* is said to move artifacts from the ground to smugglers, who then move antiquities to dealers, and from dealers to collectors. In this staging, the *tombarolo* exists in networked arrangements of patrimony capital-beyond-the-state. What the tomb robber teaches us, then, is that when the state reconstructs this figure through discourse, symbols, and law, the state is also reconstituting itself as a power. The historical vicissitudes of their cultural and legal standing tell us more about how antiquities have been politicized and valorized than about unauthorized excavators themselves. With each new interpretation of tomb robbers' persistence, the state has offered legal and policing instruments as the logical solution. "Our patrimony is under attack" is entrenched in cultural politics, and it has served as the pretext for nationalization, market restrictions, criminalization, and reliance on private capital. If tomb robbers are always active, they are always available for scapegoating and counterattacking.

Digging for artifacts may well be Italy's oldest profession, as one informant quipped, but it emerged as an urgent social problem—one requiring specific and intensive legal and political remedy—only in the second half of the twentieth century. Instead of tackling the range of threats to cultural heritage sites and objects—including unchecked industrialization and urbanization—the Italian government chose to create an art police unit and focus narrowly on the illicit antiquities market. Consistent with the state's deployment of law enforcement more generally during this period, the problems that received the most attention were those that could be framed as conflict between divergent perspectives. I posited a combination of international and national political pressures that instigated the Art Squad's establishment. The model the government chose tells us more about the state's aspirations to power—*what kind of power it wanted to exercise*—than about the actual scope and scale of tomb robbing.

What kind of power was the state aspiring to? To answer this question we need to reflect again on the generative authority of *Homo autotelus* and its relationship with the patria. Mussolini's muscular performances of destruction, excavation, and renewal embodied the power to create a new Italy from ancient materials. Borrowing from the visual and physical repertoire of tomb robbers, he suggested his own participation in the mythical autochthony of the ancient patria. Whereas "state" is a construct centered on mechanisms and rational bureaucracy, and "nation" is a construct centered on a community of people, "patria" is the land—more precisely, a way of looking at the land to make it ideologically connected to the nation-state. With Mussolini gone, and styles of leadership altered after Fascism, the connective power of patria had no obvious surrogate in successive individual leaders. *Tombaroli* fill this void. They represent themselves as locals who are more authentically "Italian" than the state officials who advocate global culture and metropolitan inclusion. In this sense they are at home in the national sensorium—one's subcognitive, embodied affiliations with one's cultural community.[4] When they describe the smell or taste or feel of the soil, which *tombaroli* say they can assess with unparalleled mastery, or when they claim to be descended from ancient peoples and thus rightful heirs to their artifacts, *tombaroli* are appropriating the politics of state patrimony.

In the rhetorical register of "patria," one can impute to the land a want, or a purpose: *This land was meant for* us, *the natural order of things means we are here, with our landscape and our things.* It is the space of managed interplay between rational and irrational.[5] The threat imputed to *tombaroli* goes deeper than the capacity to supply artifacts to the antiquities trade. It is their mastery of the very terrain that birthed the modern nation-state. When artifacts' symbolic and financial value are inscribed in the project of materially populating the patria, their protection and control through military-police mechanisms becomes natural and logical. Reducing the ideology of national culture to treasure, patriots, and deviants simplifies the complicated reality of artifacts and digging, which are shot through with internal diversity and heterogeneous ideology. Blaming *tombaroli* for bleeding the nation of its patrimony is a crucial move because it masks state inefficiency and widespread mistrust of the government's process of cultural power.

Archaeological looting is universal; the Art Squad has made its reputation as the force best equipped to fight it. As I wrote this book, the Syrian civil war (2014–19) pushed looting to the level of a geopolitical crisis: "blood antiquities" was used to describe artifacts extracted and smuggled by insurgent groups to fund their violent exploits. Many questions about the scope and impact of that tragic episode remain unanswered, including what to do about destroyed museums, ancient towns, and archaeological sites in the war zone. Whatever that future holds, it will bear the imprint of Italy's Art Squad. In the midst of the Syrian conflict, the Italian government, working with UNESCO, formed a new Task Force to be deployed "in favour of countries facing emergencies that may affect the protection and safeguarding of culture and the promotion of cultural pluralism."[6] The Art Squad had already spread its influence in Iraq, having established a unit in Baghdad in 2003 to support recovery efforts after the National Museum of Iraq was looted that April.[7] In 2015 its brief expanded to counterterrorism. The Art Squad would now provide training and direct action to prevent archaeological materials from falling into the hands of militant groups. The director of UNESCO, Irina Bokova, praised the Art Squad for its effective policing and urged other nation-states to follow its lead. European heads of state once mocked Italy as the extra wheel of the chariot. In cultural politics, Italy now drives the chariot.

Coda to the World's Greatest Cultural Power

In 2013, in a break with bureaucratic custom, the Ministry of Culture offered Italian citizens a role in directing patrimony capital. Through a nationwide initiative called L'Arte Aiuta l'Arte (Art Aiding Art), people were asked to vote on a short list of artworks in need of conservation.[8] The project was one of selective preservation; only a portion of the damaged works could be saved. The money for the conservation did not come from the Ministry of Culture. Instead, it was raised by a special event titled "Night at the Museum," when art museums offered late-night viewings for donors. Ministry officials selected eight paintings as candidates, and for three weeks Italians were invited to vote online for the one they thought most deserved conservation. A majority of the voters chose to spend the money on a painting of the Madonna and holy child, attributed to Pietro Perugino. Government officials praised the democratic nature of L'Arte Aiuta l'Arte, citing among other things the use of social media to raise public awareness of the plight of artworks. They noted that 73 percent of the voters were women and 21 percent were from Campania. This was noteworthy because, according to the Ministry of Culture, women and southern Italians have historically been underrepresented in government decision making. Speaking to National Public Radio in the United States, Dr. Anna Maria Buzzi, director of the initiative, said, "The strength of a democratic institution is listening to its citizens. Giving people the right to choose makes them more invested in their own heritage. It makes them care more. If you give people the responsibility, they are more likely to participate."[9]

The minister of culture, Massimo Bray, was similarly effusive: "I am very happy with the successful outcome of this project, which has revived interest among many young people who are active on the Web and in social networks. The many comments of citizens encourage each other to work in this direction, creating ever more choices for how to share our cultural patrimony."[10] Bray and Buzzi did not address archaeologists' criticisms that other EU countries spend billions more euros per annum on their cultural patrimony. Nor did they respond publicly to concerns that the government was diverting badly needed resources from Italy's heritage sites to the cultural crisis in Syria and Iraq. L'Arte Aiuta l'Arte was a success because it permitted, however briefly, the idea that cultural power is a democratic endeavor. It offers a clear example of the state's setting the agenda for national patrimony by determining what counts as a masterpiece, adding a veneer of public enfranchisement to the fait accompli of state disinvestment in archaeology and art.

The episode highlights the inconsistencies of the "timeless fictions of national culture."[11] The fiction here is the permanence, the fated inevitability of those treasured masterpieces. Without money the masterpieces fade and rot. The limited choice given to the public reminds us that the concept of state cultural property rests on "a homology between the oneness of the group of 'people' and certain kinds of objects in which they see their identity as residing."[12] When public spending on the arts dwindles and the list of possible rescues is winnowed to eight paintings, the homology becomes an overdetermined outcome of bureaucratic compromise. "Extremely demagogic" was how one Roman archaeologist described the program.[13] The L'Arte Aiuta l'Arte episode shows, too, how selective preservation is related to cultural destruction. The government pledged to restore the losing seven works sometime in the future, but similar promises have gone unfulfilled by previous administrations. Art and artifacts are managed in a way that fits the needs of the state in a given moment. What ensues is a form of cultural destruction, as Françoise Choay (2001) has phrased it, in material, spatial, and intellectual terms.

Constructing Cultural Heritage

The Art Squad's global influence and the rise of private patrimony capital tie together the main threads of this book. State patrimony is a sociopolitical construct. In its earliest iterations in Italy, it imagined cultural heritage as nation-state property and framed a relationship between state and public in which the former protected cultural treasures and the latter enjoyed and admired them. As markets and geopolitics changed, however, so did this relationship. Cultural heritage is back to being a monetized market good managed by the state and firms to maximize value for both parties. Public enjoyment is not a constitutional right; it is a strategic goal, a corporate vision. The logic of shared governance allows any aspect of life in the nation-state "to be imagined as an object, that is, bounded in time and space, or (amounting to the same thing) associated as property with a particular group, which is imagined as territorially and historically bounded."[14]

Heritage is not history.[15] Ancient monuments and artifacts enrich our study of history, but they do not constitute a neutral or self-evident data set that can give us a full account of what happened in the past. What makes up any given body of cultural heritage, whether at the national or the local level, tells us as much about present-day values and interests as about the past. This is because cultural heritage is the outcome of present-day actors' selecting sites, objects, and practices from an imagined past, asserting them as an inheritance of the "patria," and obliging present-day members of the community to protect that inheritance for an imagined future community.[16] An object, site, or practice does not become a state cultural good or heritage product until an institution or a group of people with adequate social and economic capital categorizes it as such.[17] Some things are discarded while others are retained: there is discretion involved, and decisions must be made about what to preserve and how to do so. These decisions inevitably involve a complex of issues: politics, money, aesthetics, ethnic and religious identities, and scientific interests. Not everybody has the power to make and enforce decisions about what objects will be classified as heritage, so we must attend to present-day power relations when we engage with this subject.

There is nothing inevitable about the exemplary status of Italian art. This is not a comment on the genius or significance of individual works. Many scholars before me have made the case that Italian art is technically proficient and aesthetically compelling in ways that made it coveted by collectors all over the world. I have focused instead on the confluence of social, economic, political, and geographic factors by which the disparate cultural milieus of the Italian peninsula, spanning three millennia and hundreds of ethnic groups, were stitched together into a structure of statecraft.[18] To borrow from Bruce Kapferer's study of divergent nationalisms coexisting in Sri Lanka and Australia, the production of culture is "the reification of culture [and] the production of culture as an object in itself."[19] In other words, in this sphere of production a group of people cannot exist as a community without a recognizable material essence that signifies their coherence. As such, the objects within that culture take on determinative properties for the group's members.[20] In Italy these developments can be traced deep into antiquity, when Rome was the center of empire and the capital city was resplendent with artistic commissions that set the standard for public and private image making across the Roman Empire and beyond.[21]

The richness of the country's material culture—indeed, its status as a homeland of civilization—is widely accepted as fact. When public figures and scholars put a percentage value on Italy's share of the world's cultural treasures—say, Berlusconi telling reporters in London that Italy has 72 percent of the world's artistic patrimony—they participate in a lively and recurring discourse that asserts not just cultural richness but cultural *supremacy*.[22] The discourse of cultural superiority is highly effective in mobilizing and sustaining a set of legal and bureaucratic practices that demarcate licit from illicit engagements with the nation's cultural goods. This book set out to explore that discourse, situating it within the concept of cultural power and the relational activities of bureaucrats, archaeologists, tomb robbers, market actors, and the Roman and Etruscan archaeological materials that sit beneath and at the center of it all.

A broader contribution has been to theorize cultural power as a distinct form of state power that is constituted by control over cultural materials but is not limited to the cultural sphere. It is the tensile strength of state patrimony, not its hardness or softness, that provides us with a richer understanding of how Italy extends its sovereignty through cultural objects. When the government negotiates a trade agreement and makes statistical claims about cultural supremacy, or trains foreign law enforcement agencies in tactics and codes developed by the Art Squad, or aligns the state's cultural property with luxury brands, the influence of the state is extended further. In a 2020 ruling on a case involving the Greek government and Sotheby's auction house, which possessed a Greek artifact of disputed origins, the court found that Greece had sovereignty over its cultural patrimony objects because its state is constitutionally obligated to protect them. It was as a sovereign state, not a commercial competitor, the court ruled, that Greece should be recognized as claimant to the object. Legal experts heralded it as a watershed case. "The enactment and enforcement of such patrimony laws are archetypal sovereign activities," the opinion read.[23] The implications for the Italian model of cultural patrimony were unambiguous. The case effectively validated what the Art Squad has been doing for fifty years—namely, wielding authority on foreign sovereign territory through artifacts and other cultural objects.

In the realm of state patrimony, the logic of accumulation gives priority to the massification of artworks and archaeological materials. This is done both figuratively, through metaphors and rhetorical claims, and literally, as when artifacts are densely packed at repatriation press conferences or fill museum basements and superintendents' offices for storage, study, and occasional display. Possessing heaps of antiquities strengthens the state's claim to cultural superiority and gives it leverage to act in adjacent cultural areas including private-sector contracts and diplomatic negotiations. In this light, when the Italian government repatriates antiquities, it is staging artifactual relations in two frames: as a bond between the state and a foreign entity, and as a bond between the Italian state and the Italian nation. At a basic level, it acknowledges shared interest in a body of culture. It serves as a promissory note, as when the handover is part of a Memorandum of Understanding that brokers a multiyear cooperative agreement with a foreign government. It also confirms the state's fulfillment of its constitutional obligation to the national community and the people it consists in. This is one instance of many in which iconic heritage objects "perform" Italian state power.[24]

While characterizing artifacts as things being accumulated for reinvestment may appear to empty them of symbolic and emotional resonance, in fact it reveals an elaborate process of meaning making at work. In the logic of accumulation, the meaning is in the stockpile of artifacts, the stockpile itself being the "object" of admiration, experience, and expression. What happened after 1909 has sometimes been described as retention, a reference to the Italian state's restricting antiquities to national territory. Critics of the retentionist approach hold that the only meaning ascribed to antiquities is reduced to nationalism—specifically, a chauvinistic variant of nationalism—thereby cutting off antiquities from audiences and display settings in which alternative, perhaps more diverse, interpretative discourses would enhance their symbolic and expressive qualities. This view, however, overlooks the new configurations of admiration, audience, and artifact made possible through the logic of accumulation. The cartoon Colosseum-shoe lampooned the corporate contract by visually reimagining the form of the structure. A few fictitious additions—in the form of heel, sole, and laces—lightly altered the exterior but, in so doing, deeply shifted the meaning and symbolism of the place. Entry tickets and tourist guide materials bear the Tod's logo, and a constant stream of positive media coverage of the successful refurbishment features photos of the gleaming colonnades with quotations from Tod's and state officials. These and other practices are reshaping the way people look at Italy's ancient monuments. Further analysis could help us understand how this development is recasting culture as a visual platform for neoliberal governance.

The Tensile Power of Patrimony

Previous studies of national culture have emphasized the production and performance of national culture, whether in parades and ceremonies, statues and monuments, or anthems and symbols.[25] Scholarly works oriented toward these issues have offered important insights into how symbols and events are consecrated as "national" and how they are made visible and potent to everyday citizens.[26] Following in this tradition, tracing the historical roots of nationalized antiquities in Italy reveals the social, economic, and political factors behind the Italian state's decision to declare its custodial authority over artifacts with interest to the nation.

But as I explained in my discussion of Andrea Carandini in chapter 1, popular archaeologists show that the mythical and extrasensory forms of "knowing" antiquities and ruins are still alive and well in the field of archaeology. What this says about nationhood, identity, and cultural objects is that affective epistemologies survived the scientizing of archaeology and persist in popular and institutional discourse and practice. In this respect Carandini's divinatory power is crucial because it originates in his academic training and has been legitimized through state-sector offices and honorifics.

One of the things patrimony does is function as a device for thinking about the state. In the course of my interviews with unauthorized excavators, I encountered the perception that the state does not care equally about all antiquities but prefers certain types or categories, especially those we might call charismatic—marble statues, for example, and Etruscan pottery. Unauthorized excavators complained about state officials' obsession with appearance, pointing to the natty uniforms and "self-promoting" blitz reports. For the residents of rural Campobello, patrimony management is often the most visible and steady presence of the state. This happens every summer when the archaeology team shows up and takes over the town. It happens when Carabinieri slowly drive along the perimeter of the archaeological site, and when the museum in the neighboring village holds a heritage pride event. In these situations, patrimony management stands in for the state. It is also, as we saw in the example of the mayor and the Mozzi family, the basis for a "'politics of recognition' in which marginal groups make property claims so as to improve their situations or seek redress, using a tool—the property concept—that dominant groups provide."[27]

Metonymic practice notwithstanding, patrimony is not identical to the nation. This distinction emerged forcefully when unauthorized excavators spoke of how the intense somatic experience of excavating deepened their love for the soil *here*, in Italy. Recall that Rafal linked the feeling of the potsherds in his pockets to being part of a cultural lineage. The lineage extends not from the modern nation-state, but from the fantasized patria—an ancient precursor to the nation that offers an antidote to the complexities and frustrations of late modernity. When my subjects spoke with pride about Italian antiquities and ruins, or when they described their sensory memories of digging in the earth, they situated themselves in relation to the patria, which is, by definition, not bounded by temporal and political parameters. This is a fantasy, to be sure, that all parties participate in, but it has a powerful pull. The soil layers that mark centuries of separation between the ancients and ourselves have the additional symbolic function of obscuring the complexities and frustrations of the idealized past. But there is something else embedded in this fantasy of a better, pristine past, something equally powerful: mortality—the fear that an individual's life will be rendered insignificant by the crowded timeline of human history and the unforgiving forces of nature.

Antiquities and Social Experience

Much like the layers of sediment that make up the matrix, the book has probed cultural power at three levels: macro-, meso-, and micro-, from the halls of power in Rome to the tomb robber's living room keepsakes. I have sought to show what antiquities *do* in modernity, and why *misfatti*, misdeeds—to return to the opening comic in chapter 1—are as productive of social relations as they are destructive of cultural materials. Beyond heritage protection laws and the manufactured bravura of repatriation victories, there are criticisms and confusion, deviations and habits, and individual understandings of nationhood and belonging that do not transfer neatly onto official stories about national culture and the logic of government control.

Antiquities offer a haptic experience of knowing the state and its history. Looking at the ways my subjects engage with antiquities (digging, collecting, touching, cleaning, displaying, trading, and so forth) revealed the depth of connection people develop with their objects. This is an intriguing area of study because most national subjects do not engage with their ancient cultural heritage this way. Strictly speaking, doing so is forbidden; antiquities are not for touching. One advantage of analyzing relations between people and artifacts is that it bridges another relational constellation: people and the nation-state, as mediated by those artifacts. Smelling the earth, feeling the weight of potsherds in one's pocket, seeing a long-forgotten urn in a dimly lit shaft beneath Tarquinia—these experiences were recounted with poetic joy by my subjects, many of whom linked their sensory memories with the sense of being part of a national community. The smell of the earth was special to this soil in Italy; collecting objects for pleasure, not for profit, was presented to me as "how things are done here." The *this* and the *here* were the local, and although the local is not identical with the national, the two constructs draw meaning from each other.

Mine is not a study of local identities pitted against a national one, even though a stylized version of that tension remains important to any consideration of national culture in Italy. My evidentiary base sustains an analytical distinction between heritage and social memories as separate but related aspects of national culture. Both concern the reproduction of social life. Both create affective and cognitive landmarks, which in turn provide common references to historical change and continuity. However, one major difference between social memory and heritage is that while the former involves a range of people, events, and things concentrated in specific social spaces, the latter is a specialized branch of management that privileges professional archaeologists and art historians, scientific experts, government officials, police, the judiciary, regional and national museums, and multinational organizations, conventions, and charters. Among heritage institutions and actors, there are often misalignments because "political commitments and economic priorities may differ from—and sometimes are in conflict with—local social realities."[28]

Distinguishing between social memory and heritage protection recasts national culture as an active, multilevel site of engagement with history and identity. This move also sheds light on why the *tombarolo* is a despised social actor. The *tombarolo* stands outside "Culture" as it is constructed and legislated by the state. His stories, artifact finds, and object displays, and the circulation he sets in motion by giving away artifacts, contribute to social memory but do so outside the parameters of heritage. It would be simplistic and misleading, however, to conclude that *tombaroli* are ultra-localists who reject the state. In this sense they differ considerably from the nineteenth-century bandits who terrorized rural Italy with their violent disregard for the law. The unauthorized excavators portrayed here reproduced a discourse of superior Italian culture that is, at root, the state's own discourse.

The contraposition of social memory and heritage is one example of a gap between the discourse and institutional practices of the state and the feelings and opinions of ordinary citizens. Another gap sits between punitive legal codes and long-standing local practices. Citizens are obligated to report to police their information about stolen artworks or robbed tombs. When I reminded my Italian friends and roommates about this, they laughed. One Campobello man pointed to a Roman amphora on his patio (now being used as a planter). He explained that his grandparents had a fondness for old things, and he insisted they never stole anything. His immediate interest was in quashing any ideas I might have about his lawless relatives. But he was also showing me how it is possible to collect and use antiquities for oneself, as an act of personal self-understanding, outside state-organized heritage.

Studying Patrimony from Below

Interviews, observations, archival study, and formal and ethnographic study of artifacts in the world remind us that national culture is produced not just in marquee museums and government offices, but also in the small towns, corner shops, and nondescript bars where ordinary Italians live their lives—spend time with neighbors and friends, watch sports, and grouse about traffic and tourists. Whereas my interview subjects in museums and government responded to my questions with polished answers and careful rearticulations of official heritage rhetoric, my informants in Campobello and Vergilia departed from the heritage rhetoric while still reproducing the discourse of national culture. It was in these spaces of disjuncture that I found the boundaries between licit and illicit, local and national, honorable and dishonorable to be porous and continually revisited.

Viewing national culture as a constellation of synergistic relationships builds on a robust tradition in anthropology and sociology of studying the processes, events, and experiences of a nation from the ground up. It moves "the discussion of stereotypes [about nationalities] to the realm of practice, bringing it to bear on the totalizing iconicity . . . of nation-state ideology."[29] Backstage spaces, insider discourse, and other "shadow zones" offer interpretations and ideas about shared cultural experiences that tend to be richer than the interpretations that circulate through official channels on public stages.[30] As a scholarly approach, "nationhood from below" has its intellectual and methodological challenges. It is important not to take it as infallible evidence of true or pristine understandings of national culture from the perspective of consecrated "natives."[31] Practice- and relationship-oriented study of national culture from the vantage point of ordinary people reminds us, in Ilaria Porciani's eloquent statement, that "top-down processes of national identification were generally easier and speedier, but they always coexisted with a persistent inertia. Those voices (including those of the lower classes) that express a positive identification with the Italian nation are restricted to specific situations, defined by a geographic as well as by a social demarcation."[32] Those situations are characterized by cultural intimates'—influential local leaders or trusted neighbors—preparing the ground.

Linking macro-, meso-, and micro-practices is not a matter of shoring up one's stable evidentiary base with variables of different depth and color.[33] Bringing together these approaches and their data is risky because the data may challenge as well as support each other. This was clear in my discussion with Giovanna, the young archaeologist we met in the first chapter, who had been part of heritage management through museum employment. Giovanna understood the concerns of heritage protection and agreed with her colleagues that excavation should be done professionally. But she personally disagreed with the government's interest in the repatriation of artifacts taken from Italy illegally, when in fact there are already too many sites, objects, and monuments in Italy for the government to properly conserve and protect. She advocated leaving disputed objects in foreign collections as long as they receive the appropriate care. Giovanna turned the tables on the Art Squad by suggesting that if government officials truly loved art, they would stop acting from self-interest (to bolster national pride through repatriation "wins") and instead allow the objects to stay where they can get the material care they need. This perceptive critique of heritage management would not have come to light had I limited my research to government archives, reports, and scholarly papers on heritage (even those critical of heritage). By the same token, had I done a purely ethnographic study of archaeologists without connecting their words and actions with state-level laws and official rhetoric, I would have missed the institutional logic that Giovanna was struggling with and was always, inevitably, referring to because of its omnipresence.

Pro Patria et Cultura

Above all, I have asked why the Art Squad came into being in Italy before any other art-rich country formed a similar policing unit. Two standard answers—that tomb robbing was intensifying and that cultural internationalism triggered the move—are inadequate. By 1969, when the precursor to today's Art Squad was founded, Italy was at a challenging political point, with Left/Right ideological tensions and public demonstrations erupting into violence. The long shadow of Fascism hung over domestic policing, with public mistrust still widespread. In this climate, choosing to create a uniformed law enforcement agency to oversee material culture has to be understood as a deliberate statement of power. Those material scraps of the past sustain a vast transnational politics. Artworks and artifacts made in Italy distribute Italian power into galleries and museums across Europe and the Mediterranean and to points beyond. They will outlast us as they have outlasted two millennia of Caesars and civil servants.

There is widespread consensus that every community of people, whether grouped by ethnic, regional, or national affiliation, has the right to enjoy and preserve its own body of sites and objects. But what happens when members of that community—perhaps even a sizable share of it—reject the state's model for correct engagement with the common cultural heritage? Exploring this question with sustained ethnography permits us to chip away at the concept of *godimento pubblico,* or public enjoyment. Public enjoyment was the refrain of early twentieth-century cultural policy reformers, who argued that antiquities and other cultural treasures should be nationalized to protect the people's inheritance. Those objects were to be held in trust by the state, made available in carefully prescribed ways for the people to observe: in museums, exhibition catalogs, postcard reproductions, and traveling exhibits. Of these, the museum has emerged as *the* key site for public enjoyment. This development puts museums in a challenging relationship with the idea that a community of people has a "right" to enjoy and preserve its cultural goods. Who has agency within this relationship? Who decides what "public enjoyment" means? To answer these questions requires continued assessment of when, why, and how the current set of institutional patterns and relationships came into being. This imperative, I suggest, applies even when antiquities are targeted by groups whose practices we abhor. Critical histories of cultural policies and their politicized formulation and application hold up a powerful mirror to state power in late modernity.

Acknowledgments

My archaeologist friends reckon it takes about ten years' digging in the same spot before they really understand a site. This book was nearly a decade in the making, and my evolving understanding of its topic is thanks to a long list of colleagues and interlocutors, friends and family, and their generous gifts of time, ideas, and material support.

Properly speaking, the book has two origin points. One is in my archaeological career, during which I was able to study classical archaeology and excavate in Italy and Spain. That work gave me technical proficiency in excavation methods and stylistic and historical knowledge of artifact types. The other is in my years as a sociologist, during which I developed questions and theories about the sociopolitical place of archaeology in contemporary polities. At this point, having studied and worked in two disciplines at four universities, my debts of gratitude are considerable.

During the early stages of fieldwork, the Social Science Research Council (USA) funded my time in Italy in 2011–12. Additional fieldwork time was supported by grants from the International Institute and the Rackham School of Graduate Studies at the University of Michigan and from the University of Michigan Department of Sociology. In Oxford, the Institute for Science, Innovation, and Society in the Department of Anthropology (Oxford University) hosted me as a visiting fellow in autumn 2012, welcoming me into the fold and giving me space to share my research, conduct interviews in Italy, and access the magisterial holdings of the Bodleian Library. In Rome, the British School at Rome (BSR) kindly housed and splendidly fed me in 2013 and 2014. Further research funding, critical to the completion of the book, was generously provided by the University of Virginia Department of Sociology and College of

Arts and Sciences. In the course of this project, I spent time at three excavation sites in Italy. Working in the trenches was invaluable in forming my thinking about antiquities. To those who made that work possible, but whom I haven't named owing to confidentiality agreements, thank you: you know who you are.

Many libraries and institutions helped me find archival material and secondary literature. For their patient help, I thank the archivists and librarians at the Archivio di Stato di Roma, the Biblioteca Nazionale Centrale di Roma (BNCR), the Istituto Archeologico Germanico (Rome), the American Academy in Rome, the Library of the Camera dei Deputati (Rome), and the British School at Rome. In Ann Arbor, Beau Case, the Italian studies librarian at the Hatcher Graduate Library, procured Italian-language books that were hard to find outside Italy. In Charlottesville, Christine Slaughter and her colleagues at the University of Virginia's Alderman Library worked their magic to find digitized archival material with astonishing speed, proving once again that librarians keep the flame of knowledge burning no matter what is happening in the world.

In 2016–17, I participated in the Radcliffe Institute for Advanced Study seminar "Laying Up Treasure," organized by Dan Smail and Andrew Shryock. I benefited from conversations with all my fellow seminarians. For their thoughtful engagement with my draft material—some of which is published here—I particularly thank Andrew and Dan, Andrew Bevan, Emily Osborn, John Robb, Natasha Schull, Mary Stiner, and Julia Adeney Thomas.

At the University of Michigan, fellow graduate students provided ideas and helpful feedback, and also laughter, commiseration, and warm companionship. I give thanks to Elizabeth Armstrong, José Bortoluci, Jamie Budnick, Patricia Chen, Amy Cooter, Mariana Craciun, Mathieu Desan, Marco Garrido, Dan Hirschman, Camilo Leslie, Zakiya Luna, Atef Said, Claire Whitlinger, and Elizabeth Young for friendship and unstinting support.

Geneviève Zubrzycki supervised my dissertation and did so much more. Her incisive observations profoundly influenced my approach to the study of culture and nationalism, while her precise and supportive criticism, from embryonic proposal to finished product, greatly enhanced its quality and nuance. Fatma Müge Göçek discussed drafts of things over many cups of strong coffee. Rob Jansen pushed me to think more carefully and precisely about theories of states and culture, and it was through our long discussions that I ventured into new domains of social theory. Nic Terrenato sparked my interest in the project in the first place, explaining the complexities of this sphere through many office hours visits back in Ann Arbor. Through stimulating conversations in the Michigan Social Theory seminar, Margaret Somers and George Steinmetz helped me see the interrelations of power and identity in the field of antiquities. Amir Baghdadchi read drafts and commented perceptively, always finding a twist or a puzzle and teaching me to write with clarity and humor.

At the University of Chicago, I was fortunate to spend three years at the Neubauer Collegium for Culture and Society, doing postdoctoral research for the Past for Sale project. It was a wonderfully productive period, and I am grateful for the supportive friends and colleagues during my time there: Josh Beck, Elspeth Carruthers, Jonathan Lear, David Nirenberg, Larry Rothfield, and the remarkable Collegium staff.

Italians joke that their artifact-rich country is like an instant-win lottery ticket: scratch in the right place and you might find treasure. I had my lottery win with the editorial staff at the University of Chicago Press. Susan Bielstein read each draft and drew the story out of every nook and cranny of the text. I am grateful to her and James Whitman Toftness for their timely advice and guidance, and to three anonymous reviewers for their insightful comments.

I am grateful to Anne Cherry for editing early drafts and keeping me going. For their top-notch research assistance, I thank Nicole Bonino, Miriam Muccione, and Vasfiye Toprak.

Friends and colleagues on two continents provided feedback on chapters or offered insights into my project that greatly helped my analysis: Jeffrey C. Alexander, Joshua Arthurs, Jennifer Bair, Stefan Bargheer, Claudio Benzecry, Neil Brodie, Larissa Buchholz, Sarah Corse, Mira Debs, Cathy Draycott, Jas' Elsner, Lene Faust, Dario Gaggio, Peter Galison, Elaine Gazda, Patty Gerstenblith, Richard Handler, Tracey Heatherington, Michael Herzfeld, Caroline Jones, Elene Kekelia, Morag Kersel, Krishan Kumar, Richard Lachmann, Peggy Levitt, Ekaterina Makarova, Isabella Clough Marinaro, James Marrone, Jordanna Matlon, Terence McDonnell, Milena Melfi, Ben Merriman, Alfonso Moreno, Heidi Nicholls, Christena Nippert-Eng, Jeffrey K. Olick, Davide Orsini, Cristiana Panella, Shobita Parthasarathy, Simone Polillo, Isaac Ariail Reed, Anna Skarpelis, R. R. R. Smith, Gil Stein, Oya Topçuoğlu, Tasha Vorderstrasse, Amy Whitaker, and Caitlin Wylie.

As though cheering me on through the first doctoral degree weren't enough, friends and family enthusiastically cheered me on through the second. Heartfelt thanks to Claudia Allen, Jill and Mike Folan, Becca Katzman, McRoberts-Daveys, Pytels, Griffin Reames. Gail Altenburg, Nick Roumel, Steve and Sandy Rose, Kate and Ryan Roberts and family, Olivia Roumel, Aaron, Steve, and Tim Rose and their families, Lintz siblings and families, Jan and Fred Ranger, News and Georgiadeses, Janet Greenland, Ellie and Luke McLaughlin: Thank you. I wish very much that my grandparents had lived to see this book. May their memory be eternal. Will, Alasdair, and Abigail: for your love and understanding through the peaks and valleys, I give my deepest gratitude to you.

Appendix

METHODOLOGY: DATA COLLECTION AND ANALYTICAL STRATEGIES

When I began this project, I meant to study something I thought of as the black market in antiquities. After ten years' training and employment as a classical archaeologist and assistant museum curator, I thought I had a good sense for how it worked: looters extract artifacts from the ground and sell their finds to middlemen, who then smuggle the objects to dealers at border crossings and international freeports. I understood "black market" as a coherent, bounded social sphere with a profit-oriented logic drawn from the so-called white or legitimate market. I thought, too, that the moral parameters were clear. I had long ago concluded that participants in the black market are lawbreakers who are fundamentally hostile to archaeological science and method and, more broadly, to the public-minded spirit of sharing and appreciating antiquities through museums and books. All that was left, I thought, was to find a cast of characters to interview or observe and then skillfully shed light on their procedures for finding and evaluating antiquities and smuggling them across borders. I chose Italy because I had worked there as a field archaeologist, and because it is routinely held up as an exemplary case of how the national government is effectively fighting the black market in antiquities. Once I began my fieldwork, however, I had to revise those presumptions and adjust my research methods accordingly.

PLANNING THE STUDY: PRINCIPLES OF DESIGN AND METHOD

My data draw from four groups of subjects in Italy: state actors (including archaeologists and museum professionals employed in the public archaeological or museum service, as well as employees of the Art Squad); archaeologists working in Italy but not in the state archaeological service (as at the field schools in "Vergilia" and "Campobello"); unauthorized excavators; and everyday citizens and residents of the towns where I conducted fieldwork. Because their illegal activities heightened their risk in taking part in the study, the unauthorized excavators required specific methodological protocols and ethical considerations. I will explain my study design and data collection strategies for them later in this section.

For the interviews with state actors, non-state archaeologists, and citizens/residents, I used the data collection model I first employed in 2010 and 2011 during a project on team dynamics among archaeologists in Italy. For that study I used a combination of semi-structured interviews and observations while I was allowed to join in the work of the dig team. As I explain at length in "Seeing the Unseen," the journal article I published about that project (Rose-Greenland 2013), I studied three archaeological field schools in Italy over the course of two summers. I conducted fifty-eight semi-structured interviews, with questions focused on teamwork, knowledge building, tools, and the nature of discovery. The structure of the dig sites provided a ready-made sample pool: since I was inquiring into team dynamics, I chose to interview only team members. Everybody on the dig team was university-trained and familiar with interviews and qualitative study, and their curiosity about research into their own discipline predisposed them to speak to me. Accessing the study sites and their personnel was relatively easy, moreover, because of my professional training in the discipline and my project's endorsement by other archaeologists.

From the point of view of the Institutional Review Board (IRB) at the University of Michigan, the field school study was exempt from IRB oversight because it presented little or no risk to the subjects. Because I was interviewing men and women in the context of the workplace and about matters related to the normal course of their jobs, I was not further risking their reputations or safety. Talking about digging was something they did all day, and my interview questions were a natural extension of that. I was able to expand my inquiry to a wider pool of participants for the *Ruling Culture* research. The state officials, archaeologists, and scholars I planned to interview would be approached through the ordinary course of their work and given the option of refusing questions they felt uncomfortable answering. The earlier study, in short, provided the methodological groundwork for data collection for the current book. I used professional contacts and people I knew through my various periods of residence in Italy to recruit additional archaeologists to the sample set for *Ruling Culture* and diversified my sample beyond the confines of field archaeology. Some of the material from "Seeing the Unseen" that did not make it into the journal article was kept aside and incorporated into this book.

It was the "Seeing the Unseen" fieldwork that led me to the present study. After artifacts were stolen from "Vergilia," one of my study sites, I watched officers from the local Carabinieri arrive to perform an inspection and write a report. The field director at Vergilia was not impressed by the officers' conduct, telling me afterward that they were "always too little, too late," and that she herself could have determined who had been behind the theft "in about five minutes" after talking with locals. The episode alerted me to the practical and ideological complexities of dealing with antiquities theft, and it was then that I sketched out the questions and design ideas for *Ruling Culture*. But I concluded early that the methodological approach I used for the field school study—personal introductions, participating in the excavation, living with the team, and conducting a series of one-on-one interviews and follow-up discussions—would not be transferrable to my study of unauthorized excavators.

IRB PROTOCOL, ETHICS, AND STUDY DESIGN

The Institutional Review Board at the University of Michigan set the parameters for my fieldwork with unauthorized excavators, and their strictures continued to inform my work as I reported back to them on subject recruitment, changes in study sites, and any adverse events (there were none). The IRB had two main concerns: my subjects' privacy and my personal safety. The risks I was willing to undertake in the course of my work were largely my own to assess and negotiate. After speaking at length with the IRB manager assigned to my study, I discerned two types of personal risks: imminent physical ones (potentially encountered, for example, by meeting an unknown interviewee in an isolated place) and future professional ones. Professional risks include acquiring data about crimes, past or ongoing, that could be of interest to legal authorities and lead to subpoena. I wished to avoid subpoena because releasing my data could point police officials and prosecutors back to my interview subjects. Even if there was a very low risk of that, I was ethically bound by the IRB's human subjects study protocol to inform participants that they might incriminate themselves by talking to me about specific acts of looting or looted artifacts they possessed. I addressed the imminent physical risks by following a few procedural rules. First, I met interview subjects in public spaces (bars, cafés, parks, business offices, and piazzas) and during daylight hours. Second, I visited private homes only when it was clear that other family members would be present. Third, I scrubbed my Web profiles of my home address and my children's names. I did not pull my Web profiles—Academia.edu, Facebook, the University of Michigan Department of Sociology page—entirely, however. I wanted potential subjects to be able to go online to verify my institutional affiliations and look at my previous academic publications.

Protecting subjects' privacy was a key piece of my study design. Unauthorized excavation of archaeological sites is illegal in Italy, and unauthorized diggers are regularly arrested and criminally prosecuted. Further, subjects who were "outed" as unauthorized diggers might face social censure and loss of standing in the community. I mitigated these risks by strictly protecting interview subjects' identities: assigning pseudonyms; refraining from snowball sampling; minimizing interview "spillage"; and storing my handwritten notes and typed transcripts in secure places (on spillage of information from one interview to another, see Holstein and Gubrium 1995).

The IRB approval process also involved close examination of my interview questions and consent protocol. I shared my interview questions with the IRB committee's resident anthropologist. His feedback persuaded me to change the content of several questions to leave them both open-ended and sufficiently structured to guide my subjects away from implicating themselves or others in criminal acts that could jeopardize us all. Before embarking on my fieldwork, I hired a native Italian speaker to coach me on pronunciation and conversational style. I did not mind that I speak Italian with an American accent; in fact, I saw that as an asset for establishing myself as a friendly outsider. The objective of practicing the interview was to refine my pitch and delivery so as to avoid pitfalls (such as wrongly placed emphases that could insult my subjects or imply false knowingness) and clarify my meaning.

DATA COLLECTION AND ANALYSIS

By the time I started my second summer of fieldwork for this project, I accepted that interviewing smugglers, thieves, and dealers would not be possible as long as I was looking for people who fit my preconceived categories of "smuggler," "thief," and "dealer." The problem was not just semantic. Naturally most people do not like to be called smugglers or thieves. I was not so naive as to think that I could post study subject solicitations for *tombaroli* (tomb robbers) online or in local Italian newspapers and wait for the calls to roll in. But I did think that through sustained efforts to win trust with small groups of people in one or two communities over a long period, I could meet smugglers and antiquities thieves and thereby gain insight into the secret world of the black market.

Targeting participants in the black market was the wrong way to think about it. What I came to understand, and what I analyze in depth across the book, is that there is no single, bounded black market in antiquities. While illicit transactions *do* occur—sometimes conducted by the same individuals working through a network—there is also a vigorous social space of "gray" artifactual relations. This space contains behaviors that many archaeologists and law enforcement authorities would label illegal—for example, digging for archaeological materials or finding them with metal detectors, then keeping or trading the artifacts. It also contains behaviors that are technically illegal but culturally tolerated and even supported: among other practices, inheriting artifacts from family members, keeping accidental finds without reporting them to the authorities, or purchasing small items with local or regional historical origins but no established legal provenance. In light of these complexities, labels such as *tombarolo* are not sufficient for examining the complicated values, roles, and ideas at play in the circulation, use, and evaluation of antiquities. My focus shifted from markets to matrices as a way to think about the sociocultural lives of artifacts once they leave the ground and are absorbed into the spaces of cultural intimacy found in every national community. Eventually I put "market" in quotation marks to suggest my unease with using the word in this context. There is indeed an illicit market in Italian antiquities today. Part of my fieldwork involved getting to know people who are actively fighting it. But the trade, I learned, involves much more than envelopes of cash handed over for Etruscan urns. I met people who traded coins for pots or pots for votive statues; who gave informal lectures on bucchero ware to neighbors and fellow archaeology buffs in exchange for bottles of homemade wine; and who gave artifacts as gifts at weddings and baptisms. The domestic "market," in this sense, can be better thought of as "circulation." The circulation is effectuated in "circuits," a term I appropriate from the anthropological literature because it captures the dynamism and range of actors and relationship forms that "group" does not easily accommodate.

For all my good intentions, I understood that I was asking my subjects for sensitive information. This was especially so with the unauthorized excavators. Despite their nonchalance about the prospect of police trouble, they undertook a risk by describing their digging and collecting practices to me. But the archaeologists, state officials, and neighbors of unauthorized excavators were also sharing sensitive information with me, and I treated it as such. I presented every (potential) participant with a consent form, one copy in English and one in Italian, and explained that I was studying state patrimony and the rules that guide the use and circulation of artifacts. I emphasized that looting was one aspect of my interest but that I was also studying a range of relationships and experiences that Italian people have with the material cultural heritage that populates their daily lives. Some participants signed the form; others gave oral consent, not wishing to put their legal name and signature on a form. All were given the option of commenting anonymously, and they all were informed that they had the right to decline to answer any question, for any reason or no reason, and to stop the interview at any time, for any reason. My informants were not compensated. I thanked them all for their time and ideas and supplied my name and my contact information as well as the IRB's, for follow-up, independent verification, or in case participants wanted to withdraw from the study after the fact. (None did.) At the archaeological sites I used recording devices with participants' explicit permission, but I did not use them when interviewing state officials, unauthorized excavators, or everyday subjects. The sensitivity of the research topic might have made participants wary of recordings, so I restricted myself to handwritten notes that I later typed into my laptop and stored in the secure cloud server at my university. I use pseudonyms for informants and study sites unless specified otherwise.

Notes

Introduction

1. I am grateful to Elene Kekelia and Yen-Yu Lin for their insightful definitions and cultural explanations of these terms.

2. Focusing on the case of Québécois nationalism and the role of Catholicism, Zubrzycki (2016) shows how sensory experiences of cultural objects are constructive of new collective identities even as participants have divergent understandings of what those experiences mean. This is an important corrective to scholarly assumptions that the power of national patrimony resides in its ability to confer unified meaning. See also Dickie (1999). On the persistence of marginalizations within Italy, see Forgacs (2014).

3. As Moe (2002) demonstrates, southern Italians have long been stereotyped as socioeconomically "backward" and culturally stagnant. But similar beliefs have been applied to Italy as a whole by northern and western Europeans, with the result that modern Italy's economic and political dysfunctions are blamed on inherent, collective "flaws" in Italian people. The same dysfunctions in other countries, by contrast, tend to be attributed to structures and ideologies. See also Patriarca (2001).

4. "L'Italia è la potenza culturale più grande del mondo." The phrase is attributed to former president of the republic Carlo Azeglio Ciampi by Lieutenant Colonel Ferdinando Musella of the Tutela del Patrimonio Culturale ("Art Squad"), in an interview with Federico Guiglia for *Secolo d'Italia*, April 1, 2004. It is reprinted here: http://www.patrimoniosos.it/rsol.php?op=getarticle&id=5316 (accessed 7/2/2020).

5. Buchholz (2018) provides an important corrective to the model of artistic centers and peripheries by demonstrating the innovation and resistance that occurs in so-called peripheral spaces of creativity. On soft power's subversive politics during the Cold War, see Stonor Saunders (2013).

6. Williams (1976, 87).

7. Inventories and lists of protected cultural objects have a long history in Italy. In 1624, Cardinal Aldobrandini's edict prohibited the extraction of metal or marble statues, antiques, or similar objects (Cogo 1995). Sixty years later, in the edict of Cardinal Altieri, the list had grown and become taxonomically fastidious: "statues, figures, intaglios, medallions, inscriptions on marble, metals, gold, silver, jewelry, and similar

things both ancient and modern . . . antique pictures, or any other works sculpted, painted, carved, commissioned, processed, or otherwise made [in Rome], or having been found in caves within Rome and outside Rome" (Emiliani 2015, 61–66). The list covers dozens of object types from small to large. Such edicts encoded cultural artifacts as though they were a vanishing species, and the number of categories of protected object types expanded as political and economic power in the Italian city-states waned (Natali 2004).

8. Victoria Reyes (2014) demonstrates that didactic materials at UNESCO World Heritage sites make reference to culturally dominant countries, notably Italy, to explain the significance of the site—even those with no documented connection with Italy. This perpetuates cultural heritage bias while allowing the list itself to remain seemingly impartial.

9. For example, on the state politics of the French national inventory of significant historical sites, see Kowalski (2007).

10. Proulx (2013, 111).

11. On the legal, political, and economic entanglements of the antiquities market, see the introduction and papers in Greenland (2019b). On the ambiguous legal and ethical status of the "gray" art market, see Mackenzie and Yates (2016) and Proulx (2008).

12. In the early years of state patrimony protection, the Ministry of Education held this responsibility, art and archaeology having been regarded as having a pedagogical value for the Italian public.

13. My translation from the Italian. "La Repubblica promuove lo sviluppo della cultura e la ricerca scientifica e tecnica. Tutela il paesaggio e il patrimonio storico e artistico della Nazione." www.senato.it/documenti/repository/istituzione/costituzione.pdf.

14. Rago (2004, n. 3).

15. Influential critiques of the reliance on private capital for cultural heritage projects are Settis (2002, 2017) and Montanari (2018). Settis, a prominent archaeologist, has argued that the changes have transformed patrimony from a public resource for nation building and citizenship to a private equity opportunity. For a broader discussion of the content and direction of Italian cultural policy, see Bianchini, Torrigiani, and Cere (1996).

16. "Restituiti dagli Usa eccezionali reperti archeologici di provenienza furtiva e da scavo illecito in Italia," press release from the Ministero per i Beni e le Attività Culturali, January 20, 2012, http://www.beniculturali.it/mibac/export/MiBAC/sito-MiBAC/Contenuti/MibacUnif/Comunicati/visualizza_asset.html_7901052.html (accessed 5/9/2013).

17. For expanded discussion of the Italian model and its legal underpinnings, see DiFonzo (2012).

18. For contrasting views and further background discussion, see Greenland (2016b).

19. Carver (1996); Hamilakis and Yalouri (1996).

20. Askew (2010); Meskell (2018).

21. Chapters in the edited volume by Bandelj and Wherry (2011) demonstrate important variations in heritage value mechanisms across temporal, material, national, and political lines.

22. Aronczyk (2013).

23. Zubrzycki (2011, 2013).

24. Nora (1989). "Realms of memory" is a complex term that Nora associated with events, historical periods, spaces, and objects. For further analysis of the term and the questions it raises about collective and individual cultures of memory, see Olick (1999).

25. The concept of "idioms of relatedness" is developed by Ben-Yehoyada (2017) in his study of long-term cultural and economic ties between southern Italians and North Africans.

26. On idioms of nationhood in nineteenth-century Italian politics, see Chabod (1996). For the specific case of how Italians have thought about the country's ancient past in conjunction with its modern condition and goals, see De Francesco (2013).

27. Another way to think about this is to situate artifacts in the question posed by Chris Gosden (2005): "What do objects want?"

28. Greenland (2013, 2016a).

29. Reed (2020) has greatly expanded Gell's theory in his analysis of power and agency in modern polities. For Reed, the embodiment and distribution of personhood has implications for the bounded relations between rulers and ruled, or Rectors, Actors, and Others. I am grateful for his thoughts on the additional sovereign "work" done by cultural artifacts. For a broader analysis of artifacts, agency, and Gell's influence on cultural theory, see Greenland (2019a).

30. *Agreement between the Italian Ministry of Culture and the Metropolitan Museum of Art*, February 21, 2006, Point 4.1(a).

31. Bartelson (2014); Mitchell (1991).

32. Stratigraphy refers to layers in the substrate made legible by subtle color gradations and geological features and pegged to particular historical periods. Based on this concept, the Wheeler-Kenyon method (1930s to 1950s) taught archaeologists to divide excavation sites into cubic cross sections of earth. In 1973 Bermudian archaeologist Edward Harris introduced the Harris Matrix, a tool for identifying and recording depositions, or successive layers of past human activity. In chapter 2, I discuss the scientizing of archaeological excavation in further detail.

33. As I have argued elsewhere, pottery fragments are a clear case of this. Because they are made from clay, found in the earth, and taxonomically classified (in part) based on findspot and composite materials, they are "in, on, and of" the soil. See Greenland (2017).

34. The uses of cultural heritage in these and other sociopolitical projects is discussed, with reference to other historical and geographic cases, in Harrison (2013) and Winter (2015).

35. Herzfeld (2016, 6).

Chapter One

1. My reference to the Carabinieri as "police" was a mistake. As I would understand later, the Carabinieri and the Polizia di Stato are separate law enforcement agencies with distinct duties. The former is a branch of the military, and the latter is a civil force. Some Carabinieri object to being called police. I refer to them as officers.

2. "Cultural intimacy" originates with Herzfeld (2016); for elaboration of the "backstage" of social and cultural practices, see Shryock (2004).

3. The phrase is in widespread use. See, for example, text from the Ministry of Culture's website in 2017: "[L'Italia possiede] il più ampio patrimonio culturale a livello mondiale." *L'Italia è un immense museo all'aperto*, Ministero per i Beni e le Attività Culturali, press release, accessed at https://www.beniculturali.it/mibac/export/MiBAC/sito-MiBAC/Contenuti/Ministero/UfficioStampa/ComunicatiStampa/visualizza_asset.html_1005393688.html.

4. Bennett (1995); Classen (2007).

5. Duncan (1995); Leahy (2016).

6. Herzfeld (2004, 2–3).

7. The full definition is provided in article 2, point 2 of the *Codice dei Beni Culturali* of 2004: "2. Cultural treasures are those things movable and immovable . . . presenting artistic, historic, archaeological, ethnoanthropological, archival, and bibliographic interest, and all other things determined through law or based in legal codes that testify to having civilizational value [*valore di civiltà*]" (my translation).

8. Bottari and Pizzicannella (2007, 24); see also Serio (2003).

9. "Verifica dell'interesse culturale del patrimonio immobiliare pubblico: Guida introduttiva al sistema informativo," *Ministero per i Beni e le Attività Culturali, Direzione Generale per i beni architettonici ed il paesaggio*.

10. Trentini (2004).

11. Troilo (2011, 464).

12. Aronczyk (2013); Hom (2015); Rivera (2008).

13. Mukerji (2009); for Paris as the "New Rome" of Napoleon I, see Rowell (2012).

14. World Soft Power League Table for 2019, published at https://softpower30.com/wp-content/uploads/2019/10/The-Soft-Power-30-Report-2019-1.pdf (accessed July 19, 2020).

15. Hamilakis (2007).

16. Gilmour (2011); Riall (1994).

17. Gentile (2011) expands on the interpretation of fluid and multiple national identities as productive of ideas in an interview with Simonetta Fiori.

18. For classic statements on the topic, see Anderson (1991); Smith (2009).

19. Mookherjee (2011).

20. For the chauvinism critique, see Wolkoff (2010).

21. Appiah (2006, 3).

22. See especially Gaggio (2007). A comparable theory of patrimony capital is developed, in the empirical context of Italian fashion and textile production, in Rofel and Yanagisako (2019) and Yanagisako (2002).

23. A classic text remains Trigger (2006); see also Centeno, Bandelj, and Wherry (2011); Gaggio (2011).

24. Spencer (2012, 150–51). For a critical history of the concept of patria, in particular its relation to categories of civic membership in antiquity, see Kantorowicz (1950). Key works in the discussion are Stiebing (1994) and Trigger (2006).

25. Agnew (2011).

26. Here, consistent with my previous publications on the topic, I refer to the field school by a pseudonym, "Campobello."

27. For a helpful overview of the controversies surrounding Carandini's work, see Wiseman (2001).

28. R. Suro, "Newly Found Wall May Give Clue to Origin of Rome, Scientist Says," *New York Times*, June 10, 1988.

29. See especially Carandini (1979, 1997).

30. Carandini (1997, 633).

31. Ginzburg and Davin (1980, 5).

32. Hamilakis (2007, 146).

33. Hamilakis (2007, 146), citing Manolis Andronikos, "Archaeology and Time," *To Vima*, October 12, 1972.

34. Hamilakis (2007, 147), citing Manolis Andronikos, "The Human Face of Archaeology," *To Vima*, December 18, 1988.

35. The concept of milk kinship is borrowed from Altorki (1980).

36. Elias (1982, 242–43).

37. Reed (2020, 52–57).

38. Lahire (2019, 164–65).

39. Schnapp (1997).

40. Moshenska (2012).

41. Delaney (1991) makes a similar point in her ethnographic study of a Muslim village in central Anatolia. She shows the linkages between women and soil, which are both capable of sustaining life with the right seed and cultivation. The soil, in this cultural system, is the organizational basis of the family.

42. Herzfeld (2016, 198).

43. Meskell (2002).

44. Greenland (2013).

45. In her study of archaeology and memory in New Orleans, Dawdy (2016) argues that surface textures and the appearance of age (patina) are also critical in forming embodied knowledge of the antique.

46. "Carabinieri TPC, Operazione Achei. Smantellata un'organizzazione criminale dedita al traffico nazionale e internazionale di reperti archeologici calabrese," Comando Carabinieri Tutela Patrimonio Culturale, Reparto Operativo, November 18, 2019.

47. "Operazione *Andromeda* Comunicato Stampa," Comando Carabinieri Tutela Patrimonio Culturale, Reparto Operativo, July 16, 2010, accessed at www.beniculturali.it/mibac/multimedia/MiBAC/documents/1279288486544_comunicato.pdf.

48. Note especially the work of Donatella della Porta and Herbert Reiter (2006) on the Carabinieri's decision to arrest protesters at the G8 summit in Genoa on the pretext that the protests were a threat to public order. The force used to deter protesters was gradually elevated to massive use of force, even against peaceful protesters. Important parallels exist in the illegalization of migrants; see De Genova (2002).

49. Alexander (2004, 145).

50. Troilo (2012).

51. Gell (1998, 21).

52. Gell (1998, 104).

53. Gell (1998, 98).

54. Domanico (1999).

55. Gell (1998, 230).

56. "*Sampietrini* come souvenir, l'ultima moda dei furti tra turisti [Cobblestones as souvenirs, the latest trend in tourist theft]," *La Stampa*, June 23, 2012.

57. MiBAC stands for Ministero per i Beni e le Attività Culturali e per il Turismo. Responsibility for state administration of cultural activities has been vested in various ministries since nation-state unification. The acronym has changed over time to

reflect institutional rearrangements. For ease of translation, at the cost of organizational precision, I use "Ministry of Culture" throughout the book.

58. As the Ministry of Culture was called at the time of our interview.

59. Zuboff (2015, 77).

60. Zuboff (2015, 77).

61. Rofel and Yanagisako (2019, 16).

62. Wolkoff (2010).

63. Significant contributions to this discussion can be found in Daniel Miller's edited 2005 book, *Materiality*. Subsequent work has explored various spatial, temporal, biographical, and emotional relationships between and among people and physical things. See further Keane (2003), McDonnell (2016), Zubrzycki (2016).

64. Gumbrecht (2004, 2).

65. Wali (2020, 149).

66. Tilley (1996, 173–74; 2004).

67. Gumbrecht (2004, 107).

68. Reyes (2014, 55).

69. Bandelj and Wherry (2011).

70. On the interface between "heritage" culture and tourist culture, and their mutual synergies, see Hom (2015).

71. Reinart (2010).

72. Quatremère de Quincy ([1796, 1836] 2012, 104).

73. "Diviser c'est détruire," Quatremère de Quincy (2012, 200–201).

74. Soresina (2018, 7–9).

75. Lowe and Mazari (1975, 4).

76. Snowden (2006).

77. In the mid-nineteenth century, government officials chose not to allow industrial development in the city of Rome, in order to preserve its antiquarian fabric. This stunted the development of urban infrastructure. For more on this point, and its broader sociopolitical context, see De Francesco (2013).

78. Herzfeld (2009).

79. Michael Day, "Down Pompeii? The Ruin of Italy's Cultural Heritage," *Independent*, December 4, 2010, accessed at https://www.independent.co.uk/news/world/europe/down-pompeii-the-ruin-of-italys-cultural-heritage-2150976.html

80. Shryock (2004, 3).

Chapter Two

1. Saki [H. H. Munro], "The Background," from *The Chronicles of Clovis* (1911), republished in *The Complete Saki* (London: Penguin, 1976), 121–23.

2. Emiliani (2015, 5–6).

3. Feigenbaum (2014, 5).

4. Furlotti (2019, 40).

5. Levi (2008, 108).

6. Emiliani (2015, 130–45).

7. Curzi (2004); Troilo (2005).

8. De Francesco (2013).

9. Ridley (2009) argues that the reforms Fea were pushing were too radical for

many of his contemporaries. Papal support for his work was steady but did not necessarily result in the tangible changes Fea sought.

10. Campana's family connections were important to his professional and museological achievements and should be read against the tight social world of Roman elites in the early nineteenth century. For his cultural and banking links, see Pianazza (1993). For a detailed treatment of his life, antiquities networks, and the embezzlement scandal, see Sarti (2001).

11. Borowitz and Borowitz (1991, 1).

12. Borowitz and Borowitz (1991, 43).

13. Borowitz and Borowitz (1991, 59), citing the *Causa Campana* part 3, 5–18.

14. Archivio di Stato, Collection: Ministero del Commercio e dei Lavoro Pubblici, Provincia di Roma, sezione 5, titolo 1, fascicolo 5. File name: Ministro del Belgio Estiazione di oggetti d'arte, num. del protocollo 8461, December 1862 (Archivio di Stato di Roma, Ministero dei Lavori Pubblici, Commercio, Belle Arti, Industria e Agricoltura [1855–70], busta 420). Document: Letter from the Belgium delegation (Légation de Belgique) to the minister for commerce and public works, Rome, December 19, 1862.

15. Cremona (2013).

16. Archivio di Stato, Collection: Ministero del Commercio e dei Lavoro Pubblici, Provincia di Roma, sezione 5, titolo 1, fascicolo 5. File name: Ministro del Belgio Estiazione di oggetti d'arte, num. del protocollo 8461, December 1862 (Archivio di Stato di Roma, Ministero dei Lavori Pubblici, Commercio, Belle Arti, Industria e Agricoltura [1855–70], busta 420), Document name: A Sua Eccellenza il Signor Barone Commend. P. D. Costantini Baldini Ministro del Commercio e lavori pubblici, December 24, 1862.

17. McLean (2007, 58).

18. Cotta (1992, 152); cf. Müller (2013).

19. Pentini (2005, 68–69).

20. The evidentiary basis for this assertion consists of two sets of documents in the Archivio di Stato in Rome: the Fondo Castellani papers and papers from the Ministry of Commerce and Public Works (Ministero del Commercio e dei Lavori Pubblici). The Fondo Castellani collection features private letters, bills of sale, government papers, excavation permits, and bank statements. In short, it is a gold mine of information about the antiquities that passed through the hands of Fortunato Pio, Augusto, and Alessandro from the 1830s to the 1910s.

21. Moretti Sgubini (2000).

22. Developments included considerable confusion and jockeying for position within the new national cultural administration. For example, the Commission for the Protection of the Monuments of Rome was a three-man commission that, without substantive powers, asserted itself as the new authority over the Vatican Museum.

23. Troilo (2011, 476–77).

24. See, among other studies, the papers published in Feigenbaum (2014). On the specific case of British social networks and prestige invested in the consumption of antiquities and art through the Grand Tour, see Sweet (2012). On Italy's place in the Grand Tour, see Black (2003).

25. A foundational text for this argument is Haskell and Penny (1982). For a theoretical treatment of culture at the center of systems of power, see Blanning (2002).

26. Ceserani (2012, 194).

27. On the situation and significance of Croton, see Orsi (1911) for notes on his first field season there.

28. Frothingham (1887, 389).

29. Orsi (1911, 77).

30. This point is elaborated by Paoletti (2005).

31. Ceserani (2012, 194).

32. Marchand (1996); Trigger (2006); Vašíček and Malina (1990).

33. Rasmussen (1979).

34. Walters (1905, 2:301).

35. Walters (1905, 2:303).

36. The "poor man's silver" quotation appears in Brown (1968, xix).

37. Dennis (1848, 1:410).

38. Körner (2009, 139–42).

39. Birch ([1857] 1873); Walters (1905).

40. On Eduard Gerhard's intervention, see Marchand (1996); see also van Wijngaarden (1999).

41. Marchand (1996, 97).

42. For a more comprehensive discussion of how British archaeologists used Etruscans as a counterpoint to Greek cultural supremacy, see Izzet (2007).

43. Birch ([1857] 1873, 5).

44. Walters (1905, 1:491).

45. Marchand (1996, 97).

46. Körner (2009).

47. Zannoni (1871, xlix). In Zannoni's time, *race* and *nation* were used interchangeably. For further discussion of this point, see Smith (1987).

48. Körner (2009, 138).

49. Anderson (1991, 195–96). Anderson is referring to European nations generally in this period: "In Europe, the new nationalisms almost immediately began to imagine themselves as 'awakening from sleep,' a trope wholly foreign to the Americas. . . . Read as late awakening, even if an awakening stimulated from afar, [the trope] opened up an immense antiquity behind the epochal sleep."

50. Rajala (2006).

51. Grab (1995, 40).

52. Hobsbawm ([1969] 2000).

53. Ceserani (2012); Marchand (1996).

54. Ott (2008, 150). On American purchasing power in the closing decades of the nineteenth century and its impact on the market in Italian art, see Boime (1979).

55. Helstosky (2009, 813).

56. See Van Laar and Diepeveen (2013, 27–30) on the creation of prestige through rarity. Lucien Karpik (2010, 70) makes a similar point through the concepts of rarefaction and scarcity in the market for artworks and other "singularities."

57. In the city of Florence, for example, the Association for the Defense of Ancient Florence articulated a philosophy of guardianship rather than ownership (Balzani 2003, 15). They argued that the city's cultural patrimony needed preservation and protection from the harms of daily life, and they initially identified private philanthropy as an essential source of support. Wealthy city residents were courted for monument restoration and art conservation, such objects constituting the fabric of Florence and

an integral part of Florentine identity. The group's political position, then, was one of collective moral and fiscal obligation, rooted in private benefaction for public benefit (Maggini and Tosetto 1998).

58. Elaborating on this point, Gundle (2000) argues that notions of beauty shaped the collective sense of national purpose and identity in the nineteenth and twentieth centuries.

59. Alberto Bergamini, "Politica d'arte," *Giornale d'Italia*, September 10, 1903.

60. "Discussione del disegno di legge per le Antichità," Atti Parlamentari Camera Deputati, sessione 1909, vol. 234, discussioni 2, May 24–July 18, 1909, pp. 1405–30.

61. A key example is the Campana collection and scandal, with the fallout from that and collective suspicions about the motives and ethics of powerful collectors. See Sarti (2001).

62. Morris (1905).

63. Bottari and Pizzicannella (2007, 145).

64. Hon. Luigi Rava, Camera dei Deputati, Rome, May 27, 1909. *Discussione del disegno di legge per le Antichità, Atti Parlamentari Camera Deputati*, sessione 1909, discussioni 2, 24 maggio–18 giugno 1909, no. 234. The quotation is from p. 1410.

65. Hon. Giovanni Rosadi, Camera dei Deputati, Rome, May 27, 1909, *Discussione del disegno di legge per le Antichità, Atti Parlamentari Camera Deputati*, sessione 1909, discussioni 2, 24 maggio–18 giugno 1909, no. 234. The quotation is from p. 1413.

66. Hon. Giovanni Rosadi, Camera dei Deputati, Rome, May 27, 1909. *Discussione del disegno di legge per le Antichità, Atti Parlamentari Camera Deputati*, sessione 1909, discussioni 2, 24 maggio–18 giugno 1909, no. 234. The quotation is from p. 1415.

67. Bottari and Pizzicannella (2007, 144).

Chapter Three

1. *The Futurist Manifesto* was first published on February 5, 1909, in the Italian newspaper *Gazzetta dell'Emilia*. It was published in French in *Le Figaro* on February 20, 1909. All quotations here are taken from the English-language translation published in full, as a separate appendix, in Joll (1960, 179–84).

2. Rejecting world peace as the naive and foolish obsession of anarchists, Marinetti affirmed futurism's commitment to "the continuous development and unending progress, both bodily and intellectual, of man" through war. The quotation is from Marinetti's 1911 *War, the Only Hygiene of the World*, in Rainey, Poggi, and Wittman (2009, 84).

3. Hughes-Hallett (2013, 261–62).

4. Images of poison, sickly nostalgia, and the absurdity of antique "mania" are scattered across futurist writings, Marinetti's and others'. See Rainey, Poggi, and Wittman (2009, part 1).

5. Marinetti, *The Futurist Manifesto*, quoted in Joll (1960, 182–83).

6. For earlier articulations of this link, via Nietzsche and Georges Sorel, see Joll (1960, 135–36).

7. Gentile (2003); Conversi (2009).

8. Marinetti, *Noi Futuristi*, published in Milan in 1907, quoted in Joll (1960, 141).

9. Lista (1995).

10. Sociologists of nationalism frequently refer to authority struggles over meaning and interpretation. Such discussions approach "authority" as influence or sway

over the symbolic dimensions of an artifact. In the case of Fascist Italy, however, authority took on repressive dimensions. The Fascist regime used the force of the state to arrest, interrogate, and imprison cultural dissenters. It's important to keep sight of the very real stakes in authority struggles. For the repression of dissenting cultural practices and interpretations, see Ben-Ghiat (2001), particularly chapter 1. On commandeering public space to broadcast Fascist cultural authority, see Falasca-Zamponi (1997). In Italian, de Felice (1983, 2008) offers an authoritative analysis.

11. Berghaus (2009).

12. Ravetto (2001, 22).

13. Ben-Ghiat (2001, 5–6).

14. Mussolini (1922). The quotation comes from 17:161; the translation is from Gentile (2009, 169).

15. For sociological interpretations of Fascist symbols and practices embodied in everyday life, see Berezin (1997); and Falasca-Zamponi (1997). On the history of Fascist appropriation of archaeological materials and knowledge, see Arthurs (2012). The susceptibility of archaeological science and practice to political ideas is assessed through multiple case studies in Diaz-Andreu and Champion (1996); and Kohl and Fawcett (1995).

16. Mussolini, *Opera Omnia*, 27:269, quoted in Arthurs (2012, 125).

17. Arena (2015, 314).

18. For an in-depth description of the maps' physical construction and display, see Minor (1999). Important discussions of Fascist display spaces and techniques are found in Stone (1993, 1999); Marcello (2011); and Baxa (2010).

19. Ben-Ghiat (2001, chapter 5). On the African colonies as Fascist Italy's "fourth shore," see Segrè (1974). For the repression of Libyan and Ethiopian social and cultural practices to justify Italian domination, see Ottolenghi (1997).

20. Luzzatto ([1998] 2005, 14).

21. *Scritti e discorsi*, 2:163–64; reprinted in Falasca-Zamponi (1997, 115).

22. The quotation is from *Opera omnia* 29:52–53; reprinted in Falasca-Zamponi (1997, 116). "Lictorial generation" can here be understood as the cohort of Italians born into or growing up with Fascist symbols and mentality. Literally, they make up the generation of *fasces* bearers.

23. For the pickax quotation, see Gamboni (2007, 262). The policy of slum clearance was referred to as *sventrimento* ("disembowelment"): Taylor, Rinne, and Kostof (2016, 329). For additional discussion of the renovation of central Rome, and the reconfiguration of urban space to accommodate Fascist *romanità* projects, see Agnew (1998); Arthurs (2012); Kallis (2014).

24. *Domenica del Corriere*, March 3, 1935, 39 (9): illustrated supplement. The original caption reads, "Il Duce vibra il primo colpo di piccone per liberare l'area destinata alla Mole Littoria che, fra Quattro anni, di fronte alle glorie monumentali dell'Urbe, simboleggerà la Potenza dell'Italia fascista."

25. Burgio (1999); Michaelis (1978). As Francesco Cassata shows, there was no single racist ideology in Fascist Italy, but rather three main lines of thought that were woven into official policy. See Cassata (2011, chap. 5).

26. For an excellent discussion of the history of corporatism in Italy and its operationalization through specific government bodies, see Salvati (2006).

27. "Discussione del disegno di legge: Riordinamento delle Soprintendenze alle

antichità e all'arte," Commissioni Legislative, 20 Aprile 1939–XVII, XXX Legislatura, Prima della Camera dei Fasci e Delle Corporazioni, 7.

28. Baioni (2006).

29. "Discussione del disegno di legge: Riordinamento delle soprintendenze alle antichità e all'arte," Commissioni Legislative, 20 Aprile 1939–XVII, XXX Legislatura, Prima della Camera dei Fasci e Delle Corporazioni, 7.

30. "Discussione del disegno di legge: Riordinamento delle Soprintendenze alle antichità e all'arte," Commissioni Legislative, 20 Aprile 1939–XVII, XXX Legislatura, Prima della Camera dei Fasci e Delle Corporazioni, 7. For a recent scholarly discussion of the complex history of Italian cultural and political entanglements with its former African colonial holdings, see Palumbo (2003).

31. Camera dei Fasci e delle Corporazioni, Commissione Legislativa Educazione Nazionale Lavori Pubblici Comunicazioni, Lavori Pubblici Comunicazioni, Discussioni 20 Aprile 1939–13 Luglio 1943. The remarks are from April 22, 1939.

32. Adler (2008) argues that property seizure from Italian Jews was driven as much by outside, non-Italian forces as by domestic politics.

33. "Commentators widely agree that the legislation drawn up under the Fascist Regime, although linked to ideological propaganda, was innovative and farsighted in its understanding of the importance of institutionalising the nation's cultural heritage and also the role that the State should take in this regard" (Ryde 2013, 92).

34. Falasca-Zamponi (1997, 78).

35. Billig ([1995] 2004); Gumbrecht (2004).

36. Stone (1998) argues that patronage played a significant role in Fascist cultural influence, and that commissioning new works from a range of styles and artistic movements was more important than attempting to form a monolithic Fascist aesthetic.

37. Falasca-Zamponi (1997, 67).

38. Buck-Morss (1992, 7).

39. Arendt (2018, 160).

40. Arendt (2018, 168).

41. Arendt (2018, 166–67).

42. Reed (2017, 95).

43. Buck-Morss (1992, 8).

44. Benito Mussolini, *Scritti e discorsi*, 10:29.

45. Luzzatto ([1998] 2005, 116).

46. Diary entry of Giuseppe Bottai written in 1946. Quoted in Luzzatto ([1998] 2005, 130).

47. Belco (2010, 41–43).

48. Olick (2005, 95).

49. Belco (2010, 13–14).

50. The fasces and she-wolf symbols have ancient origins and persisted through the early Middle Ages and the modern period. Fascist iconography appropriated them and re-presented them in 1920s and 1930s visual style.

51. Maiuri (1954, 48), quoted in De Francesco (2013, 213).

52. Arthurs (2012, 152).

53. Patriarca (2010, 192). The quotations are originally from the pro-Fascist journal *Italia e civiltà* 3 (January 1944).

54. Croce (1944, 1:153).

55. Fogu (2006).

56. Siviero's numerous books argue for more active state engagement in the pursuit of purloined works of art, as a matter of postwar justice and the principle of cultural intactness. His 1948 monograph was one of the first to offer systematic discussion of the illegality of the Nazis' mass appropriation of art across Europe. See Siviero (1948).

57. Jakubowski (2015, 103).

58. Agreement between Italy and Ethiopia concerning the Settlement of Economic and Financial Matters Issuing from the Treaty of Peace and Economic Collaboration, signed March 5, 1956, and entered into force on July 4, 1956, 267 UNTS 190.

59. The 1947 Peace Treaty with Italy (February 10, 1947, UNTS 167) declared: "Within eighteen months from the coming into force of the present treaty, Italy shall restore all works of art, religious objects, archives and objects of historical value belonging to Ethiopia or its nationals and removed from Ethiopia since October 3, 1935." Those terms were not met. For an in-depth analysis of the Axum obelisk repatriation: Jakubowski (2015).

60. Jakubowski (2015, 147).

61. Forgacs and Gundle (2007).

62. Ricciardi (2012).

63. Hom (2015).

64. Lambert (2010); see also Barbati, Cammelli, and Sciullo (2011).

65. Meskell (2018, 11).

66. Batisse and Bolla (2005).

67. Handler (1991); Verdery and Humphrey (2004).

68. Matthes (2015).

69. Meskell (2018, 32).

70. Meskell (2018, 30).

71. Säve-Söderbergh (1987).

72. Jakubowski (2015, 138).

73. An excellent discussion of pre-Hague Convention international agreements to protect and secure cultural property in wartime is offered by Gerstenblith (2019).

74. There is a robust literature on the passage and content of the 1954 Hague Convention. See Droit (2005) for the debate and compromises; Eriksen (2001) for evolving notions of cultural heritage and universalism among UNESCO participants.

75. By Convention definition, cultural property was

> (a) movable or immovable property of great importance to the cultural heritage of every people, such as monuments of architecture, art or history, whether religious or secular; archaeological sites; groups of buildings which, as a whole, are of historical or artistic interest; works of art; manuscripts, books and other objects of artistic, historical or archaeological interest; as well as scientific collections and important collections of books or archives or of reproductions of the property defined above; and
>
> (b) buildings whose main and effective purpose is to preserve or exhibit the movable cultural property defined in sub-paragraph (a) such as museums, large libraries and depositories of archives, and refuges intended to shelter, in the event of armed conflict, the movable cultural property defined

in subparagraph (a). (Convention for the Protection of Cultural Property in the Event of Armed Conflict, The Hague, May 14, 1954, chapter 1, article 1)

76. Across the participating national governments, there was disagreement about their obligations to specific sites. For the specific conditions of the United States' ratification of the 1954 agreements, see Gerstenblith (2014).

77. Convention for the Protection of Cultural Property in the Event of Armed Conflict, The Hague, May 14, 1954, chapter 1, article 7.2.

78. Anatole-Gabriel (2016).

79. 1972 UNESCO Convention, Article 11, paragraphs 1 and 2.

80. *Discendemo* is a regional variation on the standard Italian word *discendiamo*.

81. Balzani (2003) provides an extensive history of twentieth-century cultural patrimony management in Italy, including ministerial politics. As he points out, the Ministry of Education (which had responsibility for patrimony affairs in the early 1900s) and then the Ministry of Culture were seen as professional dead-ends by career civil servants. This continued well into the 1990s.

82. Balzani (2003, 4945–46).

83. Balzani (2003, 4947).

84. Balzani (2003, 4952).

85. Lambert (2010).

86. *Atti della Commissione d'indagine per la tutela e la valorizzazione del patrimonio storico, archeologico, artistico e del paesaggio* 1967, declaration 16, 4–5. Original: "Per i provvedimenti d' ufficio e per l'esecuzione dei propri provvedimenti, il Soprintendente si avvale del Servizio di Sicurezza dell'Amministrazione autonoma, provvedendo con propri ordini di servizio ad impartire le prescrizioni opportune."

87. Such changes were not confined to Italy. In the sphere of international cultural politics, definitions of protected objects were broadening from fine arts and public monuments to ethnographic, artifactual, and natural features. For a full discussion in the context of international cultural property law, see Gerstenblith (2019).

88. *Tempo*, May 23, 1965. The brief article recounts the charges against the men and discloses their sentences. To put the piece in perspective, it is given less column space than the adjacent discussions of society weddings and a new auto show.

89. Pallottino (1987); Rush and Benedettini Millington (2015, 7).

90. Italian journalist Fabio Isman has referred to the 1960s and 1970s as "the great raid" in recognition of a vast increase in the number and impact of tomb robbers in Italy (Isman 2009). Others have argued that it was at this moment that tomb robbers became professionalized in their skill set and network specialization (Balcells 2018).

91. Comando Carabinieri Tutela Patrimonio Culturale: Origini, funzioni e articolazioni (Rome: CCTPC, 2008), part 5, "Il Comando Carabinieri Tutela Patrimonio Culturale," 10.

92. Della Porta (1995).

93. The full name of the unit was the Organizzazione per la Vigilanza e la Repressione dell'Antifascismo (Organization for the Vigilance and Repression of Anti-Fascism). Founded in 1927, it specialized in domestic espionage, targeting suspected dissidents. It was the precursor to the German Gestapo. See further Dunnage (2012).

94. Dunnage (2012, 211).

95. See especially Reiter and Weinhauer (2007, 383).

96. The idea of the "strategy of tension" in the context of Italian policing and public violence is developed by Franco Ferraresi (1995).

97. MiBACT Budget 2020, Ministero dell'Economia e delle Finanze, p. 20.

98. Foucault (1980).

99. *Gli anni del Drago* film, produced by the Comando Carabinieri Tutela Patrimonio Culturale.

100. The announcement was made in Parliament by MP Michael Fallon on April 18, 2018, and subsequently confirmed in a UNESCO statement, https://hansard.parliament.uk/Commons/2016-04-18/debates/1604186000014/Daesh#contribution-CB101E39-C902-48EC-B5E9-65993311DF4B.

101. "Army, Smithsonian to Train Next Generation of 'Monuments Men,'" US Army press release, November 1, 2019.

Chapter Four

1. Note that the default gender of *tombaroli* I use in this book is male, reflecting the broader social discourse as well as the prosecution record. *Tombaroli* are almost exclusively men. Note Marc Balcells's comment (2018): "Regarding *tombaroli,* there is only one account in the existing literature about the involvement of women in this kind of illicit activity (Perticarari and Giuntani 1986)."

2. Tagliaferri and Rupi Paci (1992).

3. Tagliaferri and Rupi Paci (1992, 15–16).

4. Tagliaferri and Rupi Paci (1992, 16).

5. "L'arte sotto il mare," Legambiente 2010, 2.1. Legambiente is one of Italy's leading environmental nonprofit advocacy group. https://www.legambiente.it/sites/default/files/docs/Dossier_Mare_-_Salvalarte_0000000254.pdf.

6. Rush and Benedettini Millington (2015, 91, 111).

7. Isman (2009, 67).

8. Studies of illicit diggers in other parts of the world reveal a range of motives and criminal intent. No single characterization is apt. On the necessity of global and comparative perspectives, see Proulx (2013).

9. This position differs from cases in which corrupt state actors tolerate tomb robbing for personal gain. For this perspective, see Yates (2014).

10. Chippindale and Gill (2000). For a broader perspective on the harms associated with illegal archaeological digging and its associated trade, see Brodie, Doole, and Renfrew (2001) and Gill (2010).

11. Graepler and Mazzei (1996).

12. The critical material and symbolic properties the *spillone* holds for *tombaroli* are corroborated by interviews conducted by Marc Balcells (2018).

13. At American institutions all fieldwork with human subjects is regulated by a national system of rules and strict oversight. Fieldwork with vulnerable populations requires additional procedures for ensuring the safety of subjects and protecting them from any deleterious consequences for participating, including community censure and legal reprisals. Tomb robbers can be considered a vulnerable population on the grounds that in Italian law the removal and possession of archaeological materials are punishable by fines and imprisonment.

14. Nistri (2011, 186).

15. Nistri (2011, 187–89).

16. Mahmud (2014, 28).

17. Brodie, Doole, and Watson (2000, 8–10).

18. Alexander Stille, "Art Thieves Bleed Italy's Heritage," *New York Times*, August 2, 1992.

19. Lobay (2016).

20. Isman recounts that on a single night at the archaeological site of Campi, Lake Bolsena, thirty-five teams of diggers—over one hundred men all told—were working simultaneously (Isman 2009, 69).

21. Balcells (2018, 24).

22. For a full discussion of the history of looting at Etruscan sites and the market for Etruscan antiquities today, see Lobay (2016).

23. Thoden van Velzen (1996, 112).

24. Nistri (2011, 183–93).

25. *Codice dei Beni Culturali e del Paesaggio* [Codex of cultural heritage and landscape]. See chapter 3 for a discussion and analysis of the 2004 law.

26. Bottari and Pizzicannella (2002). See in particular the authors' discussion in chapter 1 of the basic definition of *patrimonio* and *beni culturali* in Italian law.

27. Bottari and Pizzicannella (2002, 44–47).

28. Perticarari and Giuntani (1986); cf. Balcells (2018, 185).

29. Bottari and Pizzicannella (2002, 45).

30. Tribunale Ordinario di Roma, December 5, 2007. Judge Salvatore Iulia, Penal Section IV.

31. Rossano and Rossano (2002).

32. "Un elevato grado di ossidazione ed evidenti concrezioni da interramento ipogeo che ne denunciano la provenienza da scavo archeologico," Tribunale Ordinario di Roma, December 5, 2007. Judge Salvatore Iulia, Penal Section IV, paragraph 7.

33. Tribunale Ordinario di Roma, December 5, 2007. Judge Salvatore Iulia, Penal Section IV, paragraph 8.

34. For a comparable and insightful discussion of the construction of Malian "looters" through images and discourse, see Panella (2014) (and Panella 2011 for additional social and political context of looting).

35. Morag Kersel's fieldwork with looters in Jordan and antiquities dealers in Jerusalem, for example, demonstrates the value of everyday conversation about tomb robbing, artifacts, and cultural identity for tracing patterns of thought among disparate stakeholders. See Kersel (2007).

36. *Gli anni del Drago* (2012), promotional film produced by the Tutela del Patrimonio Culturale. The dialogue occurs at minute 21.

37. http://www.legambiente.it/temi/ecomafia/archeomafia (accessed 3/17/2014).

38. While *-aiolo* is the preferred spelling in mainstream Italian, it varies by region and can turn up as *-arolo* in written and spoken speech in central and southern Italy. The *-rolo* ending in *tombarolo* is the reason linguists suggest the word emerged from central-southern Italian dialect. See related commentary in Cortelazzo and Zolli (1988).

39. Consistent with note 1 above, I refer to the *tombarolo* in the masculine form because I found no instance of its application to a woman, and the ideal figure it describes is specifically male. This narrative decision should not be read as dismissing the possibility that women participate in clandestine excavating.

40. Hollowell-Zimmer (2003, 46).

41. Thompson (2016).

42. Corte Suprema di Cassazione, Sezione II Penale; sentencing on October 29, 1973. Case notes reprinted in *Giurisprudenza Penale. Parte Seconda*, 396–404.

43. Bourdieu (1991, 37).

44. Bourdieu (1991, 42).

45. De Genova (2002, 420).

46. With this terminological decision, I acknowledge that I, too, play a role in constructing the *tombarolo* as a social figure. Similarly, Kersel (2012) demonstrates the role of social location in generating distinctive valuations of the antiquities trade.

47. Omero Bordo, *L'Ultimo Etrusco* online biography (section 1997–98), http://www.ultimoetrusco.it/biografia-int/testo4.htm (accessed 6/13/2016).

48. Scholarly studies of the postwar period in Italy corroborate the broader themes of Bordo's recollection of collective suffering. For sociohistorical analysis of the period, see Legnani (1973); and Piscitelli ([1905] 1975). In English, see Ginsborg (1990).

49. Cecchelin (1987, 23–24).

50. Omero Bordo, *L'Ultimo Etrusco* online biography (section 1975–77), http://www.ultimoetrusco.it/biografia-int/testo3.htm (accessed 6/13/2016).

51. Cecchelin (1987, 166).

52. Omero Bordo, *L'Ultimo Etrusco* online biography (section 1993–96), http://www.ultimoetrusco.it/biografia-int/testo.htm (accessed 11/16/2012).

53. Frances D'Emilio, "Grave Robber Creates an Etruscan Theme Park," *Los Angeles Times*, November 2, 1997, http://articles.latimes.com/1997/nov/02/news/mn-49350 (accessed 6/13/2016).

54. For the legacy of Cesare Lombroso's work: Gibson (2002). On the persistence of stereotypes about rural Italians and their supposed deficiencies: Sorge (2015, 50).

55. I called the Etruscopolis information line in November 2012, hoping to schedule an interview with Bordo. The man who answered the phone did not identify himself as Bordo but spoke with a voice strikingly similar to the one I'd heard from Bordo in television interviews. He explained that Bordo was unavailable for interviews and that if I wanted to visit Etruscopolis I would need to return next summer. I attempted to visit in July 2013 and was told that Etruscopolis was closed indefinitely.

56. Frances D'Emilio, "Grave Robber Creates an Etruscan Theme Park," *Los Angeles Times*, November 2, 1997, http://articles.latimes.com/1997/nov/02/news/mn-49350 (accessed 6/20/13).

57. A. Marianna, "L' Etrusco strega ancora. Ricostruzioni 'fedelmente false': Così facciamo rivivere la storia," *Corriere della Sera*, March 4, 2001, 57.

58. For a historical treatment of the bandit in Italian sociopolitical context, see Hobsbawm (1969). Hobsbawm argued that banditry is a universal social phenomenon. Bandits fulfill a specific role as "peasant outlaws," regarded by the state as criminals, "but who remain within peasant society, and are considered by their people as heroes, as champions, avengers, fighters for justice, perhaps even leaders of liberation, and in any case as men to be admired, helped and supported" (20). Scholars have criticized Hobsbawm's characterization for romanticizing bandits and overlooking the resentment they generated in other peasants. See, for example, Duggan's argument that in late nineteenth-century Italian anthropology bandits were not admired but were denigrated as degenerate and "atavistic": Duggan (2007, 267–68).

59. "È morto Omero Bordo: Addio all'Ultimo Etrusco," Civonline.it, Novem-

ber 8, 2018, http://www.civonline.it/articolo/e-morto-omero-bordo-addio-allultimo-etrusco.

60. Marín-Aguilera (2012). See also Thoden van Velzen (1996) on the masculine honor code of clandestine digging.

61. Smith (2005, 151).

62. Omero Bordo, *L'Ultimo Etrusco* online biography (section 1969–72), http://www.ultimoetrusco.it/biografia-int/testo4.htm (accessed 6/15/2016).

63. Thoden van Velzen (1996, 114) (quoting Perticarari and Giuntani 1986, 32).

64. Vašíček and Malina (1990, 14). On "ceraunites" and flint tools as thunderbolts, see Schnapp (1997, 151).

65. Barkan (1999, 19).

66. Barkan (1999, 17).

67. Zubrzycki (2011, 34).

68. Zubrzycki (2011, 35).

Chapter Five

1. Galbo (2019, 293).

2. On the definition of governance, and its centrality in neoliberalism, see Harvey (2007, 76). On the heritage game: Galbo (2019, 299).

3. Throsby (1999).

4. Globally, repatriation encompasses a number of practices, legal measures, and social contexts. See Greenfield (1996); Kersel and Luke (2015); Miles (2008).

5. For further analysis of the institutional process, see Rush and Benedettini (2015, 35). Wagner-Pacifici's (2005) theory of mutuality in surrender has interesting applications to repatriation.

6. For the legal perspective on this position, see Merryman (2006).

7. Cuno (2010, 39).

8. N. Gage, "How the Metropolitan Acquired 'The Finest Greek Vase There Is,'" *New York Times*, February 19, 1973. https://www.nytimes.com/1973/02/19/archives/how-the-metropolitan-acquired-the-finest-greek-vase-there-is-how.html.

9. Watson and Todeschini (2007).

10. R. Berman, "Met Chief to Discuss 'Hot Pot' in Rome," *New York Sun*, November 11, 2005, http://www.nysun.com/new-york/met-chief-to-discuss-hot-pot-in-rome/22903/ (accessed November 2012).

11. Waxman (2008, 198).

12. Quoted in Randy Kennedy and Hugh Eakin, "Met Chief, Unbowed, Defends Museum's Role," *New York Times*, February 28, 2006.

13. Montebello was speaking to the meeting of the Association of American Museum Directors (AAMD), West Palm Beach, Florida, in February 2006.

14. "Agreement between the Italian Ministry of Culture and the Metropolitan Museum of Art, New York," February 21, 2006. Available in full in *International Journal of Cultural Property* 13 (4): 427–34.

15. E. Povoledo, "Ancient Vase Comes Home to a Hero's Welcome," *New York Times*, January 19, 2008, http://www.nytimes.com/2008/01/19/arts/design/19bowl.html (accessed November 2012). The scene exemplifies the dramaturgy of repatriation; see Jacknis (2000).

16. Hoving (1994); Nørskov (2002).

17. “Passaggio dal demanio al patrimonio dello Stato della statua marmorea acefala di Afrodite, c.d. Venere di Cirene,” GU Serie Generale n. 190 del 14-08-2002.

18. Scovazzi (2009).

19. *Italia Nostra* vs. *Ministry of Cultural Heritage*—TAR Roma Lazio sez. II, April 20, 2007, n. 3518. The quotation is from the section titled “Fatto” (Facts of the case), note 3. The entire text of the decision can be found here: file:///Users/fg5t/Downloads/Italia%20Nostra%20v.%20Ministry%20of%20Cultural%20Heritage%20-%20TAR%202007.pdf.

20. Ibid.

21. Chechi (2014, 54–55).

22. Alessandro Chechi, Anne Laure Bandle, and Marc-André Renold, “Case Venus of Cyrene—Italy and Libya,” Platform ArThemis, http://unige.ch/art-adr, Art-Law Centre, University of Geneva, sec. V.1.

23. “Caro amico Muammar, ti ho riportato a casa la ragazza,” Elsa Muschella, “E la Venere di Cirene torna in aereo con Silvio,” *Corriere della Sera*, August 30, 2008.

24. “Il 72% del patrimonio culturale europeo si trova in Italia e almeno il 50% del patrimonio mondiale è situato nel nostro Paese,” Silvio Berlusconi, press conference, London, September 10, 2008. Reported by Salvatore Settis in “La tutela del patrimonio e del paesaggio in Italia: Una lunga storia, una crisi di grande attualità,” presentation given at the Festival of Art History in the Fontainebleau Palace, May 29, 2012.

25. Casanova (2007) argues that consecration in cultural systems follows institutional patterns of production and assent. The same principle obtains in systems of global patrimony, with different actors and institutional interests.

26. Rush and Benedettini Millington (2015, 179).

27. “Axum Obelisk Unveiled by Secretary of State Alfredo Mantica,” press release, Ministero degli Affari Esteri e della Cooperazione Internazionale, September 5, 2008.

28. “Obelisk Returned to Ethiopia after 68 Years,” *Guardian*, April 20, 2005, https://www.theguardian.com/world/2005/apr/20/italy.ethiopia.

29. Pietro Veronese, “Il viaggio di ritorno dell’obelisco di Axum,” *La Repubblica*, February 21, 1998, https://www.repubblica.it/online/cultura_scienze/arte/obelisco/obelisco.html.

30. Massimo Alberizzi, “Torna a casa l’obelisco di Axum: Un’operazione da sei milioni di euro,” *Corriere della Sera*, September 4, 2008.

31. The visual lexicon is not unique to artifact repatriation press conferences. There are performative parallels with American ATF agents displaying confiscated narcotics and cash after drug busts. What is interesting is how both performances—the drug bust and the looting blitz—convey state power. Both suggest that the size of the haul justifies law enforcement intervention.

32. “Operazione Teseo: Il più grande recupero di beni archeologici della storia,” January 21, 2015, Panorama. https://www.panorama.it/operazione-teseo-grande-recupero-beni-archeologici-storia (accessed June 29, 2020).

33. “TPC: Restituiti al patrimonio culturale italiano 5361 reperti archeologici,” press release by the Italian Carabinieri, January 21, 2015, http://www.carabinieri.it/cittadino/informazioni/eventi/tpc-restituiti-al-patrimonio-culturale-italiano-5361-reperti-archeologici (accessed January 2019).

34. *Gli anni del Drago* (2012), promotional film produced by the Tutela del Patrimonio Culturale, minute 21.

35. Text from the website of the Comando Carabinieri per la Tutela del Patrimonio Culturale, http://Art Squadweb.carabinieri.it/Art Squad_sito_pub/ (accessed 5/20/2013).

36. Eagleton ([1990] 2000, 64).

37. Duncan (1995); Hooper-Greenhill (1992); Zolberg (1994).

38. Shryock (2004, 11).

39. Thornton (2004) elaborates on this point in asserting that artifact repatriation can heal community trauma. On the family metaphor: Leoussi (1998).

40. Greenland (2013).

41. As of 2020, its full name is the Ministry of Cultural Heritage and Activities and Tourism (MiBACT). Budget figures come from statista.com.

42. Note Integrative DLB 2020–2022: Ripartizione spese di personale. Missione 1—Tutela e valorizzazione dei beni e attività culturali e paesaggistici (021), page 29. MiBACT Budget 2020, Ministero dell'Economia e delle Finanze.

43. Ibid., 19. MiBACT Budget 2020.

44. "Total General Government Expenditure on Recreation, Culture and Religion, 2018 (% of GDP)," Eurostat (gov_10a_exp), https://ec.europa.eu/eurostat/statistics-explained/index.php/Government_expenditure_on_recreation,_culture_and_religion (accessed July 2020).

45. "Io Sono Cultura 2019: L'Italia della qualità e della bellezza sfida la crisi," Symbola/Fondazione per le qualità italiane, https://www.symbola.net/ricerca/io-sono-cultura-2019/ (accessed July 15, 2020).

46. Napolitano and De Nisco (2017, 102).

47. Dec. lgs. 31 maggio 2014, n. 83. The entire text of the law is published at http://www.gazzettaufficiale.it/eli/id/2014/5/31/14G00095/sg.

48. Ignazio Marino, quoted in Gaia Pianigiani and Jim Yardley, "Corporate Medicis to the Rescue," *New York Times*, July 15, 2014, https://www.nytimes.com/2014/07/16/arts/design/to-some-dismay-italy-enlists-donors-to-repair-monuments.html (accessed 1/21/2019).

49. Vivian Chen, "Why Tod's Renovated the Colosseum, and Why Bulgari Repaired the Spanish Steps, While Fendi Threw Millions into a Fountain," *South China Morning Post*, August 4, 2016.

50. Massimo Consorti, "Alemanno non è Totò, il Colosseo non è la Fontana di Trevi ma Della Valle è Tod's," *Paperblog*, April 4, 2011, http://it.paperblog.com/alemanno-non-e-toto-il-colosseo-non-e-la-fontana-di-trevi-ma-della-valle-e-tod-s-323348/ (accessed 1/21/2019).

51. Tomaso Montanari, "Mr. Tod's e il Colosseo," *Minima e moralia*, August 8, 2013, http://www.minimaetmoralia.it/wp/diego-della-valle-colosseo/ (accessed 1/21/2019).

52. Galbo (2019, 299).

53. Chen, "Why Tod's Renovated the Colosseum."

54. Napolitano and De Nisco (2017, 102).

Chapter Six

1. Daniele Aiello Belardinelli, "Se non ci fosse stato lui gli Etruschi sarebbero meno conosciuti," *Tuscia Web*, November 8, 2018.

2. "È morto Omero Bordo: Addio all'Ultimo Etrusco," *Civonline.it*, November 8, 2018, http://www.civonline.it/articolo/e-morto-omero-bordo-addio-allultimo-etrusco.

3. Ibid.

4. On the concept of the national sensorium, developed in connection with Polish nationalism and Catholic traditions, see Zubrzycki (2011).

5. For an extensive analysis of how patria shaped understandings of individuals' obligations to the newly unified Italian state, see Stewart-Steinberg (2007, 8–11).

6. Memorandum of Understanding between the Government of the Italian Republic and UNESCO on the Italian National "Task Force in the Framework of UNESCO's Global Coalition Unite4Heritage," 2016, http://www.beniculturali.it/mibac/export/MiBAC/sito-MiBAC/Contenuti/MibacUnif/Comunicativi/visualizza_asset.html_65556661.html, quoted in Foradori (2017, 1).

7. Foradori (2018).

8. http://www.valorizzazione.beniculturali.it/it/archivio-sondaggi/424-arteaiutaarte.html.

9. C. Livesay, "Which Artworks Should We Save? Cash-Strapped Italy Lets Citizens Vote," *All Things Considered*, National Public Radio, January 21, 2014, podcast, http://www.npr.org/2014/01/21/263502871/which-artworks-should-we-save-cash-strapped-italy-lets-citizens-vote.

10. "La Madonna con il Bambino del Perugino sarà restaurata grazie al progetto 'L'arte aiuta l'arte,'" press release of the Ministero dei Beni e delle Attività Culturali e del Turismo, November 19, 2013, http://www.beniculturali.it/the Ministry of Culture/export/The Ministry of Culture/sito-The Ministry of Culture/Contenuti/Ministero/UfficioStampa/ComunicatiStampa/visualizza_asset.html_314365184.html.

11. Herzfeld (2016, 29).

12. Humphrey and Verdery (2004, 7).

13. Gabriele Cifani speaking to National Public Radio, "Which Artworks Should We Save?"

14. Handler (1988, 141–42).

15. Lowenthal (1985).

16. Tunbridge and Ashworth (1996).

17. Labadi (2007); Meskell (2002).

18. See especially Kaufmann (2004) on the persistent geographic associations with Italian art.

19. Kapferer (2012, 96–97).

20. "Possession of a heritage, of culture, is considered a crucial proof of national existence" (Handler 1988, 142).

21. Rutledge (2012) points out that even in the early imperial period, the profusion of old monuments and artworks made it difficult for officials to allocate conservation resources and determine what was historically significant for the principate.

22. Settis ([2002] 2007).

23. *Barnet et al. v. Ministry of Culture and Sports of the Hellenic Republic*, 19-2171 (2d Cir. 2020).

24. On iconicity and the performance of objects, see Alexander, Bartmanski, and Giesen (2012).

25. Hobsbawm (1983).

26. Billig ([1995] 2004); Edensor (2002).

27. Humphrey and Verdery (2004, 7).

28. Arantes (2007, 290).

29. Herzfeld (2016, 29).

30. Shryock (2004, 12).

31. On the unhelpfulness and insulting nature of the term "native," see Herzfeld (2016).

32. Porciani (2012, 74).

33. Krause (2013).

References

Adler, Franklin Hugh. 2008. "Jew as Bourgeois, Jew as Enemy, Jew as Victim of Fascism." *Modern Judaism* 28 (3): 306–26.

Agnew, John. 1998. "The Impossible Capital: Monumental Rome under Liberal and Fascist Regimes, 1870–1943." *Geografiska Annaler*, ser. B, *Human Geography* 80 (4): 229–40.

Agnew, John. 2011. "Landscape and National Identity in Europe: England versus Italy in the Role of Landscape in Identity Formation." In *Landscapes, Identities and Development*, edited by Z. Roca, P. Claval, and John Agnew, 37–50. Ashgate, UK: Aldershot and Burlington.

Alexander, Jeffrey C. 2004. *The Civil Sphere*. Oxford: Oxford University Press.

Alexander, Jeffrey C., Dominik Bartmanski, and Bernhard Giesen. 2012. *Iconic Power: Materiality and Meaning in Social Life*. New York: Palgrave Macmillan.

Altorki, Soraya. 1980. "Milk-Kinship in Arab Society: An Unexplored Problem in the Ethnography of Marriage." *Ethnology* 19 (2): 233–44.

Anatole-Gabriel, Isabelle. 2016. *La fabrique du patrimoine de l'humanité: L'UNESCO et la protection patrimoniale (1945–1992)*. Paris: FMSH.

Anderson, Benedict. 1991. *Imagined Communities*. London: Verso.

Appiah, Kwame Anthony. 2006. *Cosmopolitanism: Ethics in a World of Strangers*. New York: Norton.

Arantes, Antonio A. 2007. "Diversity, Heritage and Cultural Politics." *Theory, Culture and Society* 24 (7–8): 290–96.

Arena, Giovanni. 2015. "The Last Exhibition of the Italian Colonial Empire: Naples, 1938–1940." In *Cultures of International Exhibitions, 1840–1940: Great Exhibitions in the Margins*, edited by Marta Filipova, 313–32. London: Routledge.

Arendt, Hannah. 2018. "Culture and Politics." In *Thinking without a Banister: Essays in Understanding, 1953–1975*, edited by Jerome Kohn, 160–84. New York: Schocken Books.

Aronczyk, Melissa. 2013. *Branding the Nation: The Global Business of National Identity*. Oxford: Oxford University Press.

Arthurs, Joshua. 2012. *Excavating Modernity: The Roman Past in Fascist Italy*. Ithaca, NY: Cornell University Press.

Askew, Mark. 2010. "The Magic List of Global Status: UNESCO, World Heritage and the Agendas of States." In *Heritage and Globalisation*, edited by Sophia Labadi and Colin Long, 19–44. London: Routledge.

Baioni, Massimo. 2006. *Risorgimento in camicia nera*. Arezzo: Carocci.

Balcells, Marc. 2018. "Contemporary Archaeological Looting: A Criminological Analysis of Italian Tomb Robbers." PhD diss., CUNY Academic Works, 2018.

Balzani, Roberto. 2003. *Per le antichità e le belle arti: Le legge n. 364 del 20 giugno 1909 e l'Italia giolittiana*. Rome: Mulino.

Bandelj, Nina, and Frederick Wherry, eds. 2011. *The Cultural Wealth of Nations*. Stanford, CA: Stanford University Press.

Barbati, Carla, Marco Cammelli, and Girolamo Sciullo, eds. 2011. *Diritto e gestione dei beni culturali*. Bologna: Mulino.

Barkan, Leonard. 1999. *Unearthing the Past: Archaeology and Aesthetics in the Making of Renaissance Culture*. New Haven, CT: Yale University Press.

Bartelson, Jens. 2014. *Sovereignty as Symbolic Form*. London: Routledge.

Batisse, Michel, and Gérard Bolla. 2005. *The Invention of "World Heritage."* Paris: Association of Former UNESCO Staff Members.

Baxa, Paul. 2010. *Roads and Ruins: The Symbolic Landscape of Fascist Rome*. Toronto: University of Toronto Press.

Belco, Victoria. 2010. *War, Massacre, and Recovery in Central Italy, 1943–1948*. Toronto: University of Toronto Press.

Ben-Ghiat, Ruth. 2001. *Fascist Modernities: Italy, 1922–1945*. Berkeley: University of California Press.

Bennett, Tony. 1995. *The Birth of the Museum: History, Theory, Politics*. New York: Routledge.

Ben-Yehoyada, Naor. 2017. *The Mediterranean Incarnate: Region Formation between Sicily and Tunisia since World War II*. Chicago: University of Chicago Press.

Berezin, Mabel. 1997. *Making the Fascist Self: The Political Culture of Interwar Italy*. Ithaca, NY: Cornell University Press.

Berghaus, Günter, ed. 2009. *Futurism and the Technological Imagination*. New York: Rodopi.

Bianchini, Franco, Massimo Torrigiani, and Rinella Cere. 1996. "Cultural Policy." In *Italian Cultural Studies: An Introduction*, edited by David Forgacs and Robert Lumley, 291–308. Oxford: Oxford University Press.

Billig, Michael. (1995) 2004. *Banal Nationalism*. Reprint, London: SAGE.

Birch, Samuel. (1857) 1873. *History of Ancient Pottery: Egyptian, Assyrian, Greek, Etruscan, and Roman*. Reprint, London: John Murray.

Black, Jeremy. 2003. *Italy and the Grand Tour*. New Haven, CT: Yale University Press.

Blanning, T. C. W. 2002. *The Culture of Power and the Power of Culture*. Oxford: Oxford University Press.

Boime, Albert. 1979. "America's Purchasing Power and the Evolution of European Art in the Late Nineteenth Century." In *Saloni, gallerie, musei e loro influenza sullo sviluppo dell'arte dei secoli XIX e XX*, edited by Francis Haskell, 123–39. Bologna: CLUEB.

Borowitz, Helen, and Albert Borowitz. 1991. *Pawnshops and Palaces: The Fall and Rise of the Campana Art Museum*. Washington, DC: Smithsonian Institution Press.

Bottari, Francesca, and Fabio Pizzicannella. 2002. *L'Italia dei tesori: Legislazione dei beni culturali, museologia, catalogazione e tutela del patrimonio artistico*. Milan: Zanichelli.

Bottari, Francesca, and Fabio Pizzicannella. 2007. *I beni culturali e il paesaggio: Le leggi, la storia, la responsabilità*. Bologna: Zanichelli.

Bourdieu, Pierre. 1991. *Language and Symbolic Power*. Cambridge: Cambridge University Press.

Brodie, Neil, Jenny Doole, and Colin Renfrew, eds. 2001. *Trade in Illicit Antiquities: The Destruction of the World's Archaeological Heritage*. Cambridge: McDonald Institute.

Brodie, Neil, Jenny Doole, and Peter Watson, eds. 2000. *Stealing History: The Illicit Trade in Cultural Material*. Cambridge: McDonald Institute.

Brodie, Neil, and Kathryn Walker Tubb, eds. 2002. *Illicit Antiquities: The Theft of Culture and the Extinction of Archaeology*. London: Routledge.

Brown, Cynthia Ann. 1968. *Catalogue of Italian Terra-Sigillata in the Ashmolean Museum*. Oxford: Clarendon Press.

Buchholz, Larissa. 2018. "Rethinking the Center-Periphery Model: Dimensions and Temporalities of Macro-Structure in a Global Field of Cultural Production." *Poetics: Journal of Research on Culture, the Media and the Arts* 71 (December): 18–32.

Buck-Morss, Susan. 1992. "Aesthetics and Anaesthetics: Walter Benjamin's Artwork Essay Reconsidered." *October* 62:3–41.

Burgio, Alberto. 1999. *Nel nome della razza: Il razzismo nella storia d'Italia, 1870–1945*. Bologna: Mulino.

Carandini, Andrea. 1979. *Archeologia e cultura materiale: Dai lavori senza gloria nell'antichità a una politica dei beni culturali*. Bari: De Donato.

Carandini, Andrea. 1997. *La nascità di Roma: Dèi, Lari, eroi e uomini all'alba di una civiltà*. Turin: Guilio Einaudi.

Carver, Martin. 1996. "On Archaeological Value." *Antiquity* 70 (267): 45–56.

Casanova, Pascale. 2007. *The World Republic of Letters*. Translated by M. DeBevoise. Cambridge, MA: Harvard University Press.

Cassanelli, Roberto, and Giovanni Pinna. 2005. *Lo stato aculturale: Intorno al Codice dei beni culturali*. Milan: Jaca Book.

Cassata, Francesco. 2011. *Building the New Man: Eugenics, Racial Science and Genetics in Twentieth-Century Italy*. Budapest: Central European University Press.

Cecchelin, Riccardo, and Omero Bordo. 1997. *Omero: La mia vita con gli Etruschi*. Rome: Mediteranee.

Centeno, Miguel, Nina Bandelj, and Frederick F. Wherry. 2011. "Political Economy of Global Cultural Wealth." In *The Cultural Wealth of Nations*, ed. Nina Bandelj and Frederick F. Wherry, 23–46. Stanford, CA: Stanford University Press.

Ceserani, Giovanna. 2012. *Italy's Lost Greece: Magna Graecia and the Making of Modern Archaeology*. Oxford: Oxford University Press.

Chabod, Federico. 1996. "The Idea of Nation." In *Nationalism in Europe, 1815–Present*, edited by Stuart Woolf, 124–36. London: Routledge. Originally published as F. Chabod, *L'idea di nazione*. Bari: Laterza, 1961.

Chechi, Alessandro. 2014. *The Settlement of International Cultural Heritage Disputes*. Oxford: Oxford University Press.

Chippindale, Christopher, and David W. Gill. 2000. "Material Consequences of Contemporary Classical Collecting." *American Journal of Archaeology* 104: 463–511.

Choay, Françoise. 2001. *The Invention of the Historic Monument*. Cambridge: Cambridge University Press.

Classen, Constance. 2007. "Museum Manners: The Sensory Life of the Early Museum." *Journal of Social History* 40 (4): 895–914.

Coccolo, Francesca. 2017. "Law No. 1089 of 1 June 1939." In *Cultural Heritage Scenarios, 2015–2017*, edited by Simona Pinton and Lauso Zagato, 195–209. Venice.

Cogo, Giampaolo Maria. 1995. "I beni culturali ed ambientali tra ordinamento ed istituzioni." In *I beni culturali: Esigenze unitarie di tutela e pluralità di ordinamenti*, edited by Luca Mezzetti, 27–40. Padua: CEDAM.

Conversi, Daniele. 2009. "Art, Nationalism, and War: Political Futurism in Italy (1909–1944)." *Sociology Compass* 3 (1): 92–117.

Cortelazzo, Manlio, and Paolo Zolli. 1988. *Dizionario etimologico della lingua italiana*. Bologna: Zanichelli.

Cotta, Maurizio. 1992. "Elite Unification and Democratic Consolidation in Italy: An Historical Overview." In *Elites and Democratic Consolidation in Latin America and Southern Europe*, edited by J. Higley and R. Gunther, 146–77. Cambridge: Cambridge University Press.

Cremona, Alessandro. 2013. "Dalla Villa Strozzi alla Villa Mérode: Una dimora per l'archeologia. Storia della prima sede dell'École française de Rome." In *Construire l'institution: L'École française de Rome, 1873–1895*. Rome: Publications de l'École française de Rome.

Croce, Benedetto. 1944. *Il dissidio spirituale della Germania con l'Europa*. Vol. 1 of *Scritti e discorsi politici*. Bari, n.p.

Cuno, James. 2010. *Who Owns Antiquity? Museums and the Battle over Our Ancient Heritage*. Princeton, NJ: Princeton University Press.

Curzi, Valter. 2004. *Bene culturale e pubblica utilità*. Bologna: Minerva.

Dawdy, Shannon. 2016. *Patina: A Profane Archaeology*. Chicago: University of Chicago Press.

de Felice, Renzo. 1983. *Le interpretazioni del fascismo*. Bari: Laterza.

de Felice, Renzo. 2008. *Mussolini il duce, 1929–1940*. Turin: Giulio Einaudi.

De Francesco, Antonino. 2013. *The Antiquity of the Italian Nation: The Cultural Origins of a Political Myth in Modern Italy, 1796–1943*. Oxford: Oxford University Press.

De Genova, Nicholas P. 2002. "Migrant 'Illegality' and Deportability in Everyday Life." *Annual Review of Anthropology* 31:419–47.

Delaney, Carol. 1991. *The Seed and the Soil: Gender and Cosmology in Turkish Village Society*. Berkeley: University of California Press.

della Porta, Donatella. 1995. *Social Movements, Political Violence, and the State: A Comparative Analysis of Italy and Germany*. Cambridge: Cambridge University Press.

della Porta, Donatella, and Herbert Reiter. 2006. "The Policing of Global Protest: The G8 at Genoa and Its Aftermath." In *The Policing of Transnational Protest*, edited by Donatella della Porta, Abby Peterson, and Herbert Reiter, 13–41. Aldershot, UK: Ashgate.

Dennis, George. 1848. *Cities and Cemeteries of Etruria*. London: Dent.

Díaz-Andreu, Margarita, and Timothy Champion. 1996. "Nationalism and Archaeology in Europe: An Introduction." In *Nationalism and Archaeology in Europe*, edited by Margarita Díaz-Andreu and Timothy Champion, 1–23. Boulder, CO: Westview.

Dickie, John. 1999. *Darkest Italy: The Nation and Stereotypes of the Mezzogiorno, 1860–1900*. New York: St. Martin's Press.

DiFonzo, Monica. 2012. "'Think You Can Steal Our Caravaggio and Get Away with It? Think Again': An Analysis of the Italian Cultural Property Model." *George Washington International Law Review* 44 (3): 539–72.

Domanico, Laura. 1999. "The Invisible Landscape: Subsoil, Environment and the Italian Legislation on the Cultural Heritage." *European Journal of Archaeology* 2 (2): 159–75.

Droit, Roger-Pol. 2005. *Humanity in the Making: Overview of the Intellectual History of UNESCO, 1945–2005*. Paris: UNESCO.

Duggan, Christopher. 2007. *The Force of Destiny: A History of Italy since 1796*. London: Allen Lane.

Duncan, Carol. 1995. *Civilizing Rituals: Inside Public Art Museums*. New York: Routledge.

Dunnage, Jonathan. 2012. *Mussolini's Policemen: Behaviour, Ideology and Institutional Culture in Representation and Practice*. Manchester: Manchester University Press.

Durkheim, Émile. (1912) 1995. *The Elementary Forms of the Religious Life*. Translated by Karen Fields. New York: Free Press.

Eagleton, Terry. (1990) 2000. *The Ideology of the Aesthetic*. Reprint, Oxford: Blackwell.

Edensor, Tim. 2002. *National Identity, Popular Culture and Everyday Life*. London: Bloomsbury.

Elias, Norbert. 1982. *Power and Civility*. Oxford: Blackwell.

Emiliani, Andrea. 2015. *Leggi, bandi e provvedimenti per la tutela dei beni artistici e culturali negli antichi stati italiani, 1571–1860*. Florence: Polistampa.

Eriksen, Thomas Hylland. 2001. "Between Universalism and Relativism: A Critique of the UNESCO Concept of Culture." In *Culture and Rights: Anthropological Perspectives*, edited by J. K. Cowan, 127–48. Cambridge: Cambridge University Press.

Falasca-Zamponi, Simonetta. 1997. *Fascist Spectacle: The Aesthetics of Power in Mussolini's Italy*. Berkeley: University of California Press.

Feigenbaum, Gail, ed. 2014. *Display of Art in the Roman Palace*. Los Angeles: Getty Publications.

Feldman, Martha. 2007. *Opera and Sovereignty: Transforming Myths in Eighteenth-Century Italy*. Chicago: University of Chicago Press.

Ferraresi, Franco. 1995. *Minacce alla democrazia: La Destra radicale e la strategia della tensione in Italia nel dopoguerra*. Milan: Feltrinelli.

Fogu, Claudio. 2006. "*Italiani Brava Gente*: The Legacy of Fascist Historical Culture on Italian Politics of Memory." In *The Politics of Memory in Postwar Europe*, edited by Richard Ned Lebow, Wulf Kansteiner, and Claudio Fogu, 147–76. Durham, NC: Duke University Press.

Foradori, Paolo. 2017. "Protecting Cultural Heritage during Armed Conflict: The Italian Contribution to 'Cultural Peacekeeping.'" *Modern Italy* 22 (1): 1–17.

Foradori, Paolo. 2018. "Cops in Foreign Lands: Italy's Role in International Policing." *International Peacekeeping* 25 (4): 497–527.

Forcucci, Lauren E. 2010. "Battle for Births: The Fascist Pronatalist Campaign in Italy, 1925 to 1938." *Journal of the Society for the Anthropology of Europe* 10 (1): 4–13.

Forgacs, David. 2014. *Italy's Margins: Social Exclusion and Nation Formation since 1861*. Cambridge: Cambridge University Press.

Forgacs, David, and Stephen Gundle. 2007. *Mass Culture and Italian Society from Fascism to the Cold War*. Bloomington: Indiana University Press.

Foucault, Michel. 1980. *Power/Knowledge*. New York: Pantheon Books.

Frothingham, Arthur. 1887. "Letter from Roma." *American Journal of Archaeology* 3 (3/4): 387–92.

Furlotti, Barbara. 2019. *Antiquities in Motion: From Excavation Sites to Renaissance Collections*. Los Angeles: Getty Publications.

Gaggio, Dario. 2007. *In Gold We Trust: Social Capital and Economic Change in the Italian Jewelry Towns*. Princeton, NJ: Princeton University Press.

Gaggio, Dario. 2011. "Selling Beauty: Tuscany's Rural Landscape since 1945." In *The Cultural Wealth of Nations*, edited by Nina Bandelj and Frederick F. Wherry, 90–113. Stanford, CA: Stanford University Press.

Galbo, Joseph. 2019. "Renovating the Roman Colosseum: Politics, Urban Restructuring, and the Value of Heritage in Neoliberal Times." *European Journal of Cultural and Political Sociology* 6 (3): 288–316.

Gamboni, Dario. 2007. *The Destruction of Art: Iconoclasm and Vandalism since the French Revolution*. London: Reaktion Books.

Gell, Alfred. 1998. *Art and Agency: An Anthropological Theory*. Oxford: Oxford University Press.

Gentile, Emilio. 2003. *The Struggle for Modernity: Nationalism, Futurism, and Fascism*. New York: Praeger.

Gentile, Emilio. 2009. *La Grande Italia: The Myth of the Nation in the 20th Century*. Madison: University of Wisconsin Press.

Gentile, Emilio. 2011. *Italiani senza padri: Intervista sul Risorgimento*. Edited by Simonetta Fiori. Rome: Laterza.

Gerstenblith, Patty. 2014. "Beyond the 1954 Hague Convention." In *Cultural Awareness in the Military: Developments and Implications for Future Humanitarian Cooperation*, edited by Robert Albro and Bill Ivey, 83–99. Basingstoke, UK: Palgrave Macmillan.

Gerstenblith, Patty. 2019. *Art, Cultural Heritage, and the Law*. 4th ed. Durham, NC: Carolina Academic Press.

Gibson, Mary. 2002. *Born to Crime: Cesare Lombroso and the Origins of Biological Criminology*. Westport, CT: Praeger.

Gill, David. 2010. "The Portable Antiquities Scheme and the Treasure Act: Protecting the Archaeology of England and Wales?" *Papers from the Institute of Archaeology* 20:1–11.

Gilmour, David. 2011. *The Pursuit of Italy: A History of a Land, Its Regions, and Their Peoples*. New York: Farrar, Straus and Giroux.

Ginsborg, Paul. 1990. *A History of Contemporary Italy: Society and Politics, 1943–88*. London: Penguin.

Ginzburg, Carlo, and Anna Davin. 1980. "Morelli, Freud and Sherlock Holmes: Clues and Scientific Method." *History Workshop* 9:5–36.

Gosden, Chris. 2005. "What Do Objects Want?" *Journal of Archaeological Method and Theory* 12 (3): 193–211.

Grab, Alexander. 1995. "State Power, Brigandage and Rural Resistance in Napoleonic Italy." *European History Quarterly* 25 (1): 39–70.

Graepler, Daniel, and Marina Mazzei, eds. 1996. *Provenienza: Sconosciuta! Tombaroli, mercanti e collezionisti. L'Italia archeologica allo sbaraglio*. Bari: Edipuglia.

Greenfield, Jeanette. 1996. *The Return of Cultural Treasures*. Cambridge: Cambridge University Press.

Greenland, Fiona. 2013. "The Parthenon Marbles as Icons of Nationalism in 19th Century Britain: From Pre-national to Supra-national." *Nations and Nationalism* 19 (4): 654–73.

Greenland, Fiona. 2016a. "Color Perception in Sociology: Materiality and Authenticity at the *Gods in Color Show*." *Sociological Theory* 34 (2): 81–105.

Greenland, Fiona. 2016b. "Cultural Internationalism and the Italian Model of Repatriation." *Brown Journal of World Affairs* 23 (1): 143–54.

Greenland, Fiona. 2017. "In, on, and of the Inviolable Soil: Potsherds and Matters of Nationhood in Modern Italy." In *National Matters: Materiality, Culture and Nationalism*, edited by Geneviève Zubrzycki, 5–57. Stanford, CA: Stanford University Press.

Greenland, Fiona. 2019a. "Material Culture and the Problem of Agency." *American Journal of Cultural Sociology* 7 (3): 412–20.

Greenland, Fiona. 2019b. "New Insights into the Antiquities Market." *International Journal of Cultural Property* 26 (3): 211–25.

Gumbrecht, Hans Ulrich. 2004. *Production of Presence: What Meaning Cannot Convey*. Stanford, CA: Stanford University Press.

Gundle, Stephen. 2000. *Il Bel Paese*: Art, Beauty and the Cult of Appearance. In *The Politics of Italian National Identity: A Multidisciplinary Perspective*, edited by Gino Bedani and Bruce Haddock, 124–41. Cardiff: University of Wales Press.

Hamilakis, Yannis. 2007. *The Nation and Its Ruins: Antiquity, Archaeology, and National Imagination in Greece*. Oxford: Oxford University Press.

Hamilakis, Yannis, and Eleana Yalouri. 1996. "Antiquities as Symbolic Capital in Modern Greek Society." *Antiquity* 70 (267): 117–29.

Handler, Richard. 1988. *Nationalism and the Politics of Culture in Quebec*. Madison: University of Wisconsin Press.

Handler, Richard. 1991. "Who Owns the Past? History, Cultural Property, and the Logic of Possessive Individualism." In *The Politics of Culture*, edited by Brett Williams, 63–74. Washington, DC: Smithsonian Institution Press.

Harrison, Rodney. 2013. *Heritage: Critical Approaches*. New York: Routledge.

Harvey, David. 2007. *A Brief History of Neoliberalism*. Oxford: Oxford University Press.

Haskell, Francis, and Nicholas Penny. 1982. *Taste and the Antique: The Lure of Classical Sculpture, 1500–1900*. New Haven, CT: Yale University Press.

Helstosky, Carol. 2009. "Art Forgery and the Market in Nineteenth Century Italy." *Journal of Modern History* 81 (4): 793–823.

Herzfeld, Michael. 2004. *The Body Impolitic: Artisans and Artifice in the Global Hierarchy of Value*. Chicago: University of Chicago Press.

Herzfeld, Michael. 2009. *Evicted from Eternity: The Restructuring of Modern Rome*. Chicago: University of Chicago Press.

Herzfeld, Michael. 2016. *Cultural Intimacy: Social Poetics in the Nation-State*. London: Routledge.

Hobsbawm, Eric J. (1969) 2000. *Bandits*. Reprint, New York: New Press.

Hobsbawm, Eric J. 1983. "Introduction: Inventing Tradition." In *The Invention of Tradition*, edited by Eric Hobsbawm and Terence Ranger, 1–14. Cambridge: Cambridge University Press.

Hollowell-Zimmer, Julie. 2003. "Digging in the Dirt: Ethics and 'Low-End Looting.'" In *Ethical Issues in Archaeology*, edited by Larry Zimmerman, Karen Vitelli, and Julie Hollowell-Zimmer, 45–57. Walnut Creek, CA: Altamira.

Holstein, James A., and Jaber F. Gubrium. 1995. *The Active Interview*. Thousand Oaks, CA: Sage.

Hom, Stephanie Malia. 2015. *The Beautiful Country: Tourism and the Impossible State of Destination Italy*. Toronto: University of Toronto Press.

Hooper-Greenhill, Eilean. 1992. *Museums and the Shaping of Knowledge*. London: Routledge.

Hoving, Thomas. 1994. *Making the Mummies Dance: Inside the Metropolitan Museum of Art*. New York: Touchstone.

Hughes-Hallett, Lucy. 2013. *Gabriele D'Annunzio: Poet, Seducer, and Preacher of War*. New York: Knopf.

Humphrey, Caroline, and Katherine Verdery. 2004. "Introduction: Raising Questions about Property." In *Property in Question: Value Transformation in the Global Economy*, edited by Katherine Verdery and Caroline Humphrey, 1–25. Wenner-Gren Foundation for Anthropological Research. New York: Berg.

Isman, Fabio. 2009. *I predatori dell'arte perduta: Il saccheggio dell'archeologia in Italia*. Milan: Skira.

Izzet, Vedia. 2007. "Greeks Make It; Etruscans Fecit: The Stigma of Plagiarism in the Reception of Etruscan Art." *Etruscan Studies* 10 (18): 223–37.

Jacknis, Ira. 2000. "Repatriation as Social Drama: The Kwakiutl Indians of British Columbia, 1922–1980." In *Repatriation Reader: Who Owns American Indian Remains?*, edited by Devon A. Mihesuah, 266–81. Lincoln: University of Nebraska Press.

Jakubowski, Andrzej. 2015. *State Succession in Cultural Property*. Oxford: Oxford University Press.

Joll, James. 1960. *Three Intellectuals in Politics*. New York: Pantheon.

Kallis, Aristotle. 2014. *The Third Rome, 1922–1943: The Making of the Fascist Capital*. New York: Palgrave Macmillan.

Kantorowicz, Ernst H. 1950. "*Pro Patria Mori* in Medieval Political Thought." *American Historical Review* 56:472–92.

Kapferer, Bruce. 2012. *Legends of People, Myths of State: Violence, Intolerance, and Political Culture in Sri Lanka and Australia*. Washington, DC: Smithsonian Institution Press.

Karpik, Lucien. 2010. *Valuing the Unique: The Economics of Singularities*. Princeton, NJ: Princeton University Press.

Kaufmann, Thomas DaCosta. 2004. *Toward a Geography of Art*. Chicago: University of Chicago Press.

Keane, Webb. 2003. "Semiotics and the Social Analysis of Material Things." *Language and Communication* 23 (2–3): 409–25.

Kersel, Morag. 2007. "Transcending Borders: Objects on the Move." *Archaeologies: The Journal of the World Archaeological Congress* 3 (2): 81–98.

Kersel, Morag. 2012. "The Value of a Looted Object: Stakeholder Perceptions in the Antiquities Trade." In *The Oxford Handbook of Public Archaeology*, edited by Robin Skeates, Carol McDavid, and John Carman, 253–72. Oxford: Oxford University Press.

Kersel, Morag, and Christina Luke. 2015. "Civil Societies? Heritage Diplomacy and Neo-liberalism." In *Global Heritage: A Reader*, edited by Lynn Meskell, 70–93. Malden, MA: John Wiley.

Kohl, Philip L., and Clare Fawcett, eds. 1995. *Nationalism, Politics, and the Practice of Archaeology*. Cambridge: Cambridge University Press.

Körner, Axel. 2009. *The Politics of Culture in Liberal Italy*. New York: Routledge.

Kowalski, Alexandra. 2007. "State Power as Field Work: Culture and Practice in the French Survey of Historic Landmarks." In *Practicing Culture*, edited by Craig Calhoun and Richard Sennett, 82–104. London: Routledge.

Krause, Monika. 2013. "Recombining Micro and Macro: The Grammar of Theoretical Innovation." *European Journal of Social Theory* 16 (2): 139–52.

Labadi, Sophia. 2007. "Representations of the Nation and Cultural Diversity in Discourses on World Heritage." *Journal of Social Archaeology* 7 (2): 147–70.

Lahire, Bernard. 2019. *This Is Not Just a Painting: An Inquiry into Art, Domination, Magic, and the Sacred*. Cambridge: Polity Press.

Lambert, Simon. 2010. "Italy and the History of Preventive Conservation." *CeRO Art* EGG 1: doi.org/10.4000/ceroart.1707.

Leahy, Helen Rees. 2016. *Museum Bodies: The Politics and Practices of Visiting and Viewing*. London: Routledge.

Legnani, Massimo. 1973. *L'Italia dal 1943 al 1948: Lotte politiche e sociali*. Turin: Loescher.

Leoussi, Athena S. 1998. *Nationalism and Classicism: The Classical Body as National Symbol in Nineteenth-Century England and France*. New York: St. Martin's Press.

Lerici, Carlo. 1962. *Italia Sepolta*. Milan: Lerici.

Levi, Donata. 2008. "The Administration of Historical Heritage: The Italian Case." In *National Approaches to the Governance of Historical Heritage over Time*, edited by Stefan Fisch. Amsterdam: IOS Press.

Lista, Giovanni. 1995. *F. T. Marinetti, l'anarchiste du futurism*. Paris: Séguier.

Lobay, Gordon. 2016. "Looting and the Antiquities Trade." In *A Companion to the Etruscans*, edited by Sinclair Bell and Alexandra Carpino, 458–74. Malden, MA: Wiley.

Lowe, C. J., and Frank Mazari. 1975. *Italian Foreign Policy, 1870–1940*. London: Routledge.

Lowenthal, David. 1985. *The Past Is a Foreign Country*. Cambridge: Cambridge University Press.

Luzzatto, Sergio. (1998) 2005. *The Body of Il Duce: Mussolini's Corpse and the Fortunes of Italy*. Reprint, New York: Metropolitan Books.

Mackenzie, Simon, and Donna Yates. 2016. "What Is Grey about the 'Grey Market' in Antiquities?" In *The Architecture of Illegal Markets: Towards an Economic Sociology of Illegality in the Economy*, edited by Jens Beckert and Matías Dewey, 70–86. Oxford: Oxford University Press.

Maggini, Benedetta, and M. C. Tosetto. 1998. "L'Associazione per la Difesa di Firenze Antica." *Bollettino d'informazione—Brigata aretina degli amici dei monumenti* 67.

Mahmud, Lilith. 2014. *The Brotherhood of Freemason Sisters: Gender, Secrecy, and Fraternity in Italian Masonic Lodges*. Chicago: University of Chicago Press.

Maiuri, Amadeo. 1954. *Saggi di varia antichità*. Venice: Neri Pozza.

Marcello, Flavia. 2011. "Mussolini and the Idealisation of Empire: The Augustan Exhibition of Romanità." *Modern Italy* 16 (3): 223–47.

Marchand, Suzanne. 1996. *Down from Olympus: Archaeology and Philhellenism in Germany, 1750–1970*. Princeton, NJ: Princeton University Press.

Marín-Aguilera, Beatriz. 2012. "Italy, a Huge Open-Air Museum: 'Tombaroli' at Cerveteri and Tarquinia." In *Proceedings of the First International Conference on Best Practices in World Heritage: Archaeology*, 563–79. Madrid: Complutense.

Matthes, Erich Hatala. 2015. "Impersonal Value, Universal Value, and the Scope of Cultural Heritage." *Ethics* 125 (4): 999–1027.

McDonnell, Terence. 2016. *Best Laid Plans: Cultural Entropy and the Unraveling of AIDS Media Campaigns*. Chicago: University of Chicago Press.

McLean, Paul D. 2007. *The Art of the Network: Strategic Interaction and Patronage in Renaissance Florence*. Durham, NC: Duke University Press.

Merryman, John Henry. 2006. *Imperialism, Arts and Restitution*. Reprint, Cambridge: Cambridge University Press.

Meskell, Lynn. 2002. "Negative Heritage and Past Mastering in Archaeology." *Anthropological Quarterly* 75 (3): 557–74.

Meskell, Lynn. 2018. *A Future in Ruins: UNESCO, World Heritage, and the Dream of Peace*. Oxford: Oxford University Press.

Michaelis, Meir. 1978. *Mussolini and the Jews: German-Italian Relations and the Jewish Question in Italy, 1922–1945*. New York: Oxford University Press.

Miles, Margaret M. 2008. *Art as Plunder: The Ancient Origins of Debate about Cultural Property*. Cambridge: Cambridge University Press.

Miller, Daniel, ed. 2005. *Materiality*. Durham, NC: Duke University Press.

Minor, Heather Hyde. 1999. "Mapping Mussolini: Ritual and Cartography in Public Art during the Second Roman Empire." *Imago Mundi* 51:147–62.

Mitchell, Timothy. 1991. "The Limits of the State: Beyond Statist Approaches and Their Critics." *American Political Science Review* 85 (1): 77–96.

Moe, Nelson. 2002. *The View from Vesuvius: Italian Culture and the Southern Question*. Berkeley: University of California Press.

Montanari, Tomaso. 2018. *Constituzione italiana: Articolo 9*. Rome: Carocci.

Mookherjee, Nayanika. 2011. "The Aesthetics of Nations: Anthropological and Historical Approaches." *Journal of the Royal Anthropological Institute*, n.s., S1–S20.

Moretti Sgubini, Anna Maria, ed. 2000. *La Collezione Augusto Castellani*. Rome: "L'Erma" di Bretschneider.

Morris, May. 1905. "Opus Anglicanum II—The Ascoli Cope." *Burlington Magazine for Connoisseurs* 6 (24): 440–48.

Moshenska, Gabriel. 2012. "MR James and the Archaeological Uncanny." *Antiquity* 86:1192–1201.

Mukerji, Chandra. 2009. "The New Rome: Infrastructure and National Identity on the Canal du Midi." *Osiris* 24:15–32.

Müller, Jan-Werner. 2013. "The Paradoxes of Post-War Italian Political Thought." *History of European Ideas* 39 (1): 79–102.

Mussolini, Benito. 1922. "Dal primo discorso alla Camera alla Conferenza di Cannes" (22 giugno 1921–13 gennaio 1922), [published as part of the *Opera omnia* series].

Napolitano, Maria Rosaria, and Alessandro De Nisco. 2017. "Cultural Heritage: The Missing 'Link' in the Place Marketing Literature 'Chain.'" *Place Branding and Public Diplomacy* 13:101–6.

Natali, Andrea. 2004. "Evoluzione dei concetti di conservazione e di tutela dei documenti grafici in età moderna nello Stato Pontificio." *Culture del Testo e del Documento* 15:103–31.

Nistri, Giovanni. 2011. "The Experience of the Italian Cultural Heritage Protection Unit." In *Crime in the Art and Antiquities World*, edited by Stefano Manacorda and Duncan Chappell, 183–93. New York: Springer.

Nora, Pierre. 1989. "Between Memory and History: *Les Lieux de Mémoire*." *Representations* 26 (Spring): 7–25.

Nørskov, Vinnie. 2002. "Greek Vases for Sale: Some Statistical Evidence." In *Illicit Antiquities: The Theft of Culture and the Extinction of Archaeology*, edited by N. J. Brodie and K. W. Tubb, 23–37. London: Routledge.

Nye, Joseph. 2005. *Soft Power: The Means to Success in World Politics*. New York: PublicAffairs.

Olick, Jeffrey K. 1999. "Collective Memory: The Two Cultures." *Sociological Theory* 17 (3): 333–48.

Olick, Jeffrey K. 2005. *In the House of the Hangman: The Agonies of German Defeat, 1943–1949*. Chicago: University of Chicago Press.

Orsi, Paolo. 1911. "Croton: Prima campagna di scavi al santuario di Hera Lacinia." *Notizie degli Scavi Antichità*, suppl., 77–124.

Ott, John. 2008. "How New York Stole the Luxury Art Market: Blockbuster Auctions and Bourgeois Identity in Gilded Age America." *Winterthur Portfolio* 42 (2/3): 133–58.

Ottolenghi, Gustavo. 1997. *Gli italiani e il colonialismo: I campi di detenzione italiani in Africa*. Milan: Sugarco.

Pallottino, Massimo. 1987. "La stagione della Commissione Franceschini." In *Memorabilia: Il futuro della memoria: Beni ambientali architettonici artistici e storici in Italia*. Vol. 1, *Tutela e valorizzazione oggi*, edited by Massimo Pallottino, 7–11. Bari: Laterza.

Palumbo, Patrizia, ed. 2003. *A Place in the Sun: Africa in Italian Colonial Culture from Post-Unification to the Present*. Berkeley: University of California Press.

Panella, Cristiana. 2011. "The Social Life of (Plundered) Things: Les Contraintes du 'Donner à Voir.'" In *Halte au pillage! Le patrimoine archéologique en péril, du détecteur de métaux au huaquero*, edited by G. Compagnon, 391–407. Arles: Errance.

Panella, Cristiana. 2014. "Looters or Heroes? Production of Illegality and Memories of 'Looting' in Mali." *European Journal of Crime and Policy Research* 20:487–502.

Paoletti, Maurizio. 2005. "Paolo Orsi: La 'dura disciplina' e il 'lavoro tenace' di un gran archeologo del Novecento." In *Magna Graecia: Archeologia di un sapere*, edited by Salvatore Settis and Maria Cecilia Parra, 192–97. Milan: Electa.

Patriarca, Silvana. 2001. "Italian Neopatriotism: Debating National Identity in the 1990s." *Modern Italy* 6 (1): 21–34.

Patriarca, Silvana. 2010. *Italian Vices: Nation and Character from the Risorgimento to the Republic*. Cambridge: Cambridge University Press.

Pentini, Stefano Aluffi. 2005. "Fortunato Pio Castellani: Fondatore della bottega e orefice dell'aristocrazia romana." In Ministero per i Beni e le Attività Culturali, Soprintendenza per i Beni Archeologici del Lazio, *I Castellani e l'oreficeria archeologica italiana*, 67–82. Rome: "L'Erma" di Bretschneider.

Perticarari, Luigi, and Anna Maria Giuntani. 1986. *I segreti di un tombarolo*. Milan: Rusconi.

Pianazza, Murielle. 1993. "Giovan Pietro Campana: Collezionista, archeologo, banchiere e il suo legame con Firenze." *Mitteilungen des Kunsthistorischen Institutes in Florenz* 37 (2/3): 433–74.

Piscitelli, Enzo. (1905) 1975. *Da Parri a De Gasperi: Storia del dopoguerra*. Reprint, Milan: Feltrinelli.

Porciani, Ilaria. 2012. "On the Uses and Abuses of Nationalism from Below: A Few Notes on Italy." In *Nationalism from Below: Europe in the Long Nineteenth Century*, edited by Maarten van Ginderachter and Marnix Beyen, 73–95. Basingstoke, UK: Palgrave Macmillan.

Proulx, Blythe Bowman. 2008. "Transnational Crimes against Culture: Looting at Archaeological Sites and the 'Grey' Market in Antiquities." *Journal of Contemporary Criminal Justice* 24:225–42.

Proulx, Blythe Bowman. 2013. "Looting at Archaeological Sites in 'Global' Perspective: Nature, Scope, and Frequency of the Problem." *American Journal of Archaeology* 117:111–25.

Quatremère de Quincy, Antoine-Chrysostome. (1796, 1836) 2012. *Letters to Miranda and Canova on the Abduction of Antiquities from Rome and Athens*. Translated by Chris Miller and David Gilks. Los Angeles: Getty Publications.

Rago, Pasquale. 2004. "Valorizzazione dei beni culturali e ambientali e Titolo V della Costituzione." *Ambiente Diritto Legislazione Giurisprudenza*.

Rainey, Lawrence, Christine Poggi, and Laura Wittman, eds. 2009. *Futurism: An Anthology*. New Haven, CT: Yale University Press.

Rajala, Ulla. 2006. "'We Would Never Have Thought to Go There': The Changing Definitions of a Site in Central Italian Archaeology." *Bulletin of the History of Archaeology* 16:19–27.

Rasmussen, Tom. 1979. *Bucchero Pottery from Southern Etruria*. Cambridge: Cambridge University Press.

Ravetto, Kriss. 2001. *The Unmaking of Fascist Aesthetics*. Minneapolis: University of Minnesota Press.

Reed, Isaac Ariail. 2017. "Chains of Power and Their Representation." *Sociological Theory* 35 (2): 87–117.

Reed, Isaac Ariail. 2020. *Power in Modernity: Agency Relations and the Creative Destruction of the King's Two Bodies*. Chicago: University of Chicago Press.

Reinart, Sophus. 2010. "Lessons on the Rise and Fall of Great Powers: Conquest,

Commerce, and Decline in Enlightenment Italy." *American Historical Review* 115 (5): 1395–1425.

Reiter, Herbert, and Klaus Weinhauer. 2007. "Police and Political Violence in the 1960s and 1970s: Germany and Italy in a Comparative Perspective." *European Review of History* 14 (3): 373–95.

Reyes, Victoria. 2014. "The Production of Cultural and Natural Wealth: An Examination of World Heritage Sites." *Poetics* 44:42–63.

Riall, Lucy. 1994. *The Italian Risorgimento: State, Society, and National Unification*. London: Routledge.

Ricciardi, Alessia. 2012. *After La Dolce Vita: A Cultural Prehistory of Berlusconi's Italy*. Stanford, CA: Stanford University Press.

Ridley, Ronald. 2009. *The Eagle and the Spade:Archaeology in Rome during the Napoleonic Era*. Cambridge: Cambridge University Press.

Rivera, Lauren. 2008. "Managing 'Spoiled' National Identity." *American Sociological Review* 73 (4): 613–34.

Rofel, Lisa, and Sylvia J. Yanagisako, eds. 2019. *Fabricating Transnational Capitalism: A Collaborative Ethnography of Italian-Chinese Global Fashion*. Durham, NC: Duke University Press.

Rose-Greenland, Fiona. 2013. "Seeing the Unseen: Prospective Loading and Knowledge Forms in Archaeological Discovery." *Qualitative Sociology* 36 (3): 251–77.

Rossano, Dario, and Francesco Rossano. 2002. *Beni, diritti, ed istituti culturali*. Naples: Giuridiche Simone.

Rowell, Diana. 2012. *Paris: The "New Rome" of Napoleon I*. London: Bloomsbury.

Rush, Laurie, and Luisa Benedettini Millington. 2015. *The Carabinieri Command for the Protection of Cultural Property: Saving the World's Heritage*. Woodbridge, UK: Boydell Press.

Rutledge, Steven. 2012. *Ancient Rome as a Museum: Power, Identity, and the Culture of Collecting*. Oxford: Oxford University Press.

Ryde, Jennifer Ann. 2013. "Church or Museums? Tourists, Tickets, and Transformation." PhD diss., University of Western Sydney.

Salvati, Mariuccia. 2006. "The Long History of Corporatism in Italy: A Question of Culture or Economics?" *Contemporary European History* 15 (2): 223–44.

Sarti, Susanna. 2001. *Giovanni Pietro Campana (1808–1880): The Man and His Collection*. BAR International Series 971. Oxford: Archeopress.

Säve-Söderbergh, Torgny, ed. 1987. *Temples and Tombs of Ancient Nubia: The International Rescue Campaign at Abu Simbel, Philae and Other Sites*. London: Thames and Hudson/UNESCO.

Schnapp, Alain. 1997. *The Discovery of the Past*. New York: Abrams.

Scovazzi, Tullio. 2009. "New Trends in the Field of Restitution of Removed Cultural Properties to the States of Origin." Paper presented at International Meeting on Illicit Traffic of Cultural Property, December 16–17.

Segrè, Claudio. 1974. *Fourth Shore: The Italian Colonization of Libya*. Chicago: University of Chicago Press.

Serio, Mario. 2003. *Istituzioni e politiche per i beni culturali: Materiali per una storia*. Bologna: Bononia University Press.

Settis, Salvatore. (2002) 2007. *Italia S.p.A: L'assalto al patrimonio culturale*. Reprint, Turin: Giulio Einaudi.

Settis, Salvatore. 2017. *Architettura e Democrazia: Paesaggio, cittá, diritti civili*. Turin: Giulio Einaudi.

Shryock, Andrew. 2004. "Other Conscious/Self Aware: First Thoughts on Cultural Intimacy and Mass Mediation." In *Off Stage/On Display: Intimacy and Ethnography in the Age of Public Culture*, edited by Andrew Shryock, 3–28. Stanford, CA: Stanford University Press.

Siviero, Rodolfo. 1948. *Sulle opere d'arte italiane recuperate in Germania*. Rome: Accademia nazionale dei Lincei.

Smith, Anthony. 1987. *The Ethnic Origins of Nations*. Oxford: Blackwell.

Smith, Anthony. 2009. *The Cultural Foundations of Nations: Hierarchy, Covenant and Republic*. Malden, MA: Blackwell.

Smith, Kimbra L. 2005. "Looting and the Politics of Archaeological Knowledge in Northern Peru." *Ethnos* 74 (2): 149–70.

Snowden, Frank. 2006. *The Conquest of Malaria: Italy, 1900–1962*. New Haven, CT: Yale University Press.

Soresina, Marco. 2018. *Italy before Italy: Institutions, Conflicts and Political Hopes in the Italian States, 1815–1860*. London: Routledge.

Sorge, Antonio. 2015. *Legacies of Violence: History, Society, and the State in Sardinia*. Toronto: University of Toronto Press.

Spencer, Vicki A. 2012. *Herder's Political Thought: A Study of Language, Culture, and Community*. Toronto: University of Toronto Press.

Stewart-Steinberg, Suzanne. 2007. *The Pinocchio Effect: On Making Italians, 1860–1920*. Chicago: University of Chicago Press.

Stiebing, William H. 1994. *Uncovering the Past: A History of Archaeology*. Oxford: Oxford University Press.

Stone, Marla. 1993. "Staging Fascism: The Exhibition of the Fascist Revolution." *Journal of Contemporary History* 28 (2): 215–43.

Stone, Marla. 1998. *The Patron State: Culture and Politics in Fascist Italy*. Princeton, NJ: Princeton University Press.

Stone, Marla. 1999. "A Flexible Rome: Fascism and the Cult of Romanità." In *Roman Presences: Receptions of Rome in European Culture, 1789–1945*, ed. Catherine Edwards, 205–20. Cambridge: Cambridge University Press.

Stonor Saunders, Frances. 2013. *The Cultural Cold War: The CIA and the World of Arts and Letters*. New York: New Press.

Sweet, Rosemary. 2012. *Cities and the Grand Tour: The British in Italy, c. 1690–1820*. Cambridge: Cambridge University Press.

Tagliaferri, Gismondo, and Luisa Rupi Paci. 1992. *Tombaroli si nasce: La vita, le avventure e le scoperte di Gismondo Tagliaferri da Vulci raccontate da Luisa Rupi Paci*. Florence: Bonechi.

Taylor, Rabun, Katherine W. Rinne, and Spiro Kostof. 2016. *Rome. An Urban History from Antiquity to the Present*. New York: Cambridge University Press.

Thoden van Velzen, Diura. 1996. "The World of Tuscan Tomb Robbers: Living with the Local Community and the Ancestors." *International Journal of Cultural Property* 5:111–26.

Thompson, Erin. 2016. *Possession: The Curious History of Private Collectors from Antiquity to the Present*. New Haven, CT: Yale University Press.

Thornton, Russell. 2004. "Repatriation as Healing the Wounds of the Trauma of History: Cases of Native Americans in the United States of America." In *The*

Dead and Their Possessions: Repatriation in Principle, Policy and Practice, edited by Cressida Fforde, Jane Hubert, and Paul Turnbull, 17–24. London: Routledge.

Throsby, David. 1999. "Cultural Capital." *Journal of Cultural Economics* 23 (1): 3–12.

Tilley, Christopher. 1996. "The Powers of Rocks: Topography and Monument Construction on Bodmin Moor." *World Archaeology* 28 (2): 161–76.

Tilley, Christopher. 2004. *The Materiality of Stone: Explorations in Landscape Phenomenology*. Oxford: Berg.

Trentini, Antonella. 2004. *Codice dei beni culturali e del paesaggio*. Rimini: Maggioli.

Trigger, Bruce. 2006. *A History of Archaeological Thought*. 2nd ed. Cambridge: Cambridge University Press.

Troilo, Simona. 2005. *La patria e la memoria: Tutela e patrimonio culturale nell'Italia unita*. Milan: Electa.

Troilo, Simona. 2011. "National Museums in Italy: A Matter of Multifaceted Identity." In *Building National Museums in Europe, 1750–2010*, edited by Peter Aronsson and Gabriella Elgenius, 461–95. Conference proceedings from EuNaMus, European National Museums: Identity Politics, the Uses of the Past and the European Citizen, Bologna, 28–30 April 2011. EuNaMus Report No. 1.

Troilo, Simona. 2012. "A Gust of Cleansing Wind: Italian Archaeology on Rhodes and in Libya in the Early Years of Occupation (1911–1914)." *Journal of Modern Italian Studies* 17 (1): 45–69.

Tunbridge, John E., and Gregory John Ashworth. 1996. *Dissonant Heritage: The Management of the Past as a Resource in Conflict*. London: John Wiley.

Van Laar, Timothy, and Leonard Diepeveen. 2013. *Artworld Prestige: Arguing Cultural Value*. Oxford: Oxford University Press.

van Wijngaarden, Gert Jan. 1999. "The Complex Past of Pottery: An Introduction." In *The Complex Past of Pottery: Production, Circulation and Consumption of Mycenaean and Greek Pottery*, edited by Jan Paul Crielaard, Vladimir Stissi, and Gert Jan van Wijngaarden, 1–19. Amsterdam: Gieben.

Vašíček, Zdenek, and Jaroslav Malina. 1990. *Archaeology Yesterday and Today: The Development of Archaeology in the Sciences and Humanities*. Cambridge: Cambridge University Press.

Verdery, Katherine, and Caroline Humphrey, eds. 2004. *Property in Question: Value Transformation in the Global Economy*. Wenner-Gren International Symposium Series. Oxford: Berg.

Wagner-Pacifici, Robin. 2005. *The Art of Surrender: Decomposing Sovereignty at Conflict's End*. Chicago: University of Chicago Press.

Wali, Alaka. 2020. "Community Destruction, Museum Collections and the Work of Resilience." In *Cultural Violence and the Destruction of Human Communities: New Theoretical Perspectives*, edited by Fiona Greenland and Fatma Müge Göçek, 141–67. London: Routledge.

Walters, Henry Beauchamp. 1905. *History of Ancient Pottery: Greek, Etruscan, and Roman*, vols. 1 and 2. London: John Murray.

Watson, Peter, and Cecilia Todeschini. 2007. *The Medici Conspiracy: The Illicit Journey of Looted Antiquities—from Italy's Tomb Raiders to the World's Greatest Museums*. New York: PublicAffairs.

Waxman, Susan. 2008. *Loot: The Battle over the Stolen Treasures of the Ancient World*. New York: Henry Holt.

Williams, Raymond. 1976. *Keywords. A Vocabulary of Culture and Society*. New York: Oxford University Press.

Winter, Tim. 2015. "Heritage Diplomacy." *International Journal of Heritage Studies* 21 (10): 997–1015.

Wiseman, T. P. 2001. "Reading Carandini." *Journal of Roman Studies* 91:182–93.

Wolkoff, Joshua S. 2010. "Transcending Cultural Nationalist and Internationalist Tendencies: The Case for Mutually Beneficial Repatriation Agreements." *Cardozo Journal of Conflict Resolution* 11:709–38.

Yanagisako, Sylvia. 2002. *Producing Culture and Capital: Family Firms in Italy*. Princeton, NJ: Princeton University Press.

Yates, Donna. 2014. "Displacement, Deforestation, and Drugs: Antiquities Trafficking and the Narcotics Support Economies of Guatemala." In *Cultural Property Crimes: An Overview and Analysis on Contemporary Perspectives and Trends*, edited by Kila Joris and Marc Balcells, 21–36. Leiden: Brill.

Zannoni, Antonio. 1871. *Sugli scavi della certosa: Relazione letta all'inaugurazione del Museo Civico di Bologna*. Bologna: Regia.

Zolberg, Vera. 1994. "'An Elite Experience for Everyone': Art Museums, the Public, and Cultural Literacy." In *Museum Culture: Histories, Discourses, Spectacles*, edited by D. J. Sherman and I. Rogoff, 49–65. Minneapolis: University of Minnesota Press.

Zuboff, Shoshana. 2015. "Big Other: Surveillance Capitalism and the Prospects of an Information Civilization." *Journal of Information Technology* 30:75–89.

Zubrzycki, Geneviève. 2011. "History and the National Sensorium: Making Sense of Polish Mythology." *Qualitative Sociology* 3:21–57.

Zubrzycki, Geneviève. 2013. "Aesthetic Revolt and the Remaking of National Identity in Québec, 1960–1969." *Theory and Society* 42:423–75.

Zubrzycki, Geneviève. 2016. *Beheading the Saint: Nationalism, Religion, and Secularism in Quebec*. Chicago: University of Chicago Press.

Index

Page numbers followed by *f* refer to images.